Transnational Whiteness Matters

Transnational Whiteness Matters

Edited by
Aileen Moreton-Robinson,
Maryrose Casey, and Fiona Nicoll

LEXINGTON BOOKS

A division of
ROWMAN & LITTLEFIELD PUBLISHERS, INC.
Lanham • Boulder • New York • Toronto • Plymouth, UK

LEXINGTON BOOKS

A division of Rowman & Littlefield Publishers, Inc.
A wholly owned subsidiary of The Rowman & Littlefield Publishing Group, Inc.
4501 Forbes Boulevard, Suite 200
Lanham, MD 20706

Estover Road
Plymouth PL6 7PY
United Kingdom

British Library Cataloguing in Publication Information Available

Library of Congress Cataloging-in-Publication Data

Transnational whiteness matters / edited by Aileen Moreton-Robinson, Maryrose Casey,
and Fiona Nicoll.
     p. cm.
  Includes bibliographical references.
  ISBN-13: 978-0-7391-2557-1 (cloth : alk. paper)
  ISBN-10: 0-7391-2557-5 (cloth : alk. paper)
  ISBN-13: 978-0-7391-3221-0 (electronic)
  ISBN-10: 0-7391-3221-0 (electronic)
  1. Whites in literature. 2. Literature, Modern—20th century—History and
criticism. I. Moreton-Robinson, Aileen. II. Casey, Maryrose. III. Nicoll, Fiona
Jean.
  PN56.3.W45T73 2008
  812'.5093552—dc22   2008033427

Printed in the United States of America

∞ ™ The paper used in this publication meets the minimum requirements of American
National Standard for Information Sciences—Permanence of Paper for Printed Library
Materials, ANSI/NISO Z39.48-1992.

Contents

PART II. GENDERING WHITENESS

Acknowledgements

As with any publication this collection has a varied history and is produced with assistance from a range of people and organizations. We are grateful for all the professional and personal support we have received for this project. We would like to thank everyone who has contributed their time, energy and support to this collection. We would like to thank Joseph Parry and the anonymous referees at Lexington Books for their constructive feedback. As editors, we would like to acknowledge and thank Lenise Prater and Jodi Gallagher for their invaluable editorial and research assistance. We would like to thank the contributors for their commitment and patience with the project. Earlier versions of some of the papers were originally presented at the 'Whiteness and the Horizons of Race Conference' in Brisbane, Australia in December 2005. The editors, as organizers of the conference, would like to take the opportunity to thank everyone involved. Thanks are due to the members of the Australian Critical Race and Whiteness Studies Association executive committee, the keynote speakers, participants and volunteers who worked together with us on this conference, especially Tina Muir and Gillian Kehoul. The conference was supported by the Australian Studies Centre at the University of Queensland and we would like to express our thanks to David Carter, then director of the Centre. Maryrose Casey would like to acknowledge the material support provided by an Australian Postdoctoral Fellowship from the Australian Research Council. Thanks are also due to the School of English, Communications and Performance Studies, Monash University for a grant to complete the manuscript. Fiona Nicoll would like to acknowledge the support of the Centre for Critical and Cultural Studies at the University of Queensland for making time available for her to work on this project. We would like to acknowledge the support of the Indigenous Studies Research Network at QUT for providing workspace to develop the introduction of the book. And finally a special thank you to friends, families and partners whose support make all things possible.

Introduction: Virtue and Transnational Whiteness

Aileen Moreton-Robinson, Maryrose Casey & Fiona Nicoll

At the beginning of the twenty-first century the world was witness to a global crisis framed by the USA in the aftermath of 9/11 as the 'war on terror.' The events of 9/11 became a catalyst for a global alliance of industrialized nations in which white people are culturally and economically dominant. The alliance consisted of nations whose wealth was built on colonizing practices. Nations such as Britain, Australia, France and the USA positioned themselves globally as the virtuous protectors of democracy. They asserted a privileged connection to 'race blind' freedoms in a 'race-blind' war on terror. Claiming moral authority these nations argued that the invasion of Iraq was required because it was governed by an oppressive dictator who possessed weapons of mass destruction that were a threat to the world. The moral rationale for these acts, highlight how transnational whiteness can mobilize virtue when there is a perceived threat to its hegemony.

A leading western scholar, Alistair Bonnett, argues that through the spread of western ideologies and practices since the fifteenth century, the 'whiteness of modernity' has been culturally produced and reproduced within different nation states around the world.[1] Bonnett asserts that what is required now is an examination of the ways in which different cultures assimilate and reproduce racial whiteness. This book responds to this challenge by considering how virtue is mobilized as part of whiteness within texts produced in different cultural contexts.

In the late twentieth century critical whiteness studies developed and proliferated. The emergence of the field extends previous studies and theories of race centered on non-white objects and subjects. This epistemological shift toward the study of whiteness occurred within the context of globalization. The early critical whiteness literature came predominantly from the Americas. However one of the effects of globalization on the study of race has been the establishment of critical whiteness studies as a field that is now international in scope. Collections such as Susan Petrilli's *Whiteness Matters*[2] and Cynthia Levine-Rasky's *Working through Whiteness*[3] offer analyses across and between borders in terms of the critical relational and contextual locations of whiteness.

The chapters in *Transnational Whiteness Matters* demonstrate that whiteness is an imperial project that has undergone change over the centuries. This book illustrates that whiteness is a transnational process of racialization, which exceeds containment within fixed boundaries of identity and nation, reinscribing social hierarchies through national imaginaries and their transgression. A key thread that weaves through this book is how notions and claims of virtue operate discursively within transnational whiteness. Virtue, the claiming of a morally superior position that at the same time denies any moral authority to others, functions as a usable property or currency that is deployed to support, defend and perpetuate white dominance. Virtue functions through reason and goodness within the conventions by which societies live and govern behavior. It serves to absolve guilt recuperating itself by rational justification.

The collection contributes to transnational whiteness debates through theoretically informed readings of historical and contemporary texts by established and emerging scholars in the field of critical whiteness studies. From a wide range of disciplinary perspectives and national locations, the book traces continuity and change in the cultural production of white virtue within texts, from the proud colonial moment through to neoliberalism and the global war on terror in the twenty-first century. Read together, these chapters convey a complex understanding of how transnational whiteness travels and manifests itself within different political and cultural contexts. Some chapters address political, legal and constitutional aspects of whiteness while others explore media representations and popular cultural texts and practices. The book also contains valuable historical studies documenting how whiteness is insinuated within the texts produced, circulated and reproduced in specific locations, from colonial India and Australia to post-Apartheid-era South Africa.

Australia has proven an extremely fertile ground for critical work on whiteness for historical, cultural and political reasons related to the ongoing legacies of the White Australia policies that shaped national identity for most of last century—on one hand—and the persistent failure to address Indigenous sovereignty claims—on the other. While most of the critical whiteness literature generated in the USA begins from the premise of slavery rather than colonization, current Australian work complicates this premise. The Australian context raises important questions about the ideological processes that enable the USA to position itself outside of relations of colonization and indigenous dispossession. Certain chapters explore ways that Indigeneity is complicated by 'blackness' and the continuing legacies of British colonization on Australian cultural texts. This is in contrast to the critical whiteness literature from Canada, which engages with Indigeneity and whiteness within different constitutional and treaty frameworks. While the book creates a dialogue with existing work in Chicano/a, Latin, Hispanic and Native American studies on sovereignty and borders, this collection contributes to the emerging critical whiteness literature addressing Australia, Asia and the Pacific.

Each chapter addresses the ways in which texts produced in these different countries depend on rhetorical strategies that implicitly or explicitly privilege or center the virtues of whiteness in texts. With its focus on literary and critical/theoretical textual configurations of whiteness, *Transnational Whiteness Matters* also contributes to the international literature on race, with particular implications for critical whiteness theory in a 'postcolonizing' world. This postcolonizing world is not, as some theoretical frameworks have optimistically defined, a project beyond and after colonializm whereby the postcolonial subject is conflated with alterity. The authors of the chapters collected within this book draw on texts from a variety of historic and geographic locations to demonstrate how race is configured through the prism of whiteness within and across borders. In different ways, all of the contributors engage with the persistence of colonizing interests and subjectivities across a range of cultural sites, moments, practices and expressions. The book is divided into two main sections. The thread woven through the first section is how whiteness functions within national imaginaries. The second section focuses on the relations between gender, whiteness and nation.

WHITENESS IN NATIONAL IMAGINARIES

This section of the book considers how virtue is redeemed and recuperated through narratives of white subjectivity, national identities and Indigenous dispossession.

In the first chapter, 'Redeeming Self: The Business of Whiteness in Post-Apartheid South African Writing' by Tony Simoes da Silva, themes of "helping and exclusion, benevolence and responsibility and complicity" in recent life-writing narratives written by white people in Africa, are examined. He is interested in the way autobiographical accounts by white authors deploy figures of self-abasement operating as signs of "*goodness*, [which are] invariably read as self-serving." Focusing on recent autobiographical writing by white authors, da Silva approaches these texts as "performative acts, concerned at once with writing a personal narrative of the self and with (re)situating the raced subject within the new discourses of national belonging." He argues that authors such as Rian Malan, Christopher Hope, Gillian Slovo, J. M. Coetzee and Breyten Breytenback use the life-narrative form to produce emotional rather than intellectual accounts of whiteness as a defense against political changes that challenge the centricity of white subjects in post-Apartheid South Africa. The chapter concludes by noting the function of these literary narratives, as a form of history writing, which recuperates virtue in ways that are conducive to a collective white amnesia about power relations under apartheid.

Chapter two, 'Managing resistance: Whiteness and the storytellers of Indigenous Protest in Australia,' by Maryrose Casey argues that the documentation of Indigenous action and the inclusion of these events within the history texts of Australia has represented and acted as an important site of change in the dynamics of cross-cultural interaction. Despite this shift, the process of documenting Indigenous political action has and continues to have an active role in affirming and repeating past narratives of white virtue. The question or issue of Indigenous rights and presence in Australia has played a pivotal role in the framing of the national identity and imaginary since the first stirrings of a white sense of Australia as home. In this context, Casey argues that Indigenous public political agitation and action, whether symbolic acts or massed action, have consistently confronted and contested white social and moral narratives of race and nation. Examining recent ways in which representations of Indigenous people, as victims or political activists, as passive or resistant, have been deployed to support competing narratives and images of the white nation and its virtues, she identifies several ways that the written and social memory of Indigenous political action and the desires and beliefs they represent are manipulated. These include silence, effectively a denial of Indigenous action, or the framing of that action as corrupt, derivative or new, all of which reinscribe the virtue of white academics as subjects of knowledge and advocates on behalf of Indigenous interests.

Virtue and whiteness are inextricably linked in the third chapter, 'Picturing Whiteness: The Events of 9/11 in Children's Story Books' by Jo Lampert. This chapter discusses the shift within Western discourses of multiculturalism and diversity since September 11 in 2001 by considering children's picture books that were produced to explain the event. Her analysis of two books in particular, *On That Day* and *There's a Big, Beautiful World Out There*, considers how imagined readers are problematically positioned to embrace racial tolerance, global harmony and diversity whilst, simultaneously they are required to accept white America as the symbol of goodness in the world. The chapter suggests that these texts are representative of the ways recent political agendas are present in texts that seem, at first glance, separate from politics.

In chapter four 'Consuming Pathologies: *The Australian* against Indigenous Sovereignties,' Fiona Nicoll demonstrates what critical race and whiteness theory as an emerging field of Australian scholarship might contribute to existing debates about ways 'race' is represented in the media. Her examination of the way virtue is deployed in over a decade of reporting, features and editorials in *The Australian*, Australia's only daily broadsheet newspaper, shows how discourses of Indigenous pathology were mobilized to discredit Indigenous rights claims in a context of 'practical reconciliation.' She demonstrates how a possessive relationship to Indigenous Australians as 'ours' works ideologically to 'domesticate' political contestations of sovereignty that Indigenous rights activists present within both national and global. This process worked in *The Australian* to construct white journalists and academics as authentic representatives of Indigenous peoples' best interests while positioning Indigenous leaders and organizations offering collective representation and promoting social justice values as anachronistic and corrupt.

The fifth chapter by Aileen Moreton-Robinson entitled, 'Writing off Treaties: White Possession in the United States Critical Whiteness Studies Literature,' explores the relationship between Native American dispossession and the critical whiteness studies scholarship that emerged in the United States during the 1990s. The epistemological shift to the study of whiteness was in response to overt acts of racist violence reported in the press and the need to reconsider the persistence of racism in light of the proposition that race was socially constructed and not biologically determined. Ironically in most of this literature, prescriptive politics assume a central role; many are committed to the abolition of whiteness through naming it, deconstructing it and resisting it yet this does not seem to include a Native American political agenda. Virtue is perpetuated in the political prescriptions offered by this literature which continually disavows Native American sovereignty by failing to challenge white Americans to consider race beyond the black/white binary and simultaneously denying America's continuing colonial history and the basis of white possession.

GENDERING WHITENESS

This section focuses on how constructs of gender are deployed to recuperate the virtue of white masculinity and femininity as the embodiment of the nation and civilization.

In chapter six entitled 'White Man's Burden: Whiteness in Rudyard Kipling's *Kim* and Rabindranath Tagore's *Gora*,' Urbashi Barat focuses on India, where color has through the centuries been the marker of race, where the terms varna, color, and jati, tribe, caste, race, are more or less synonymous in popular usage, whiteness has inevitably been associated with the conqueror and the colonizer. The respective virtues attached to a colonial masculinity, coded as white, and the resistance and independence asserted on the part of 'mother India,' coded as dark, are entangled in complicated ways. History and legend, myth and literature, have usually represented the invader and the colonizer as the white male taking over the dark unknown feminine/effeminate India, most notably and recently in the portrayals of the European/British colonization of the country from the seventeenth century onward. Urbashi Barat analyses and compares the representations of whiteness and the other in Rudyard Kipling's English *Kim*, and in the equally well-known critic of empire, Rabindranath Tagore's *Bengali Gora*. She argues that in both novels the differences between the two are not simply a matter of being located on opposing sides of the colonial divide but, rather, of being located within different interpretations of masculinity, nationhood and society. This analysis is extended using Yasmine Gooneratne's novels *A Change of Skies* and *The Pleasures of Conquest* as context, demonstrating that this gendered view of whiteness and the colonial dynamic of nationhood and identity, is something that is shared even by a once-White but now multicultural Australia.

Suzanne Lynch in chapter seven entitled 'Fictions and Truths of Racial Production in Hannah Crafts' The Bondswoman's Narrative' unsettles the racialized distribution of virtue in American literary narratives that posit racial identity in singular terms and preclude representations of enslaved subjects as individuals seeking a 'humanization of the self.' Lynch begins with reflections on why, until recently, the name Hannah Crafts meant little or nothing to many scholars of American literature. It was not until Henry Louis Gates purchased the auctioned manuscript, *The Bondwoman's Narrative*, and introduced it to the reading public that Hannah Crafts's name began to play a pivotal role in the reading of early American texts. Crafts's narrative definitively positions itself, along with those of her contemporaries Lydia Maria Child, Catherine Sedgwick, Frank J. Web, and William Wells Brown, as a narrative of racial resistance that at once acknowledges and challenges the conventions of colonial racial discourse. Lynch explicates Crafts's participation in a willingness to confront the unrealistic paradigms of race. She critiques her society, positioning herself as a woman intolerant of the conventional interpretation of experience, and in presenting herself as such she questions the limits of these conventions. She provides an alternative to racial singularity in that she not only blurs, but also resists the imagery of whiteness and blackness, historically accomplished through making meaningful the properties of racial production. By upsetting the properties of particularity she works to eliminate the categories of race and to provide an alternative means of visualization.

In chapter eight, 'Constructing Whiteness in the Australian Adventure Story, 1875–1920,' Martin Crotty examines the ways in which authors of juvenile adventure stories in the late nineteenth and early twentieth centuries manipulated "white" and "black" to construct their Australian archetype. In the 1870s and 1880s Australian adventure novels, written by English authors, always positioned the black as the enemy, to be wiped out, forced to give way to British whiteness, which was attached, in turn, to virtue. The ideal Australian was a "pure" British white. These easy dichotomies between white (good) and black (bad) worked for a time, but by the 1890s were becoming problematic. By the early twentieth century, however, the hard boundaries between good "whiteness" and bad "blackness" were being questioned and interrogated, some heroes having an element of Aboriginality, and Aborigines and Europeans sometimes acting in concert against other external enemies. Australian whiteness began to take on a faintly brown hue. This chapter elucidates a process of change from the emerging Australian nationalism to new authorial positioning which opened up a space for the continued expression of Aboriginality as part of Australian culture, in particular its manhood. It is argued that in essence, an appropriation of certain aspects of constructed Aboriginality was required to ease non-Indigenous anxieties about place, belonging and racial fitness which also provided rationales for policies and practices of Indigenous assimilation. In spite of the differences Crotty documents between 19th and 20th century literary engagements with Aboriginality, the virtue ascribed to whiteness is maintained through the profoundly unequal terms on which cultural processes of white Aboriginalization and Aboriginal assimilation are desired and demanded.

Tanya Serisier in chapter nine entitled, 'Laura Bush and Dan Brown: Whiteness, Feminism and the Politics of Vulnerability' presents a fascinating and illuminating examination of the intersection between two apparently very different cultural texts: a speech by the First Lady, Laura Bush, broadcast on national radio after the invasion of Afghanistan and Dan Brown's best selling novel *Angels and Demons*. Serisier demonstrates how 'the politics of vulnerability' in these respective texts, becomes an ideological means by which the virtues of civilization and democracy are attached to white men and women in ways that are consistent with discourses of feminism and Christianity. Racialization operates through ex-nomination and exceptionalism allowing the authors of both texts to evade charges of white racism while simultaneously conjuring images of 'a sexualized, violent, racialized masculinity, uncontrollably desirous of white women' and from the predations of which Islamic women require urgent liberation. This chapter contributes to our understanding of American cultural production within the 'global war on terror' by showing how virtue continues to be constructed in relation to broad axes of race, gender and religion to appear as constitutively 'white and western.'

In chapter ten Annie Werner in 'Marking the White body: Tattooing in the White Colonial Literary Imagination' illustrates how tattooing was represented within the colonial literary imagination as a transgressive process that indelibly marked the boundaries of corporeal and hegemonic whiteness. Within beachcomber and captivity narratives, virtue was associated with the pure, unmarked, white body of European civilization while tattooing signified savagery, primitiveness and sexual violence, all attributes of being 'native' on the colonial frontier. Descriptions of Indigenous practices of tattooing were constructed in relation to European tropes of rape so that tattooed white body appears as the product or victim of foreign invasion. These violent attributes were, in turn, displaced onto white tattooed bodies, stigmatized by virtue of simultaneously embodying attributes of whiteness and blackness. Thus the process of tattooing complicated and problematized racial categories, relegating whites who transgressed their corporeal and visceral purity to the status of insider/outsider for the remainder of their lives.

NOTES

1. Alistair Bonnett, "A White World? Whiteness and Meaning of Modernity in Latin America and Japan," in *Working through Whiteness: International Perspectives,* ed. Cynthia Levine-Rasky (Albany, USA: State University of New York, 2002), 69–70.

2. Susan Petrilli, ed., "Whiteness Matters/Il Bianco Al Centro Della Questione," *Athanor: Semiotica, Filosofia, Arte, Letteratura* Anno XVII, nuova serie, n. 10 2006/2007

3. Alistair Bonnet, "A White World?"

Part I

WHITENESS IN NATIONAL IMAGINARIES

Chapter One

Redeeming Self:
The Business of Whiteness in
Post-Apartheid South African Writing

Tony Simoes da Silva

Genuflecting before the last British governor on the soil of her beloved Kenyan farm in 1930, Karen Blixen sought desperately to persuade the Empire's last representative to allow her Black workers to remain on land excised from the coffee plantation she was about to lose.[1] Hounded by creditors and overwhelmed by an unusually uncooperative climate alike, Blixen had set out to do one last thing for her workers, believing it to be one of many acts of kindness she had bestowed on them over the years.

Whether or not she succeeded is a moot point, not least because the word of colonial governors rarely counted for much. It was always in the nature of European colonialism to remain flexibly pragmatic, if I am forgiven the tautology; the business of empire rather than social etiquette determined how the likes of Lord Delamere or Joseph Byrne behaved when in charge of the prized possessions of the British Empire. Besides, for colonial administrators being agreeable to White women was all part of a day's work. For her part moreover Blixen was merely doing what White people in Africa had long felt to be their natural mission: she was being and doing good, fighting the good fight to protect the Black workers towards whom she expressed such tender maternal feelings from the tentacles of rising economic imperatives. As she writes in the novel, in words that convey the contextual ambivalence of her request and the governor's response: "I would have liked to stay on until I could have seen the squatters installed in their new place. But the surveying of the land took time, and it was uncertain when they would be able to move on to it."[2] She could not bring herself to say it, but in her deepest heart she suspected already that the governor's acquiescence to her request might not be all it seemed.

In retrospect, of course, it is easy to mock Blixen and others like her, caught up in the ideological cauldron of imperial ideologies for which they were often seriously unprepared; certainly, such behavior is best interpreted with a fair degree of skepticism. However, it is also the case that actions such as Blixen's unleash levels of signification that are not easily explained by the shallow smugness of the enlightened reader encountering the text for the first time decades later. That said, it is not my purpose here to engage with Blixen or her work in any meaningful way, either to critique or defend it. Rather, I am interested in extrapolating from the symbolism of her act of personal commitment to Kenya and its people implicit in the above moment as a link into more recent life writing narratives by White Africans. Specifically, I want to explore Blixen's heartfelt plea to the British governor as a particularly crucial moment in the enunciation, and indeed the production, of settler Whiteness in Africa, centered round notions of belonging and exclusion, benevolence and responsibility, and complicity.[3] Blixen goes down on her knees because she feels responsible for the plight of her workers, guilty even that her failure as a coffee producer should have led to their present predicament. The request to the British Governor is in this sense an act of atonement. In seeking to guarantee 'her Africans' a less unstable future, Blixen asks forgiveness for her role in their impending dispossession, for she seems aware that as their employer she has been complicit in it.[4] That is why her behavior seems so utterly self-interested; and yet it cannot be otherwise.[5]

Blixen's dilemma is one that I argue continues to determine how the writing of White people connected with Africa is produced and received: from her perspective self-abasement is a sign of her *goodness*, yet invariably read as self-serving. Her good actions complicate her ability to narrate *out* of Africa. Focusing in this chapter on a number of life-writing narratives by White South Africans who set out to fight the apartheid regime, I examine how these works highlight what Justin Cartwright calls the "white dilemma in Africa."[6] I read the increasing adoption of life-writing forms among White South Africans as contemporary reenactments of Blixen's genuflection; performative acts concerned at once with writing a personal narrative of the self and with (re)situating the raced subject within the new discourses of national belonging. This "public rehearsal of memory," or perhaps better put, the public rehearsal of private memories, re-centers personal trauma above the collective and perfectly illustrates ongoing debates about the way White South Africans remain the principal agents in the writing of a national narrative.[7] The difficulties White South Africans struggle to negotiate in their writing constitute perfect reflections of subjectivities at the cusp of overwhelming processes of change in which the self feels undermined. This is nowhere as deeply felt as in the case of White South African liberals who believe they gave themselves passionately and generously to the struggle to defeat apartheid; to some, it seems as if their efforts now receive insufficient recognition. In a recent letter to the Editor of *The Economist*, Helen Suzman, anti-apartheid activist and former opposition MP in the South African parliament prior to 1994 complained bitterly about what she perceives as attempts by the governing African National Congress to erase the contribution of White liberal South Africans like her to the struggle against apartheid.[8]

I suggest that in the context of contemporary South Africa, the act of selective memory intrinsic to any form of life writing is increasingly crossing over into a metonym of the widespread collective amnesia through which the recent past is interpreted as Antjie Krog shows with such poignancy and humor in *Country of My Skull* and *A Change of Tongue*.[9] As I argue here, in life writing by White South Africans such postures obfuscate the relationship between knowledge, power, agency and privilege by dissociating Whiteness from the narrative weight ascribed it in the history of Southern Africa. To put it differently, by overly sentimentalizing and exaggerating the effects of Apartheid and its demise on the function and impact of Whiteness such narratives convey a kind of 'privatization of White experience' in the new African nation, privileging an emotional rather than an intellectual understanding of White subject positions. In short, such rhetorical strategies represent a rejection or at least a deferral of the need to make sense of the political and social contingencies of the present. To this extent it is possible to speculate that the emphasis on the singular pronoun 'I,' with its natural solipsistic tendency, acts as an attempt to deflect the White person's growing sense of political invisibility.[10]

In a narrative such as Rian Malan's *My Traitor's Heart*, for instance, this is literally the case, as the writer, drunk and out of his mind on drugs repeatedly falls down before his Black companions to empty out his guts.[11] Gone is Karen Blixen's fine deportment and good manners; in this post-colonial, post-modern moment White penance is all the more sincere if drenched in bodily fluids. Back from Los Angeles, where he has spent a few years as an exile of sorts, Malan brings to his writing the performativity of self typical of American culture and society: to be sorry alone is insufficient; it is crucial *to let it be known* how truly remorseful one is. Different instantiations of this practice, articulated with varying degrees of subtlety and success, are found in Christopher Hope's *White Boy Running*, J. M. Coetzee's *Boyhood* and Breyten Breytenbach's *Dog Heart*.[12] As I see it, such narratives aim to reclaim for the White person a form of re-signified Whiteness, one forever alternating between a 'Whiteness under duress,' riven by a dizzying paranoia about the end of history, and 'Whiteness as void,' a pitiful version from which all power and privilege have been evacuated. This is nowhere as clearly evidenced as in Breytenbach's text; as I demonstrate below, *Dog Heart* constitutes a crude attempt at divesting from Whiteness.

One of the central points these texts show, is that even when at its most liberal—and 'politically enlightened' might in this instance be a better way of putting it—White South African identities are faced with an internal tension that betrays the strength of those very same ideologies of race the authors themselves set out to challenge and in almost every case to combat actively. As Matthew Frye Jacobson, David R. Roediger, Toni Morrison and others have argued, Whiteness is not a natural condition, rather a kind of exclusive club to which one is admitted on the basis of fulfilling certain conditions, and then ensuring that they are carefully guarded.[13] In South Africa this is particularly obvious because the very foundations of both nation and state have been so deeply implanted in the insidious world of racist discourses. To belong in and to the apartheid nation, real or imagined, meant to be authenticated White either through discursive or actual processes.[14] In a pertinent essay specifically addressing the formation of Jewish subjectivities in South Africa, Joseph Sherman has shown how access to what might be described as 'authorized' or 'hegemonic' Whiteness was regulated by and through a range of political and economic functions.[15] As the title of his essay suggests, 'serving the natives' in out of the way places, mostly in the shantytowns where most Black South Africans lived became one of the most travelled routes pursued by earlier groups of Jewish immigrants to South Africa at the beginning of the twentieth century. Created largely in order to make Black people invisible to White South Africa, the Black shantytown functions thus as a liminal space where an incipient Whiteness can be articulated, and then assiduously and dangerously performed.[16]

In later years, as Jewish people moved on to take up a much less perilous, financially more rewarding and in many instances very influential role in South African society, the places they vacated in the service industry that supported Black South Africa were taken up by newer groups of immigrants from Portugal (primarily from the Madeira island), Greece and Lebanon. Thus even in the South Africa where Whiteness was born by the stroke of the pen, *becoming* White required a great deal of hard work. More recently, in a book entitled *People who have Stolen From Me*, David Cohen explores this strange world of shifting hierarchies and danger zones within Whiteness in post-apartheid South Africa.[17] Through the story of Harry Sher and Jack Rubin, Jewish owners of a furniture business who insist on staying put in spite of the constant dangers to which they and their employees are subjected, Cohen offers a slice of Johannesburg's social history rich in the contradictions that the apartheid regime sought to smooth over. Cohen's text is particularly interesting for its dispassionate portrait of the way South African society seesaws between the polarities of Black and White. After first pushing out the Black residents of areas such as Johannesburg's

Jules Street in the mid-20th century, White people are now once again the minority in any such settings. Moreover, just as once upon a time it was marginalized White communities who lived there, so it is that now they too are the only White people to stay behind.

THE MEMORY OF THE WHITE CHILD

This sense of flux, or lack thereof, is perhaps an appropriate point of entry into the works I want to discuss in this essay. In the context of stories emerging out of Africa—and the reference is intended—the White African child frequently tells a story of a growing up in Africa that is just as much a growing away from Africa. In texts such as Gillian Slovo's *Every Secret Thing*, Breyten Breytenbach's *Dog Heart* and Drury Pifer's *Innocents in Africa* this is literally the case.[18] The autobiographical mode thus acts simultaneously as a material and as a geographical site invested with meanings that originate in the political conditions that frame the experiences it narrates. Even J. M. Coetzee's "memoir-fictions," *Boyhood* and *Youth*, which as Van der Vlies notes are neither exclusively life writing nor fiction, serve to illustrate this point.[19] For these reasons, the thematic, political and ethical imperatives of each different work will differ on the basis of its historical setting.

While all such stories usually demand a careful (re)positioning between African identities, racial discrimination, power and privilege, for instance, it also matters whether they were produced in pre- or post-1994 South Africa. Either way, in most cases it is almost inevitable that as part of the process of storytelling, the White narrator will repeatedly draw the readers' attention to his or her position within, and critical view on South Africa's unique system of race relations. In a narrative performance that parallels Blixen's genuflection, here too White South African authors restage their Whiteness anew time and again in order to ensure that it reflects and blends in with the changing political contexts of the New South Africa. As Gillian Whitlock aptly notes, "Contemporary South African autobiography is extraordinary, unmistakably a world of its own. Tattooed across its surface is a series of political events that configure and invade the private domain."[20]

In *Every Secret Thing*, for example, Slovo wavers between recognizing that the world in which her parents circulated differs from hers and resenting their unwillingness—although she knows that it is their inability—to include her and her sisters in it. Slovo's anger betrays a degree of Puritanism that is not uncommon in the childhood memoir, the child narrator arrogating for herself a speaking position from which to judge her parents. Significantly, though, perhaps most of all she resents the way in which they kept her

outside their political lives; she knows that the respect she enjoys among
ANC cadres, in independent Mozambique in the 1980s and post-apartheid
South Africa is essentially a token recognition of her link to the great radical activists, Joe Slovo and Ruth First. If she is able to return to South Africa and have direct and immediate access to the highest levels of political
power—Nelson Mandela himself comes to visit when Joe is dying and to sit
with the family when he dies—it is largely because of who her parents were,
not because any one thinks she or her sisters have done anything particularly
significant in the struggle. Having lost her parents to the struggle against
White racism in South Africa, Slovo returns perhaps to collect her dues; it
is as if through her frequent tussles with the White people who now occupy
the house that was once her family's in Johannesburg, she seeks to secure
the political capital her parents' work to change the meaning of Whiteness
accrued. In a particularly powerful passage in the book, Slovo returns in
Johannesburg to the house she shared, intermittently, with her parents. That
so much of their time even then was taken up with the pain of others, of
Black people, endows the 'memory-scape' each visit creates for Slovo with a
unique significance. The place she returns to brings back strong impressions
of an earlier life, one she remembers as a time of emotional privation and
trauma. Unfortunately for her, the new White occupants of the house that
once belonged to her and to her parents show little desire to allow her to reclaim, symbolically, her childhood. For them, the house, which Slovo sees as
a special place, almost sacred in its web of signification, is now *their* house.
Although they are never given any voice other than as mediated through
Slovo, the new owners of Slovo's childhood home become metonymic of an
old and unreconstructed whiteness. The emphasis the narrative places on the
conflict between them and Slovo is on the one hand explained by the fact
that it tells of the trauma Slovo relives in writing. Yet, it would be foolish to
overlook how neatly it juxtaposes two very different ways of being white in
South Africa, and more importantly in post-apartheid South Africa.

I propose then that texts such as those by Slovo, Coetzee, Breytenbach,
Malan, Hope and others, produced out of remembering a childhood lived in
the world of apartheid, are all the more resonant for their discursive appeal to
innocent and unformed socialities. Here the grown-up autobiographical self
(re)encounters the evils of apartheid and faces a profoundly life-changing
decision—the rejection of all they have always associated with home, with
family, with nation and self. As I have suggested earlier, one of the central
ways in which this process takes place is through a reassessment of notions
of agency, with White people now repeatedly identifying themselves as the
underdog in profoundly changed political settings. In South Africa, this
divestment from Whiteness allows White narrators to free themselves from

its weight as signified within the rigid strictures of apartheid. Even on the odd occasions where it is assumed as the clear sign of privilege and power that it was, *and remains*, Whiteness is interpellated in an uncannily self-cancelling act. *I am White and ineradicably guilty; I need all the help and understanding I can get.*

Given that even in the post-apartheid period a White racial identity remains inextricable from privilege and power, frequently a way out of this conundrum—one of the sundry manifestations of the 'white dilemma in Africa'—involves an intricate reclaiming of markers of difference other than race. In the work of Afrikaans-speaking writers in particular, the 'White trash' label gains a new cachet. For English-speaking South Africans a long-lost claim to 'minor ethnicity' status through one's Irish, Jewish or Scottish ancestry will do just as well. Australian scholar Fiona Probyn has usefully proposed that the way the White self seeks to account for the privilege his race accrues may be usefully read in terms of "ressentiment," a speaking position predicated on an insistence that the power and function of Whiteness have been much overrated.[21] Probyn is especially concerned with her own ability to speak as a White critic in the field of Whiteness studies, and with how feminist theory may provide a way out of the ethical and theoretical quandaries she identifies.

In the case of writers such as J. M. Coetzee, Christopher Hope and Richard Jürgens,[22] this might involve an appeal to the function of class in apartheid South Africa; for Drury Pifer the attempt to step outside the dominant spaces made available to White people by apartheid is negotiated through a focus on one's foreignness (as a young boy he leaves the country to settle with his American parents back in the U.S.); in the work of Ruth First there are hints of the ways in which gender and ethnicity impact on the White self, while Gillian Slovo seeks shelter in the liminality of her position as the child of famous political activists. All, I argue, find ways of *transferring* some of the anxiety they experience as liberal thinking White South Africans onto what they insist are similarly constraining ideologies. To restate my point, such discursive manoeuvres are underpinned by a desire to chip away at the strength of Whiteness as an ideological position by implying that its power is at best exaggerated, even negligible.

None, however, does it with the verve and schizophrenia evident in Breyten Breytenbach's *Dog Heart: A Memoir*. *Dog Heart*, written post-apartheid at the behest of a German publisher for a European readership, illustrates how easy it seems to be for White South Africans to revert to type, as it were. Given the right conditions, and the appropriate political temperature, even the anti-Apartheid radical with the best pedigree will quickly dust off the vocabulary that was supposed to have been put away in 1990 (or was it

1994?).[23] For what is remarkable in *Dog Heart* is the way it draws so freely from, and then in turn feeds back into the racist discourses of Whiteness in Africa. Here Breytenbach combines the paternalism of 'we can see all the good work all going to waste' that characterizes Doris Lessing's assessment of Zimbabwe in the period immediately following independence with the inevitable propensity of White people to claim center stage.[24] The litany of the horrors suffered by White people since independence—depicted in *Dog Heart* usually as having been at the hands of Black 'criminals,' though it is unclear why he bothers qualifying what he intends as 'Blacks' *tout court*— falls neatly in this category. That is not to say that the events he recounts are untrue, or that he exaggerates the crime wave affecting the country in the last decade. One need be only remotely aware of world affairs to be familiar with the New South Africa's crime statistics, even if few people within or outside the country would be likely to know that most of the victims are Black.[25]

It is the manner of Breytenbach's treatment of this issue that I want to note here, notably his reification of a trope of 'Whiteness under duress.' Ironically, while Breytenbach himself a few years ago would have been the first to object to such biased and simplistic representations, now he happily joins in. By privileging yet again the suffering of White people, Breytenbach resorts to what George Lipsitz sees "as a rhetorical move common to many defenders of white privilege."[26] In Lipsitz' words, though spoken in a different context, Breytenbach "relegates black grievances against whites to the past while situating white complaints about blacks in the present."[27] After all, what do we remember most vividly of Blixen's *Out of Africa* if not the pain she endures in her love affair with Africa? The dispossessed villagers serve merely as backdrop and trigger to this enactment of White trauma. This is best illustrated early in Breytenbach's text through a couple of instances where the bearing of racism on the behavior of many Black people is not actually denied, rather it is obfuscated through a banal repetition of the lines "you should understand that he is a victim of racism,"[28] and "he too is a victim of racism."[29] The 'mantra of betrayal' which Whites now repeat endlessly legitimizes a reading of the post-1994 nation in which they have mastered the tools of their own invisibility. Inviolable they may no longer be, but they have yet to give up the privileged position as serving as the normative center that defines civilized forms of being.

Writing during the period of the TRC, to Breytenbach's eyes the new South Africa is a world irredeemably on its way to hell. At the risk of overdoing the point, I argue that Breytenbach's account is haunted by that ghostly presence Whites in Africa have long learned to fear, the unfathomable horror that consumed Conrad's Kurtz. In post-1994 South Africa as in post-1980 Zimbabwe/Rhodesia or in the Belgian Congo in the nineteenth century, the gaze of Whiteness cannot see much cause for optimism. Just as Doris Lessing could foresee only doom and despair for a newly independent Zimbabwe (and how right she was, you may say, but that is a different narrative), so too Breytenbach, writing almost 20 years later, presages for South Africa days of little hope and even more limited happiness. It is symptomatic that one of the most salient aspects of the book is the way in which the coming home to (South) Africa anticipated in A *Season in Paradise* is re-signified in this latest memoir largely as a farewell to (South) Africa.[30] As the writer puts it, in a line that resonates throughout the book as an uncanny unifying thread, "We (Whites) are painted in the colours of disappearance."[31] Ultimately, the autobiographical act of farewell is coaxed out of him by a German publisher whose readership likes the story of Africa best when told through the eyes and the pen of a White man; that in this case the story bears all the hallmarks of the White man's genuine devotion to Africa and Africans, and of his authentic suffering, all the better. He might have written *Dog Heart* in Danish.

Breytenbach returns in *Dog Heart* to his beloved Boland to give body to old memories, and, as the book progresses, to cover up the tracks of his past life. With each death of an old (White) friend, usually a renowned painter or poet, Breytenbach moves farther away from the world of the Rainbow Nation. In the manner of every other White South African, he is appalled by the crime wave sweeping the land and what he sees as the rampant philistinism of the Rainbow Nation. However unwittingly, in *Dog Heart* Breytenbach has devised a way of telling a story of Whiteness that lightens up both its tone and the ideological load endemic to its South African origin. *Dog Heart* is a narrative of remembering that insists on forgetting the conditions that have led to the present state of affairs in South Arica.

As if to show that when the White man talks (of) Africa he draws his vocabulary from limited sources, Breytenbach's juxtaposition of the White man's misery to that of the Xan Bushmen[32] resonates with Laurence van der Post's well-known predilection for losing himself among the indigenous peoples of South Africa. Just as J. M. Coetzee in *Boyhood* finds it easier to share his humanity with the Cape Colored people his mother employs as servants, so too Breytenbach opts for sidestepping the real dialogue White people are being asked to initiate: with Black South Africans but on their terms. That is the point Ndebele, Walaza and Magkoba make, drawing closely on views uttered earlier by Steve Biko.[33] Setting out the political aims of Black Consciousness he wrote, anticipating the *status quo* about which Krog writes in *A Change of Tongue*: "We wanted to remove [the White man] from our table, strip the table of all the trappings put on it by him, decorate it in true African style, settle down and then ask him to join us on our own terms if he liked."[34]

I would argue therefore that in Breytenbach's memoir the Xan Bushmen's achievements serve as mere backdrop to the narrative he portrays as under the threat of extinction; crucially, the narrative of their doomed existences echoes those of Afrikanerdom in the New South Africa. The stories of the Xan Bushmen frame a celebration of Afrikaner heroism and pioneer courage. Like the Karoo, they are (in) the scenery, specks in a grander narrative of national (literally) achievement: the rise and fall of the Afrikaner Empire. More topically, they are the living remnants of a world gone by, in ways that parallel the present experiences of Afrikaners. As Ndebele proposed, such narrative and rhetorical strategies operate within the broader context of the mythmaking he believes characterizes the work of Afrikaner writers.[35]

Ironically, then, such narratives might in some way be seen to write back to a 'master narrative'—though I am conscious that in this context I am abusing the phrase—that is now no longer *naturally* inflected as White. That is not to argue that the story of Whiteness as it emerges in countless childhood narratives produced by White Africans is necessarily, if at all, an attempt to usurp the movement set in place by Black Africans' *prise de parole* began in the 1960s and 1970s. However, it is possible to read such texts as unconsciously engaging in a process of resistance to a perceived 'erasure of self' initiated by the end of racial dominance by White people. In a strange reversal of an earlier phenomenon examined by Robert Fraser in *Lifting the Sentence*, it is now White people who feel the necessity to deploy the pronominal 'I' in order to retain some of the visibility that the end of apartheid brought about. As Fraser puts it: "[I]f history fails to notice you, the salutary reaction is to gesture towards yourself, wave and declaim, 'Look, here I am!' In colonial times, this was a necessary act of psychological liberation: a move towards visibility."[36] Through life writing they articulate a counter image of Whiteness—still the product of apartheid, but resisting rather than authorizing it; in sum, redeemed.

In South Africa's recent encounter with postcoloniality much life writing by White authors sets out to rewrite the power structures that were central both to the country's apartheid period and to its colonial phase. Insofar as childhood will always presuppose, indeed signify a degree of innocence from broader ideological elements, frequently it is through the voice of the small child that White South Africans seek to negotiate the past with an eye on the present. Indeed, if work such as Breytenbach's is representative of a broader White South African viewpoint, perhaps they do so with a diminishing focus on the future. Indeed we might note that in the work by authors who situate their narrative in the actual period of their anti-Apartheid political activism, such as Helen Joseph, Hilda Bernstein and Helen Suzman, for example, the adoption of life writing forms reflects a much more overt awareness of the narratives as historical texts.[37] In *Autobiographics*, Leigh Gilmore usefully remarks, via Paul de Man, on "the apparent incommensurability of autobiography's divided status as historical document on the one hand, and aesthetic artefact, on the other."[38] Therefore the works I examine here echo, if always in diverse and contrasting ways, Walter Benjamin's comment on the cultural document as at the same time potentially a document of barbarism.[39]

As I see it, the life-writing narratives of White South Africans have become a particularly relevant site for the exploration of a relationship with place and identity that is profoundly and problematically inflected by race. The repudiation of hegemonic Whiteness as a dominant identity produced by the end of apartheid has transformed both the stage on which identity politics are 'performed' in South Africa and the directions by which individuals exercise their autobiographical acts. The 'making of personal memories' in contemporary South Africa both conflicts with and complements the making of a collective national memory. Thus I contend that we might see the recent redefinition of political systems and discourses in Southern Africa as one of the catalysts for the recent growth in the 'White' memoir. Insofar as they document the period between colonial and postcolonial conditions, or, in South Africa pre- and post-apartheid, these texts alternate as nostalgic reminiscing and a coming to grips with brutal political contingencies. If I may return to Whitlock, writing in *The Intimate Empire: Reading Women's Autobiography*, "Autobiographic writing can suggest the multiplicity of histories, the ground 'in between' where differences complicate, both across and within individual subjects."[40]

Significantly, such texts are as much a personal recollection of the past, as a reflection on *and* of the collective experiences of White Southern African people; in Leigh Gilmore's cumbersome formulation, in South Africa and Zimbabwe narratives of self undertake "powerful ideological work."[41] As texts coming out of South Africa, these narratives are required to perform more than the functions associated with the form, at once a recollection of the past and often a form of 'therapy.' For if they engage with the past in the selective manner associated with life writing, they must also responsibly undertake to make sense of history's residue. To tell the story of the (White South African) self demands simultaneously an awareness of the ways in which such a narrative has in the past always overwritten other (non-White) stories. To borrow Dominic LaCapra's words, in his comment on the way texts are 'canonised'—that is, interpellated to serve specific functions— "some are particularly effective in engaging critical processes that interfere with the regeneration of ideologies and established contexts in general."[42]

The 'pure' narrative of self that constitutes the foundational level of the memoir is thus severely undermined by the historical setting of the life experiences told in such texts. To a degree that is perhaps exacerbated, and possibly blown out of proportion by the political demands of local conditions, life writing becomes a stage for the articulation and performance of new mythologies of self and place that frequently run counter to, and are disruptive of the new dominant mythology, if also inevitably subject to it. After all, as is becoming increasingly clear, for all its inclusiveness the Rainbow Nation does not offer the imaginative space for all the stories that have been marked by the 'weight of history' in such permanent ways. Not surprisingly, and here I am conscious of coming full circle on a point made above, life-writing narratives such as J. M. Coetzee's, Breyten Breytenbach's and most especially Slovo's now constitute one of the various forms of history writing in the New South Africa. In the life writing of White South Africans "memoro-politics"[43] is "above all a politics of the secret, of the forgotten event that can be turned, if only by strange flashbacks, into something monumental."[44]

NOTES

1. I have in mind here the film made of Blixen's novel, rather than the latter. In the novel the description of the travails she endured trying to secure a plot of land for the squatters who for so long had lived on her property takes up a few pages, but it has little of the visual representation. In the film, the "long pilgrimage, [a] beggar's journey which took up [her] last months in Africa" (320) is reduced to one single moment, but all the more dramatic for the way in which the White woman on her knees is framed by the gaze of both the Black squatters and the White colonial administrator and his White entourage.

2. Karen Blixen, *Out of Africa* (Harmondsworth: Penguin, 1980), 322.

3. For extensive analysis of Blixen's text, see: Gillian Whitlock, *The Intimate Empire: Reading Women's Autobiography* (Oxford: Cassell, 2000); Simon Lewis, "Culture, Cultivation and Colonialism in *Out of Africa* and Beyond." *Research in African Literatures* 31, no. 1 (Spring, 2000).

4. The irony of course is that even while living on her land they had no rights of ownership, and the dispossession she aims to stop was caused by land holdings such as her own.

5. Whiteness in African settings has always been impelled by self-interest and profit, as Frantz Fanon (1952; 1961); O. Mannoni (1956), Albert Memmi (1991), Aimé Césaire (1972) and others have shown; its meaning and function are inextricable from the wider project of colonial discourses. According to Homi Bhabha, without a spectral colonized Other there would not have been a colonizer Self (See: *The Location of Culture* (London: Routledge, 1994)).

6. Justin Cartwright, back cover of *Disgrace*, J. M. Coetzee (Harmondworth, Middlesex: Penguin Books, 2002).

7. Sarah Nuttall and Carli Coetzee, eds., *Negotiating the Past: The Making of Memory in South Africa* (Oxford: Oxford University Press, 2002): 75.

8. Helen Suzman, "Letter to the Editor," *Economist*, May 7, 2005, 16(N).

9. Antjie Krog, *Country of My Skull* (London: Jonathan Cape, 1997) and *A Change of Tongue* (Johannesburg: Random House, 2003).

10. Grant Farred, "First Stop Port-au-Prince: Mapping Postcolonial Africa through Toussaint L'Ouverture and His Black Jacobins," in *The Politics of Culture in the Shadow of Capital*, ed. David Lloyd and Lisa Lowe (Durham, NC: Duke University Press, 1997).

11. Rian Malan, *My Traitor's Heart* (London: Vintage, 1990).

12. Breyton Breytenbach, *Dog Heart: A Memoir* (Cape Town, Johannesburg, Pretoria: Human and Rousseau, 1998); J. M. Coetzee, *Boyhood* (London: Vintage, 1998); Christopher Hope, *White Boy Running* (London: Abacus, 1988).

13. Matthew Frye Jacobson, *Whiteness of a Different Color: European Immigrants and the Alchemy of Race* (Cambridge, Mass.: Harvard University Press, 1998), David Roediger, *Towards the Abolition of Whiteness: Essays on Race, Politics and Working Class* (New York: Verso, 1994) and Toni Morrison *Playing in the Dark: Whiteness and the Literary Imagination* (Cambridge, Mass.: Harvard University Press, 1992).

14. I have in mind here the myriad of tests carried out during Apartheid to determine a person's 'degree of whiteness'; in work that drew closely on nineteenth century scientific discourses of race, but with a degree of *laissez faire* that resonates with colonial readings of place and industriousness, some tests carried out in South Africa consisted of no more than a pencil inserted through someone's hair to determine their 'racial purity.' If the pencil got stuck, classification veered to Black; if it fell through there was some chance that the individual might be classified White.

15. Joseph Sherman, "Serving the Natives: Whiteness as the Price of Hospitality in South African Yiddish Literature," *Journal of Southern African Studies* 26, no. 3 (September 2000).

16. The notion of danger here invoked relates to the well-known fact that small merchants with businesses in the myriad of townships that surround all South African cities have long been at the forefront of the kind of violence Fanon wrote about so lyrically. In other words, faced with the brutality of Apartheid, Black South Africans often reacted by taking out their anger on the Whites closest to hand, and, in the instance of Jewish, Greek, Italian and Portuguese immigrants to South Africa, those closest to Whiteness.

17. David Cohen, *People Who Have Stolen From Me: Rough Justice in the New South Africa* (New York: St. Martin's Press, 2004).

18. Drury Pifer, *Innocents in Africa: An American Family's Story* (New York: Harcourt Brace & Company, 1994); Gillian Slovo, *Every Secret Thing: My Family, My Country* (London: Little, Brown, 1997), and Breytenbach, *Dog Heart*.

19. A. Van der Vlies, "The novelist has entered the room," *Times Literary Supplement*, 5344, September 2, 2005, 9(N).

20. Gillian Whitlock, *The Intimate Empire*, 146.

21. Fiona Probyn, "Playing chicken at the Intersection: The White Critic of Whiteness," *Borderlands EJournal* 3, no. 2 (2004), http://www.borderlandsejournal.adelaide.edu.au/vol3no2_2004/probyn_playing.htm (accessed June 10, 2008).

22. Richard Jürgens, *The Many Houses of Exile* (Pretoria: Clarke's Books, 2002).

23. I do not mean to be facetious, but I wonder if perhaps it is indeed the case that White South Africans will need a few generations before they let go of the templates colonialism put in place, and Apartheid patented.

24. Doris Lessing, *African Laughter: Four Visits to Zimbabwe* (London: HarperCollins, 1992).

25. A recent piece in the UK leftwing newspaper, *The Guardian*, painted a particularly bleak picture of the situation in Johannesburg, noting how the crime rate seemed unstoppable in its ever-upwards trajectory. (Saturday 15 January 2006).

26. George Lipsitz, *The Possessive Investment in Whiteness: How White People Profit from Identity Politics* (Philadelphia: Temple University Press, 1998), 222.

27. Lipsitz, *The Possessive Investment,* 222.

28. Breytenbach, *Dog Heart,* 28.

29. Breytenbach, *Dog Heart,* 36.

30. Breyton Breytonbach, *A Season in Paradise* (New York: Persea Books, 1980), translated by Rike Vaughan.

31. Breytenbach, *Dog Heart,* 151.

32. Breytenbach, *Dog Heart,* 42

33. Steve Biko, *Black Consciousness in South Africa* (New York: Random House, 1978).

34. Biko, *Black Consciousness,* 69.

35. Nhlanhla Ndebele, "The African National Congress and the Policy of Non-Racialism: a Study of the Membership Issue. Politikon" 29, no. 2 (November 2002).

36. Robert Fraser, *Lifting the Sentence: A Poetics of Postcolonial Fiction* (Manchester: Manchester University Press, 2000), 67.

37. While neither of these writers' work is part of this study, they will on occasion be referred to illustrate a contrast or a parallel; the texts in question are: Helen Joseph, *If This Be Treason* (London: Deutsch, 1963); *Tomorrow's Sun: a Smuggled Journal from South Africa* (London: Hutchinson, 1966); Hilda Bernstein, *The World that Was Ours* (London: Persephone Books, 2004); Helen Suzman, *In No Uncertain Terms: The Memoir of Helen Suzman* (Johannesburg: Jonathan Ball, 1993) with a Foreword by Nelson Mandela).

38. Leigh Gilmore, *Autobiographics: A Feminist Theory of Women's Self-Representation* (Ithaca: Cornell University Press, 1994), 70.

39. Walter Benjamin, "On the Concept of History," trans. Harry Zohn *Selected Writing, Volume 4: 1938–1940* (Cambridge: Harvard University Press, 2003), 392.

40. Whitlock, *Intimate Empire,* 5. Recent narratives by Kenyan- and Zimbabwean-born White writers have also focused on the way in which the White children of Africa are 'orphaned' as a result of the new nations' independence from their colonial masters. Among the best known examples are Alexandra Fuller's *Let's Not go to the Dogs Tonight* (London: Random House, 2002); Peter Godwin's *Mukiwa* (London:

Picador, 1996), although, unlike the previous text this is a fictionalized account, and Jeremy Gavron's *Moon* (London: Viking, 1996).

41. Leigh Gilmore, *The Limits of Autobiography: Trauma and Testimony* (Ithaca, New York and London: Cornell University Press, 2001), 10.

42. Dominick LaCapra, *History, Politics and the Novel* (Ithaca: Cornell University Press, 1987), 25.

43. Ian Hacking, *Rewriting the Soul: Multiple Personality and the Sciences of Memory* (Princeton: Princeton University Press, 1995), 21.

44. Hacking, *Rewriting the Soul,* 214.

Chapter Two

Managing Resistance: Whiteness and the Storytellers of Indigenous Protest in Australia

Maryrose Casey

Since the first stirrings of a white sense of Australia as home, the issues of Indigenous rights and presence in Australia have played a pivotal role in the framing of identity and nation. In this context, Indigenous public political agitation and action, whether symbolic acts, massed action or long-term campaigns, have consistently confronted and contested white social and moral narratives of race and nation. The documentation of Indigenous protest action, and the inclusion of these events within the history texts of Australia, has represented and acted as a potential site for positive change in the dynamics of cross-cultural interaction. However, as Aileen Moreton-Robinson argues, whiteness as an epistemological a priori is embedded in all representations of Indigenous Australian people and continues to inform racialized ways of knowing.[1] "Whiteness establishes the limits of what can be known about the other through itself," functioning in effect as "an invisible regime of power that secures hegemony through discourse."[2] Within this regime, white scholars are positioned as leading investigators of the lives, values and abilities of Indigenous people and Indigenous people are "cast as native informants who provide 'experience' as opposed to knowledge."[3] Contained within this dynamic, the process of documenting Indigenous political action often plays an active role in affirming and repeating past narratives and reestablishing the dominance and power of whiteness within the frames of reference. Representations of Indigenous people as victims or political agitators, as passive or resistant, have been deployed to support competing narratives and images of the white nation and its virtues.

This process of effectively manipulating the written and social memory of Indigenous political action, and the desires and beliefs they represent, has operated through many different strategies; strategies that silence Indigenous voices, that deny Indigenous agency, and strategies that frame Indigenous

19

activists' actions as corrupt, derivative or new practices unconnected with the past. Central to these strategies is the implicit positioning of Indigenous and non-Indigenous people and communities in relation to knowledge and agency, authenticity and authority. On February 13, 2008 the Australian government after more than ten years of argument and a change of government formally apologized to Indigenous Australians for the long-term policies of removal of children as a form of cultural containment and erasure. Though the apology has finally been made the framing of what has become known as the Stolen Generations has strongly marked political and historical writings about Indigenous Australians. In this chapter, I examine some of the ways in which whiteness has been deployed and acts discursively to frame and contain Indigenous Australian social protest action and achievements by analyzing an essay by Bain Attwood that discusses the Stolen Generations.[4]

THE STOLEN GENERATIONS INQUIRY (1995–1997)

In the late 1990s, the historiography of Aboriginal/European relations since European settlement became the focus of what has been labelled the history wars.[5] Central to these debates are questions about what happened in the past, the nature of the interactions and engagements between Indigenous and non-Indigenous communities and the sources used for the different hi/stories. As Moreton-Robinson has observed, these debates were between white men as intellectuals, Indigenous voices were "rarely represented."[6] Among the main foci of the history wars are accounts of the degree of conflict involved in European settlement, the official and unofficial policies that legitimated that conflict and the policies of containment that followed. In terms of the policies of containment, a pivotal campaign in the 1990s that provoked and fuelled much of the conservative reaction within the history wars was what has become known as the issue of the Stolen Generations.

The Stolen Generations is a general term used to denote the Australian Aboriginal and Torres Strait Islander children, usually of mixed cultural heritage, who were taken, often under duress, from their families by Australian government agencies and church missions, under various state acts of Parliament between approximately 1910 and 1970. The children were typically placed in orphanages or institutions and trained to be unskilled workers, such as domestic laborers. The policies that justified the removal of Aboriginal and Torres Strait Island children from their parents developed from a range of different discourses and motivations. The social, political and cultural contexts of the removals across the twentieth century were shaped and informed by racialized narratives that supported the formation and protection of a White Australia and framed Indigenous Australians as "childlike" and members of a "dying race" and "superseded branches of humanity fated to be displaced by a superior culture."[7] The stated aims framed the acts of removals as being for the protection of the children, or to support the processes of assimilation of children of mixed descent into the white population. Assimilation policies dominated intercultural relations in Australia for many decades in the twentieth century. The legislative terms of assimilation were very clear:

> The policy of assimilation, in the view of all Australian Governments, means that all aborigines and part aborigines are expected eventually to attain the same manner of living as other Australians, and to live as members of a single Australian community enjoying the same rights and privileges, accepting the same responsibilities, observing the same customs and influenced by the same beliefs, hopes and loyalties as other Australians.[8]

The basic premise is apparent, the absorption of difference into the unstated and assumed norm of white Australia. As Anne Haebich argues "the system removed, controlled, managed and concentrated [Indigenous children], principally to protect and promote wider community interests," where that wider community was the Euro-Australian community.[9]

In 1995, a national inquiry into the removal of Indigenous Australian children was established in response to a long-term campaign by Indigenous individuals and organizations. One of the main reasons for advocating the inquiry was that the general level of ignorance of the history of forcible removal of children of mixed cultural background from their families "was hindering the recognition of the needs of its victims and their families and the provision of services."[10]

Over a two-year period, the inquiry headed by Sir Ronald Wilson, a former High Court judge and president of the Human Rights Commission and Mick Dodson, its Social Justice Commissioner, considered 777 submissions. These submissions included public evidence from 535 Indigenous individuals and groups, forty-nine church organizations and seven government submissions.[11] The final report of the Inquiry, *Bringing Them Home: Report of the National Inquiry into the Separation of Aboriginal and Torres Strait Islander Children and their Families,* was tabled in the Federal Parliament early in 1997.

The Inquiry found: that the majority of children had been forcibly removed; institutionalized; denied contact with their Aboriginality; in some cases traumatized and abused; and that the forced separation had caused long-lasting disorders. The report argued that, according to the 1948 United Nations Convention on the Prevention and the Crime of Genocide, some state administrators of Aboriginal affairs were guilty of genocide.[12] Though the process of removal and placement of the children was not sufficiently formally documented to assess the full extent of the practices of removal, after consideration of the findings based on archival and oral evidence, the report stated:

> Nationally we can conclude with confidence that between one in three and one in ten Indigenous children were forcibly removed from their families and communities in the period from approximately 1910 until 1970. In certain regions and in certain periods the figure was undoubtedly much greater than one in ten. *In that time not one family has escaped the effects of forcible removal* (confirmed by representatives of the Queensland and WA Governments in evidence to the Inquiry). Most families have been affected, in one or more generations, by the forcible removal of one or more children. [13]

When it was tabled, the *Bringing Them Home Report* received wide media coverage and public support. In the short term, as Robert Manne argued, the overwhelming response to the *Bringing Them Home Report* was potentially culturally transformative.[14] This positive reaction was quickly overshadowed by a counter reaction against the report. Despite the detailed findings within the *Bringing Them Home* report, the nature and extent of the removals documented were disputed within Australia. The findings of the inquiry were questioned on all levels in terms of the reliability of the information, the number of children removed and the intent and effectiveness in practice of government policies. Some conservative journalists, such as Andrew Bolt, denied the very existence of the Stolen Generations.[15] Despite the extensive archival and oral evidence, Bolt described the idea as a 'preposterous and obscene' myth, claiming that there had not been any policy in any state or territory at any time for the systematic removal of 'half-caste' Aboriginal children.

The debates continued and in April 2000, the then Aboriginal Affairs Minister in the conservative John Howard Government, John Herron, submitted a report to the Senate Legal and Constitutional References Committee Inquiry into the Stolen Generation that questioned whether there had ever actually been a 'Stolen Generation.' The Commonwealth Government's explicit rejection of the findings of the inquiry in its submission, focused on the language used rather than the information collected by the inquiry, claiming that it was incorrect to use the phrase 'stolen generation' as:

> At most, it might be inferred that up to 10 percent of [Indigenous] children were separated for a variety of reasons, both protective and otherwise, some forcibly, some not. This does not constitute a 'generation' of 'stolen' children. The phrase 'stolen generation' is rhetorical.[16]

In addition to claiming that the 'stolen generations' were a rhetorical overstatement, in the submission the government argued that the treatment of the children who had been removed was "essentially lawful and benign." The submission also claimed that though "a proportion of those removed fitted within the stereotype of forcible removal," the evidence was only anecdotal and had not been subjected to proper scrutiny.[17]

"LEARNING THE TRUTH"

The year 2007 marked the 10th anniversary of the tabling of the *Bringing Them Home* report. Following the intense scrutiny of the report and its claims in the first years after it was tabled, the issue of the Stolen Generations had been discredited or sidelined with the Commonwealth Government spending millions of dollars fighting compensation claims. After ten years, the handling of the Stolen Generations within both fiction and non-fiction discussing Aboriginal and European Australian relations marks the writer's political position. In general, Australian historiography, especially in relation to Indigenous and non-Indigenous conflict, has continued to be contested within the paradigm of critique established by the history wars focused on questions about what happened during and after European settlement and what sources can be deemed reliable. In this context, historians of Aboriginal and European relations who claim the middle ground in the debates and the authority to speak hold an important and influential place.

Bain Attwood, a white academic historian originally from New Zealand, is acknowledged as a leading authority on Aboriginal history. He has authored, co-authored and edited several books and collections focused on the history of Aboriginal and Euro-Australian's interactions. Many of his books focus on Indigenous protest, including *The Making of the Aborigines* (1989), *The Struggle for Aboriginal Rights* (1999), *Rights for Aborigines* (2003) and *Thinking Black: William Cooper and the Australian Aborigines League* (2004). Among other contributions to the debates about the historiography of Australian race relations, Atwood has published a book titled, *Telling the Truth about Aboriginal History* (2005). In this book, he critiques the current practices of what he calls 'Aboriginal historiography' by which, his argument suggests, he means the historiographic approaches used by white historians writing about Indigenous Australians. The questions he raises engage with, among other elements, the role oral sources play if the Indigenous side of the story is to be included. Attwood sees the dependence on oral sources as problematic.[18] Attwood's paradigm of historiography, where authentic evidence is in the written archive, effectively erases the white orality that proceeds, informs and shapes that archive.

Telling the Truth builds on a number of articles and book chapters discussing 'Aboriginal' historiography that Attwood has published over the last fifteen years.[19] In a precursor to *Telling the Truth*, the essay "Learning about the Truth: the stolen generations narrative" Attwood critiques the historiographic problems he identifies within what he styles, the "stolen generations narrative."[20] This article critiques the underlying historiography that supports the evidence within the *Bringing Them Home* report and the discussions around the report. Attwood's stated basis for the critique is a need to refocus on the crucial role the present plays "in the constructions of accounts of the past."[21] As Attwood states, "any history is the product of both the past and the present or, more precisely, the fruit of a dialogical relationship between present and past."[22] He argues that despite the political context of attacks on the Stolen Generations, his critique will serve useful cultural and political purposes because the historicity of the "stolen generations narrative" has been obscured.[23]

In "Learning about the Truth," Attwood argues that the narrative of the Stolen Generations is a 'matter of "narrative accrual" or "narrative coalescence"' rather than "a necessary surfacing of a hitherto silenced or submerged history."[24] His fundamental argument is that "the stories that comprise what we today recognize as the stolen generation narrative: the new narrative is *not* simply an old one returned" (his italics).[25] In Attwood's analysis, the master narrative of the Stolen Generations is a new story.[26] Implicit in Attwood's argument is a singular perspective. The 'we' refers to a singular white community. The narrative is new to that community so therefore it is a new narrative. Embedded in this claim is the erasure of the Indigenous communities' experiences and knowledges. According to Attwood there is a clear distinction between the stories and practices of the removals of children and the Stolen Generations narrative, and that in the current context the two sources have become confused.[27] In his estimation this 'confusion' between the individual stories and the narrative leads to an emphasis on the similarities between the stories that have been told over time, thereby hiding the more striking differences between the stories of removal and the narrative.[28] To counter this confusion, Attwood sets out to examine "the articulation and circulation of [the Stolen Generation] narrative and the contemporary discourses that have determined" it.[29]

My argument here is not with the notion that narratives are the result of coalescence or accrual, or that narratives change over time even in terms of Attwood's unusual binary between narratives and history, or with intellectual and disciplinary arguments such as the analysis of practices of historiography. My point of interrogation and analysis is focused on some of the ways in which the terms and premises of Attwood's critical evaluation of the Stolen Generations narrative are examples of embedded whiteness in the analysis and framing of Indigenous campaigns for social justice.

Attwood's argument is a powerful performative act that functions to contain both the voices of Indigenous protest and the achievements of a century of Indigenous agitation against the removal of children. He frames the Stolen Generations as 'Aboriginal' history and so identifies the history as separate from the history of European Australians both in the distant and the recent past, rather than as in part a shared history to be investigated. He aggregates the white audience at the same time as he seeks to disaggregate the Indigenous experience. His selective argument is not so much about the processes of narrative accrual as an argument that frames Indigenous people as reactive rather than active and negates collective experiences of racism and racist policies. In this way his essay reaffirms what Fiona Nicoll calls the "performative assumption of perspective" by claiming the subject position Moreton-Robinson calls the "white know-all."[30] As the 'academic' and objective historian, implicitly positioned as white, Attwood assumes the perspective of a detached and disinterested subject to present and judge representations of the Indigenous people involved in the Stolen Generations campaign as the measure of Indigenous authenticity.

Attwood bases his evaluation of the 'stolen generations narrative' on:

> who and what has been involved in the production of its stories; when and where it has been constructed; the reasons why it has been created; how it has been circulated; the ways in which it has changed over time; and the various outcomes of its telling.[31]

Attwood frames the narrative around the Stolen Generations as 'new,' speaking repeatedly of "the creation of the stolen generations narrative," which he declares occurred in the 1980s.[32] The idea of a moment of creation is central to his argument. In the Australian context, the act of creating or making a new object carries resonances of *terra nullius*, the myth of beginning in an empty place. 'Create' also carries resonances of invention and fiction that are central to the denial of Indigenous accounts of their experiences as histories.

After framing the narrative as new, Attwood claims that for new historical narratives "to emerge and become prominent" requires one or more necessary conditions. These conditions, as defined by Attwood, are that there must be:

- authoritative figures who offer conceptual and moral frameworks that interpret the past in new ways

- and/or a group of vulnerable or embattled people who suffer a range of confusing problems and who are subsequently attracted by new narratives that offer satisfying explanations of and resolutions for their plight and posit a right of entitlement
- and/or a group of ambitious people who aspire to an unprecedented degree of power and status and are therefore drawn to narratives that can legitimize their new position
- and/or political and cultural environments that enable, even demand, that particular narratives reach and be accepted by a large number of people.[33]

Attwood states that he is drawing on Elaine Showalter's work in the construction of these 'necessary' conditions. The source he quotes is a study of hysterical epidemics where Showalter, in a chapter titled "Defining Hysteria," argues that "hysterical epidemics require at least three ingredients: physician-enthusiasts and theorists; unhappy vulnerable patients; and supportive cultural environments."[34] The authoritative figure must "first define name, publicize the disorder, and then attract patients and the community." Showalter argues that in practice "hysteria was 'rendered visible by the medical presence'" that offered "a unified theory of a vague syndrome, providing a clear and coherent, explanation for its many confusing symptoms." The medical practitioner grants legitimacy to the illness and the patients who suffer, and at the same time builds their own social authority. This process is only possible when patients collaborate, that is the patients present the symptoms "as the doctors expect them." This "interactive and evolving process" of a disease begins with social and cultural recruitment, as troubled individuals respond to the prototypes. Once suffering people are confronted with the prototype, they fit their experience within it and come to believe "that the laws of the disorder describe their lives." The supportive social and cultural environment for these hysterical epidemics, in Showalter's analysis, depends on a widespread sense of alarm about social change, where people are looking for external causes and solutions for their fears.

Attwood's linking the testimony of the members of the Stolen Generations to hysteria is not an isolated incident, though he does not state that he is presenting the argument in this frame or acknowledge in the text Showalter's original context. However, hysteria has been used to describe both the Indigenous testimony and the broader non-Indigenous response to that testimony. Conservative critics argued that the testimonies exemplified 'false memory syndrome,' whereas Manne contended that Aboriginal witnesses had become "the object of a 'collective hysteria.'"[35] The framing of problems facing, and actions taken, by Indigenous people as a product of individual pathology or dysfunction rather than the result of or response to systemic white behavior also reflects the broader approach of government policies since the election of the Howard conservative government in the mid 1990s.[36]

Attwood analyses the Stolen Generations narrative, within the conditions he presents, through a selective lens that constructs the formation of the narrative as a hysterical disease or pathology that only exists because it is named. After first establishing the notion that the narrative was created in the 1980s, Atwood places a white historian, Peter Read, in the position of the authoritative figure who offers conceptual and moral frameworks that interpret the past in new ways. Attwood identifies Read as playing the "crucial role in defining and naming and, thereby, creating a historical event — 'the removal; of children.'"[37] Read's work is centralized in isolation as the act of creation even though the archival and oral research that led to his published work is acknowledged. Read, rather than seeing himself as the creator of a narrative, has stated:

> In the 1970s I interviewed a number of Aboriginal people who had been separated, but I listened to them as individuals . . . [and saw their stories] as individual tragedies; it took a long time for the penny to drop.[38]

For Read it was archival research in the files of the Aborigines Welfare Board, in particular the register of the Aboriginal wards of the state that changed his perspective:

> When at length I reached the end of those 700 files, I at last understood that the red herrings of missionary zeal, malnutrition, parental neglect, the best interest of the child and the standards of the day, concealed a violent attack not only on Aboriginal family structure but on the very basis of Aboriginality.[39]

For Attwood, it is Read who is responsible for the construction of "a historical event," the naming of the narrative and "assumption of intent" not the result of the stories that were told by Indigenous people to Read or the archival material that supported their stories or government policies.[40] Read's initial usage of the words "lost children" and then later making the move to using the words 'stolen' children, is presented as if this were exclusively Read's usage and initiative. This claim not only erases the history of changes in Indigenous activists' rhetoric over the twentieth century, it also erases the usage of the word 'stolen' in relation to the forcible removal of Indigenous children. For example, rather than being first used in the 1980s, the word stolen was used within the archival record in discussions of the removal of Indigenous children as early as the mid 1920s. A letter published in an

Adelaide newspaper in 1924 discussing the removal of an Indigenous child argues for the use of stolen in that context.

> Reader: 'I Want my Baby,' Aboriginal Mother's Plaintive Cry—State's Shameful Steal
>
> There is at present in Adelaide a young Aboriginal mother breaking her heart because a heartless Parliamentary Act has enabled the servants of the Chief Protector of Aborigines to figuratively, if not literally, drag a babe out of the arms and from the breast of its mother.
>
> The word 'stolen' may sound a bit far-fetched, but by the time we have heard the story of the heart-broken mother, we are sure the word will not be thought out of place, especially by women who know the instincts of motherhood.[41]

Attwood critiques Read's work and arguments around the Stolen Generations on the basis that Read depends on Aboriginal testimony. Roseanne Kennedy has engaged with Attwood's critique of oral testimony, analyzing an earlier version of "Learning about the Truth" published in the *Financial Review*.[42] Kennedy suggests that the shifts in production reflect the expanded historical reach and significance of the narratives of separation. Drawing on Hayden White, Kennedy argues that the "shift Attwood traces can be described as a shift from chronicle to interpretive narrative." Testimonies produced in collaboration with historians chronicle events and experiences and as such are evidence for historians. Once the historian is no longer part of the process, the "narrative becomes interpretive (with the implications of fiction) rather than evidence." Attwood argues that this interpretive element "gives a false meaning to the past because it obscures or neglects details and events that do not fit the narrative pattern . . . rather than telling what really happened in the past, with all the inconsistencies and particularities of individual experience, the narrator instead produces a predictable moral tale of innocence and culpability." In singling out oral testimony and autobiography in this way, Attwood is denying "the metaphorical discourse of historical discourse itself," in effect arguing that historians write unmediated fact despite his own recognition of the role of the present in the telling of the past.

On the basis of his separation between the act of the historian as writer and the Indigenous witness as writer, Kennedy argues that Attwood undermines the witnesses' position as an interpreter of events and that his essay can be read "allegorically as a story about the declining status of academic history as the guardian of the 'truth' of the past."[43] She argues that the central issue for Attwood is:

> who is producing historical meaning. He claims that autobiographies are not simply recording the effects of practices of separation, but are now "telling the broader, collective history about the past." Witnesses are no longer offering

their testimony as evidence to be interpreted by the historical expert. Rather, they are themselves active producers of historical meaning, which Attwood apparently finds unsettling.[44]

Further, according to Attwood, Read went beyond depending on oral testimony, he effectively created and shaped the testimony through his naming and defining of the Stolen Generations. Read created the framework that "struck a chord among a particular group" and the people who had been removed responded by identifying with Read's framework. To demonstrate this process, Attwood constructs an account of biographies, autobiographies and drama written by or in collaboration with Indigenous people over a forty-year period focused on the experiences of members of the Stolen Generations. This account paints a picture of the members of the Stolen Generations as fulfilling the second condition for establishing a historical narrative: that is that the people who were removed are a group of vulnerable people who suffer a range of confusing problems as individuals, who are attracted by the new narrative that offers explanations of and resolutions for their plight, and provides the basis for a right of entitlement.

To support the framing of Indigenous life stories as the result of, and adaptations to, the Stolen Generations narrative, Attwood argues that Aboriginal oral stories given to non-Aboriginal ethnographers focused on the positive elements within their lives rather than exclusively on the negative effects of oppression.[45] This is the striking difference that Attwood identifies between the stories of removal and the narrative of the Stolen Generation. In his analysis, the mediated stories on the record had a stronger focus on the positive ways in which the Indigenous Australians coped with their oppression. These 'softer' stories are presented in contrast to the harder edged stories of the 1990s written by Indigenous writers with their own access to presses and publication.

Attwood acknowledges that for "generations Aboriginal people have told stories about the removal of children"; he cites the published story of Margaret Tucker's removal in 1917 recalled in the late 1930s.[46] However, as proof of adaptations to Read's authority, he points out that in the versions told by Tucker, her mother and her daughter over decades, though the factual content remains the same, the form of the story varies in terms of the details that are foregrounded by the different individuals at different times.[47]

Further, he states that: "Between the late 1930s and the late 1970s, the removal of children was, as far as we know, neither the subject of many stories told in Aboriginal communities nor central to their historical consciousness." This major claim that for nearly 30 years the subject was not a point of focus is justified on the basis that there is little written documentation in the Euro-Australian controlled archives. Therefore, 'we,' white historians, cannot really know.[48] This claim places the new white narrative in the position of being the sole narrative in relation to the widespread campaigns of removal and institutionalization of Indigenous children.

Attwood's analysis, based on the conditions he adapts from the conditions for a hysterical epidemic, denies any collective experience of removals. He claims a discrete binary between individual experiences and collective accounts of these experiences. Through the terms of the second and third conditions that he defines, Attwood denies meaningful Indigenous participation and contribution to the campaigns that the narrative represents. Overall, within Attwood's argument Indigenous people who were forcibly removed are framed as opportunistic, reactive or as effectively dominated by a form of psychological transference. Further, reflecting an unstated concept of, and demand for, authenticity in relation to Indigenous people, Attwood negates the Aboriginality of the members of the Stolen Generations, or as he would have it, "the children who were removed."[49] They are described as identifying with Aboriginality because being Aboriginal has social value.

The process of narrative accrual and shaping that Attwood presents does not take into account changes in rhetorical strategies over the century or the changing conditions of Indigenous access to publication except in terms of the fourth condition of narrative making, the virtue of white people in desiring to know more about Aboriginal stories.[50] In the Australian context, as Moreton-Robinson and Nicoll have argued, virtue operates as a "usable property" that is claimed by white people in order to dispossess Indigenous Australians of moral rights.[51] Attwood's focus on the desire of white people to hear Indigenous stories as the single critical factor in Indigenous articulations, disempowers Indigenous writers and activists within the scenario placing all power and virtue, as with historians like Read, and with the white audience for the stories. This viewpoint casts Indigenous people as merely taking advantage of the opportunity presented and therefore lacks virtue. Further, as Moreton-Robinson contends, central to the arguments within the history wars presented by writers such as Windschuttle, is a "fixation on protecting the virtue of the white Australian nation."[52] Attwood's framing of the role of white Australians as generous and virtuous in face of Indigenous distortion in response to the narrative effectively reproduces the same fixation.

Apart from erasing Indigenous input into the acts of establishing the social and cultural context, this generalized view of the white response erases the ways in which Indigenous people continue to be forced to negotiate with the wide variety of white agendas and desires in relation to their stories. Attwood presents an account of the situation that suggests that Indigenous people are free to produce and publish their stories because white people want to hear and accept them. Yet in practice, the terms on which Indigenous people can be heard are restricted. There are many instances that demonstrate the restrictions placed on Indigenous people in order to tell their stories. For example, Fiona Nicoll recounts the story of curating an exhibition focused on the life of Nancy De Vries, an Indigenous woman, who had been removed from her family and community, institutionalized and sexually and physically abused as a child whilst in protective care.[53] In the name of protecting all parties involved, nothing could be included in the exhibition that identified the perpetrators of the sexual and physical violence and her "testimony" was "effectively reduced to a series of allegations."[54]

Equally, an examination of the texts by Indigenous writers in the 1990s that Attwood cites as demonstrating the same negative approach, does not support his sweeping claims; rather, like the example of the Aunty Nance Exhibition, they demonstrate a more complex situation. In Attwood's analysis, he lists a number of literary examples that he states represent the process of homogenizing and shaping performed by the narrative created by Read. He includes in his examples *Stolen* (1998) by Jane Harrison and *Box the Pony* (1997) by Leah Purcell in collaboration with Scott Rankin. In this context it is useful to look at these two examples of homogeneity that Attwood describes as prompted and shaped by the process of narrative accrual.

In 1991, Ilbijerri Aboriginal and Torres Strait Islander Theatre Co-operative decided to initiate work on a play about the 'lost children,' as members of the Stolen Generations were known at the time. Jane Harrison, a descendent of the Muruwari people of New South Wales, was commissioned to research and write a play based on the experiences of members of the Koori community in Victoria. The initial title of the project was *The Lost Children* (the title was later changed to *Stolen*). In 1991 there was little knowledge or understanding about the 'lost children' outside the Indigenous communities.[55] At that time Read and others' work on the removal of children was contained within the academy. The period of development of *Stolen* runs parallel with the ongoing campaigns by Indigenous activists to gain recognition and a voice for the generations of Indigenous Australian children taken forcibly from their families. In a sense, the transition of the title from 'lost' to 'stolen' can be suggestive of Attwood's argument that the narrative supporting and surrounding the stories shapes the outcome. However, it also represents a shift in rhetoric that places responsibility with the people who removed the children rather than with the victims of the policies.

There are many different layers within the project of *Stolen* that counter Attwood's conditions. One of Attwood's repeated objections to the narrative is his claim that it collectivizes individual stories.[56] Further because of this collectivizing and homogenizing of the stories around the narrative the removals, in his opinion, assume a central place in Aboriginal collective memory and identity.[57] The 'Lost Children' project, following the policies of Ilbijerri, aimed to give a public voice to the experiences of the local Koori community. The other major aim was to produce a play that reflected the variety of Koori stories, experiences and reactions aimed at countering the representations of Koori people as a "homogenous people who all feel the same way."[58] The script development process for *Stolen* began formally in 1992. Harrison, like the members of the Human Rights and Equal Opportunity Commission's National Enquiry into the Separation of Aboriginal and Torres Strait Islander Children from their Families, heard countless stories from stolen children about abuse, refusal of access to archives and information about their families, the trauma of parents who were told their children were dead and children who were told their families were dead or had abandoned them. The Inquiry dealt with stories on a national level whereas the stories Harrison drew on came from the Victorian community.[59] In *Stolen*, Harrison weaves together the stories of five Aboriginal children removed from their families and institutionalized. On a series of different levels, the narrative traces each child's individual journey and experience of grief and abuse as they struggle to play as children and live their lives.

Ilbijerri presented public workshopped readings of the play over a three-year period from 1993 to 1996. A lack of financial resources and administrative infrastructure made covering the costs of a full production difficult for the company.[60] The company utilized the public readings as a showcase to garner interest in the project. The artistic directors and dramaturges attached to the mainstream white-controlled companies were an important focus of this process. Within the dynamic between Indigenous practitioners and non-Indigenous artistic directors there are general specific practices that limit and contain Indigenous cultural production in an environment where funding and decision-making are primarily in the control of the non-Indigenous community. As I have discussed elsewhere, in "the spirit of solidarity and cultural sensitivity, Indigenous theatre work is often 'hijacked' on behalf of the 'educative' potential for non-Indigenous audiences inherent in the work."[61] To some extent, this process would be difficult to avoid since non-Indigenous critics and producers often assume that the non-Indigenous audience, particularly the white audience, is the primary, often sole, focus of the material. One result is that the non-Indigenous decision makers and critics in effect appropriate the work of Indigenous artists; unaware of the roles the work plays in specific Indigenous communities and by default downgrading other responses. This process has two main results: firstly, the type of work that is produced by non-Indigenous controlled companies is limited to what is perceived as fulfilling this consciousness raising function for the normative white audience; and secondly, discussions and perceptions of the work are limited to the ways in which it fulfills this function.

Despite Attwood's claims that the Stolen Generation narrative received widespread acceptance this was not the case. From the 1980s onwards, even though Stolen Generation's testimonies of removal were published in the 1980s such as the anthology, *The Lost Children* (1989), the stories of separation only became highly visible in Australia in 1997 after the publication of *Bringing Them Home.*[62] As an example, reflecting this lack of awareness, prior to the release of *Bringing Them Home,* the response of the non-Indigenous companies to the play *Stolen* was tepid. *Stolen* was not perceived as an 'Aboriginal' play, but rather as a 'white' play.[63] Many works at the time were described as 'black' or 'white' according to individual Euro-Australian reader's understandings of what was Indigenous Australian in form rather than any reference to the cultural experience and identity of the writer informing and shaping the work. Once the report was released, the media attention it received changed the white Australian theater managements' view of the play. In the context of the aftermath of the *Bringing Them Home Report,* Ilbijerri negotiated with Playbox, a state funded mainstream white controlled company, to co-produce *Stolen* in 1998. Ilbijerri's approach was not to present the production as effectively part of the report. In the first production, directed by Wesley Enoch, at the end of the play each member of the cast stepped out of character and told their own story. Some cast members, like the characters in the play, had tragic stories to tell, others did not. This moment aimed to engage with the reality of these stories and at the same time to contest the tendency to generalize all Indigenous people as having the same experiences. In accord with Ilbijerri's policies, Koori communities were the focus of the regional tour of Victoria that followed the Melbourne season. On the tour, Indigenous Australian people would come up after the show and share their stories with the cast. It was an occasion and a forum for healing.

Box the Pony does not deal with the Stolen Generations. *Box the Pony* is a semi-biographical one-woman show based on Purcell's life as a young Murri woman with her family and community in a small Queensland town. I can only speculate, but I assume that Attwood may have meant another one-woman show that was first presented at the same time as *Box the Pony,* Deborah Cheetham's *White Baptist Abba Fan* (1997) which does focus on the experience of a stolen child.

Cheetham's *White Baptist Abba Fan* draws on her personal experiences. Like many other members of the Stolen Generations, Cheetham had been falsely told that she was an abandoned child, that her "mother didn't want" her. "She put you in a cardboard box and left you in a field."[64] Cheetham's story explores the difficulties of becoming acquainted with her birth mother when she had been raised in a different context and met with her mother for the first time as an adult as "strangers full of prejudices on both sides." In the text, Cheetham does not present her white family as abusive; rather she described the experience as like having a beautiful pair of shoes that are too small. No matter how much you love them, they never quite fit and always rub.[65]

According to Attwood, the stories told in the 1990s had been reshaped to fit a homogenizing narrative. Yet these two examples demonstrate multiple stories in the texts, in the process of production and in the contrast provided by the actors' own stories revealed after performances. Attwood's point about the willingness of Euro-Australians to hear the stories being critical for both shows getting produced and presented to wide audiences is true to some extent. In Attwood's system this constitutes part of "political and cultural environments that enable, even demand, that particular narratives reach and be accepted by a large number of people." However, the white audience, like the white historian, is not neutral and separate from the emotional complexities of the situation or open to accepting any possibility as Attwood suggests. Neither are they singular. Attwood objects to any collective identification on the part of Indigenous victims of removal yet combines all non-Indigenous readers and audiences as a collective with the same agenda with a marked slippage between non-Indigenous and Euro-Australians. The particular narratives that are demanded and accepted are not necessarily those that Attwood implies.

Attwood, from the position of the all-knowing white subject defending the importance of the white historian and his interpretive function, recenters whiteness in relation to Indigenous stories and acts to silence Indigenous stories about white people and whiteness in Australian history. Using the conditions defined by Showalter as necessary for the development of hysterical epidemics, Attwood separates the stories of removal from the individuals involved and their historical context in order to claim that they and their authority are derivative, corrupt and new. He also separates the Stolen Generations narrative from the white Australians who participated in the systemic racism from the abusive and violent to the people who owned or used the Indigenous domestic child labor that the policies of removal provided. The Human Rights Commission called for submissions from people involved in the process from every side. However, the people who benefited from the policies of removal did not come forward and contribute their stories. In the telling of the history of Indigenous/Euro-Australian relations, it is the Indigenous people whose stories are put on display and who must prove their stories are authentic. In the studies of the Stolen Generations, only the Indigenous stories are interrogated. When the history of the Stolen Generations is identified solely as Aboriginal history, then the white stories are left in the dark. They do not need to be brought out and examined or investigated. If the Indigenous stories can be understood solely as the result of a hysterical epidemic, then there is limited value even in examining them.

Performative acts such as Attwood's analysis and reduction of the Stolen Generations narrative contains the Indigenous stories that inform the narrative and frames Indigenous people only as informants. In this type of framing there is an implicit argument that the white stories of enacting violence and abuse do not need to be told. The basis of Attwood's interrogation of the Stolen Generation narrative demonstrates through the questions he does not ask, the ways in which whiteness operates discursively within the arguments on both sides of the history wars, functioning to protect white virtue and frame Indigenous people as reactive and hysterical. Changes in government and policy, such as in 2008, that support performative acts of acknowledgement and reconciliation, continue to operate within these narratives.

NOTES

1. Aileen Moreton-Robinson, "Whiteness, Epistemology and Indigenous Representation," in *Whitening Race: Essays in Social and Cultural Criticism*, ed. Aileen Moreton-Robinson (Canberra: Aboriginal Studies Press, 2004), 75–89.

2. Moreton-Robinson, "Whiteness, Epistemology and Indigenous Representation," 75.

3. Moreton-Robinson, "Whiteness, Epistemology and Indigenous Representation," 85.

4. I would like to thank Aileen Moreton-Robinson, Jodi Gallagher and Fiona Nicoll for their generous feedback and suggestions on drafts of this paper.

5. The provocation for the debates known as the history wars is usually taken as the publication of Keith Windshuttle, "The Myths of Frontier Massacres in Australian History," Parts 1, 2 and 3 *Quadrant October*, 44, nos. 10–12 (November and December, 2000); followed by *The Fabrication of Aboriginal History* (Paddington, NSW: Macleay Press, 2002). See Henry Reynolds and Keith Windshuttles debates such as Reynolds, "From Armband to Blindfold," *Australian Review of Books* (March 2001), 8–9, 26; Bain Attwood, "The Burden of the Past in the Present," in *Reconciliation: Essays on Australian Reconciliation*, ed. Michelle Grattan (Melbourne: Bookman Press, 2000); Robert Manne, *Australian Quarterly Essay: In Denial the Stolen Generations and the Right* (Melbourne: Schwarz Publishing, 2001).

6. Aileen Moreton-Robinson, "Indigenous History Wars and the Virtue of the White Nation," in *Ideas Market*, ed. David Carter (Carlton, VIC: Melbourne University Publishing, 2004), 219–35: 221.

7. Janeen Webb and Andrew Enstice, *Aliens & Savages* (Sydney: Harper Collins, 1998), 61.

8. Statement in the House Of Representatives, Canberra, by the Minister for Territories the Hon Paul Hasluck MP, April 20, 1961; Statement Aug 14, 1963, in Henry P. Schapper, *Aboriginal Advancement to Integration: Conditions and Plans for WA* (Canberra: Australian National University Press, 1970), 56 fn.

9. Anna Heabich, "The Noongar stolen generations" (notes for paper presented to Albany seminar *Impressions—Albany's History and Heritage* April 24, 1997) http://wwwmcc.murdoch.edu.au/ReadingRoom/CRCC/fellows/haebich/stolen.html (accessed April 24, 2001).

10. Human Rights and Equal Opportunity Commission, 'Bringing Them Home: The "Stolen Children" Report' http://www.hreoc.gov.au/social_justice/stolen _children/index.html (accessed April 24, 2001), 1.

11. Bringing Them Home: The 'Stolen Children' Report: 2.

12. Bringing Them Home: The 'Stolen Children' Report: 2.

13. Bringing Them Home: The 'Stolen Children' Report: 2.

14. Manne, *Quarterly Essay*: 5–6.

15. Andrew Bolt, "Stolen Generations: My Melbourne Writers' Festival Speech," *Andrew Bolt Blog* September 5, 2006 <http://blogs.news.com.au/heraldsun/ andrewbolt/> (accessed May 28, 2008).

16. Senator the Hon John Herron, Minister for Aboriginal and Torres Strait Islander Affairs. Quoted in Commonwealth, Senate Legal and Constitutional References Committee, *Healing: A Legacy of Generations* (Senator J. McKiernan Chair), Commonwealth Parliament, 2000, 292.

17. Senator the Hon John Herron, *Healing: A Legacy of Generations,* 292.

18. Bain Attwood, *Telling the Truth about Aboriginal History* (Crows Nest, NSW: Allen & Unwin, 2005), 159.

19. For example Bain Attwood, "Aborigines and Academic Historians: Some Recent Encounters," *Australian Historical Studies* 24, no. 94 (April 1990); Bain Attwood, "The Paradox of Australian Aboriginal History" *Thesis Eleven* 38, no.1 (1994); Bain Attwood, "Making History, Imagining Aborigines and Australia," *Prehistory to Politics; John Mulvaney, the Humanities and the Public Intellectual*, ed. Tim Bonyhady and Tom Griffiths (Carlton, VIC: Melbourne University Press, 1996); Bain Attwood, ed., *In the Age of Mabo: History, Aborigines and Australia* (St. Leonards, NSW: Allen & Unwin, 1996); Bain Attwood, "The Past as Future: Aborigines, Australia and the (Dis)course of History," *Australian humanities Review* Issue 13 (April–June 1996); Bain Attwood and Andrew Markus, "(The) 1967 (Referendum) and All That: Narrative and Myth, Aborigines and Australia," *Australian Historical Studies* 29, no. 111 (Oct. 1998); Bain Attwood, "The Burden of the Past in the Present," *Reconciliation: Essays on Australian Reconciliation*, ed. Michelle Grattan (Melbourne: Bookman Press, 2000).

20. Bain Attwood, "Learning about the Truth: The Stolen Generations Narrative," in *Telling Stories: Indigenous History and Memory in Australia and New Zealand*, ed. Bain Attwood and Fiona Magowan (Crows Nest, NSW: Allen and Unwin, 2001), 183–212.

21. Attwood, 'Learning about the Truth,' 188.

22. Attwood, 'Learning about the Truth,' 188.

23. Attwood, 'Learning about the Truth,' 184.

24. Attwood, 'Learning about the Truth,' 183.

25. Attwood, 'Learning about the Truth,' 188.

26. Attwood, 'Learning about the Truth,' 191–93.

27. Attwood, 'Learning about the Truth,' 188.

28. Attwood, 'Learning about the Truth,' 188.

29. Attwood, 'Learning about the Truth,' 188.

30. Fiona Nicoll, "Reconciliation in and out of Perspective: White Knowing, Seeing, Curating and Being at Home in and against Indigenous Sovereignty," in *Whitening Race: Essays in Social and Cultural Criticism*, ed. Aileen Moreton-Robinson (Canberra: Aboriginal Studies Press, 2004) 17–31.

31. Attwood, 'Learning about the Truth,' 183.

32. Attwood, 'Learning about the Truth,' 185.

33. Attwood, 'Learning about the Truth,' 189.

34. Elaine Showalter, *Hystories: Hysterical Epidemics and Modern Culture* (London: Picador, 1998), 17–19. The following quotes are taken from this discussion

35. Rosanne Kennedy, "Stolen Generations Testimony: Trauma, Historiography, and the Question of 'Truth,'" *Aboriginal History* 25 (2001): 116.

36. Fiona Nicoll, "De-facing *Terra Nullius* and Facing the Public Secret of Indigenous Sovereignty in Australia," *Borderlands eJournal* 1, no. 2 (December 2002). http://www.borderlandsejournal.adelaide.edu.au/vol1no2_2002/nicoll_defacing.html (accessed May 28, 2008); Aileen Moreton-Robinson, *Talkin' Up to the White Woman: Indigenous Women and Feminism* (St. Lucia, QLD, University of Queensland Press, 2000), 13. For further examples see: "Bringing them Home—The Report" *Australian Welfare Systems* http://www.austlii.edu.au/au/special/rsjproject/rsjlibrary/hreoc/stolen/stolen47.html (accessed May 28, 2008).

37. Attwood, 'Learning about the Truth,' 189.

38. Attwood, 'Learning about the Truth,' fn 23, 245.

39. Attwood, 'Learning about the Truth,' fn 23, 245.

40. Attwood, 'Learning about the Truth,' 189.

41. Tom Morton, *Adelaide Sun*, April, 1924.

42. Roseanne Kennedy, "The Affective Work of Stolen Generations Testimony: From the Archives to the Classroom" *Biography* 27, no. 1 (2004). The earlier version of Attwood's 'Learning the Truth' was published in *Financial Review, Friday 15 December 2000, Review, 1–7*.

43. Kennedy, 'Stolen Generations Testimony,' 116.

44. Kennedy, 'Stolen Generations Testimony,' 119.

45. Attwood, 'Learning about the Truth,' 187.

46. Attwood, 'Learning about the Truth,' 184.

47. Attwood, 'Learning about the Truth,' 184–85.

48. Attwood, 'Learning about the Truth,' fn 7, 242.

49. Attwood, 'Learning about the Truth,' 190–91.

50. Attwood, 'Learning about the Truth,' 196–97.

51. Moreton-Robinson, 'Indigenous History Wars and the Virtue of the White Nation,' 219.

52. Moreton-Robinson, 'Indigenous History Wars and the Virtue of the White Nation,' 222.

53. Nicoll, 'Reconciliation in and out of Perspective,' 24.

54. Nicoll, 'Reconciliation in and out of Perspective,' 24.

55. For further discussion of *Stolen* see Maryrose Casey, *Creating Frames: Contemporary Indigenous Theatre* (St. Lucia, QLD: University of Queensland Press, 2004).

56. Attwood, 'Learning about the Truth,' 190.

57. Attwood, 'Learning about the Truth,' 195.

58. Bev Murray, 'A History of the *Stolen*,' unpublished typescript (1998).

59. Anna King Murdoch, 'Seeing Things in Black and White,' *Age*, October 13, 1998, 17(N).

60. Ilbijerri operated with one part time administrator and no ongoing funding.

61. Casey, *Creating Frames*: passim.

62. Roseanne Kennedy, 'The Affective Work of Stolen Generations Testimony,' 48.

63. Personal conversations with artistic directors and dramaturges attached to subsidized theatre companies in Melbourne 1995–1997.

64. *Wimmin's Business* Brochure, Festival of the Dreaming (Sydney, 1997).

65. Deborah Cheetham, 'White Baptist Abba Fan,' *Wimmin's Business* Festival of the Dreaming, Opera House (Sydney, September 27, 1997).

Chapter Three

Picturing Whiteness: The Events of 9/11 in Children's Storybooks

Jo Lampert

Although in some ways 9/11 already seems to have happened a long time ago, it is commonly heralded as having signalled an instant of significant change. It would be difficult to say how the attacks on the World Trade Center directly affected the way anyone in the Western world thinks or performs, and the consideration of whether this change has occurred or not has been publicly contested and indeed scorned by some cultural critics who see this proposition as part of a "media hype."[1] Nonetheless it is common to describe 9/11 as "the day that shook the world."[2] Scholarly books and papers continue to be written that take seriously the claim that 9/11 heralded cultural shifts.[3] It seems useful, then, to look at such literary artefacts as children's books about 9/11 to see what kind of evidence they provide for this popular belief. In this chapter, I examine two picture books about 9/11 for the ways the multicultural discourses common in the West in the years *preceding* 9/11 are now troubled in these texts *about* 9/11.

Significantly, children's picture books were amongst the first texts published about 9/11, presumably because of the speed at which they could be written (with so little text) and the eagerness of the publishing and educational communities to address 9/11 quickly. To date, more than 50 books have been written for children about 9/11. Amongst the first to be published were the two picture books discussed in this article, *On That Day: A Book of Hope for Children*[4] and *There's a Big, Beautiful World Out There!*,[5] which have much in common. This chapter is an attempt to understand the ways in which discourses of multiculturalism have shifted, how the American subject is constructed in these books and how children are constituted as readers of these texts. I am interested, also, in the dialogic relationship between these multicultural discourses prior to 9/11 and new versions of them after 9/11, especially with reference to racial 'tolerance,' global 'harmony,' and diversity, which Cope and Kalantzis identify as having been the key positions of the 1990s.[6] Implicit in this textual analysis is an interest in how political agendas are fulfilled by these texts; for instance, whose purposes do these discourses serve?

On That Day and *There's a Big, Beautiful World Out There!* can be identified as part of a corpus of 9/11 literature that potentially "coerce[s], control[s], colonise[s]."[7] If we understand 9/11 partially as an event about competing cultural and national agendas we may be reminded that texts such as these seemingly simple picture books are formative (in constituting the good American citizen) as well as being reactive to a historical moment.[8] In other words, it is through texts like these, produced in specific historic sites, that knowledges and identities are produced and re-worked, and cultural meanings are negotiated. The two books both overtly and implicitly provide a way for children to perform as good citizens in an increasingly complex, uncertain and problematic community, where unity is privileged over diversity and good must fight against an axis of evil. The post 9/11 imaginary community is produced through books such as these.

THE BOOKS

On That Day: A Book of Hope for Children, and *There's a Big, Beautiful World Out There!* are two of the very first books that were written for children about 9/11. Andrea Patel's *On That Day* was, in fact, written one week after 9/11. It is a book for pre-schoolers that proposes to explain why "bad things" (5) happen (to good people) and what children can do to make the world safe again. Proceeds from the book are donated to September 11th scholarship programs. The author explains her urgency in writing this book: she felt immediately compelled, she says, to explain 9/11 to children. The book is published and promoted by Reading Rainbow, a literacy program that began with Barbara Bush's campaign to bring high quality books to disadvantaged children. In this publication detail it is possible to examine ideological conditions that are inseparable from the ideologies in the text itself. We already learn much about the American subject: goodness is not only within the American child, but within the very act of reading itself.

The second book, Nancy Carlson's *There's a Big, Beautiful World Out There!* was produced with equal haste. One line of text, which sits beneath an illustration of an American flag at half-mast, states that "the book was written on September 12, 2001," the day after 9/11. The use of the flag as a national symbol arouses, as always, a strong emotional passion.[9] These are both quickly produced texts, allowing us a glimpse into some very immediate ways in which the events of 9/11 were represented to children. Consequently these seemingly simple books provide a wealth of material for analysis.

The examination of children's picture books for their role in cultural production is, as children's literary critic Roderick McGillis suggests, both serious and useful, in that "everything our culture produces communicates in ways we would do well to try and understand, and everything our culture produces works upon us in some fashion that we ought to be aware of."[10] Hence these two picture books, whether or not they sold well or remained in print for long, may reveal to us the ways discourses of tolerance and multiculturalism, with all of these terms' understandings of ethnic and cultural differences[11] may or may not have begun to shift very soon after 9/11.

SUMMARIES: *ON THAT DAY* AND *THERE'S A BIG, BEAUTIFUL WORLD OUT THERE!*

Briefly, *On That Day* is directly *about* the events of 9/11, which is explained to its readers in this way: the world is a big, beautiful and mostly peaceful place. One day a terrible thing happened and 'the world' got badly hurt. Many people died and everyone was sad. Sometimes bad things happen for no good reason, and this is very frightening. We can make the world better by helping and sharing. Goodness will always win out over badness. The humanist understanding this book constructs of the world is illustrated by the last page of the book, with the following text:

> When bad things happen, only a small piece of the world breaks, not the whole world. Goodness is in the world, and it's stronger than badness.
> There will always be good things in the world.
> You are one of those good things. (12)

The second book, *There's a Big, Beautiful World Out There!* Does not refer to September 11 at all in any direct way, but declares itself to have been written *because* of 9/11. It presumes that children have been left fearful by the attacks, and reassures the reader that the world is not as frightening as it suddenly seems. The book begins with the line, "There's lots to be scared of, that's for sure" (1) and ends with the positive affirmation that "There's a big, beautiful world out there just waiting for you!" (29) The first half of the book lists the kinds of things that might frighten children: a mean dog, a thunderstorm, roller coasters, stories in the news, public speaking, insects, clowns, shadows and even "people who look different from you" (12). But the text then states that "After a while, hiding under your covers can get pretty boring"(14). Each of those previously named fears is then reexamined for its positive side. For instance, "Maybe that scary dog only looks mean" (15). The happy, smiling, culturally diverse group of children in the final illustration reminds readers that there is much to look forward to.

MULTICULTURALISM AFTER 9/11: HOW THE TERRAIN IS TROUBLED

Since the 1970s, sociocultural concerns including race and class have taken center stage in critical cultural studies,[12] and this indeed has been the case in literary criticism of children's literature as well.[13] This concern with social justice and equity as it relates to ethnicity and race is still visible in the two texts analysed in this paper. However, it has been proposed that after 9/11 a "new normal"[14] has begun to emerge whereby the (contested) multicultural discourses pre 9/11 are continued, but with increasing discomfort after the attacks on the Twin Towers.

This complication of the multicultural agenda has not gone unnoticed by others as well. Anouar Majid for instance, has claimed that the field of postcolonial studies was one of the casualties of 9/11, in which the West was no longer sure how it felt about the fantasized globalized world of multiple and hybrid identities,[15] and Judith Butler suggests that even American public intellectuals have backed off from social justice issues since 9/11.[16] In the following section, the two picture books will be analyzed in how they struggle with these discourses.

AMERICA CONFLATED: HOW WHITE AMERICA BECOMES THE WHOLE WORLD

A complicated competition emerges in the two picture books between the urge to represent an idealized culturally diverse world and a White American desire for centrality and dominance within that world. For example, on the one hand *There's a Big, Beautiful World Out There!* contains numerous illustrations of people of many colors holding hands. *On That Day* illustrates global relationships in a similar way—the globe represented as one big world where we all live happily together in peace. And yet in both texts, the hybridized identities, which were heralded prior to 9/11 seem reduced back to a single identity; that which defines the 'good' American. This is especially true in *On That Day* where a blue-eyed child's face takes up its rightful position in the center of the globe on the last page of the book.

In both books, the central character is almost certainly White, and although in each the protagonist makes friends with the 'Other' (as signified mostly by people of color), the reader is positioned to identify most strongly with the white American, who is conflated not only as the 'normal' American subject, but is equated in each text with goodness, morality and courage. This can be illustrated further by reading two additional images from *There's a Big, Beautiful World Out There!*

In suggesting that there is something 'natural' about the fear we might have other "people who look different" from us, the reader is compelled to look upon a group image of these potentially frightening others. In the discursive choice of the word 'you' the reader is also clearly identified as being *unlike* the sullen, menacing (or at least sad) faces in this illustration. This is, indeed, a mildly threatening mob, with a particular blond girl looking suspiciously to her left, towards a black boy at the center. *There's a Big, Beautiful World Out There!* attempts to address the racial targeting that was inevitable after 9/11, or to explain it to children in a way that both satisfies the liberal-minded multiculturalist who wants children to make friends with those who are 'different,' and also to address the ways they might now scare them. This is a hugely difficult task: to acknowledge fears about race *whilst* embracing racial difference. So, despite the conclusion of *There's a Big, Beautiful World Out There!*, where the readers are told to make friends with all those scary people who are different from them, it is significant that there is not one 'normal' white face in that frightening mob. Instead, these potentially fear-inducing faces include, in the illustration, several black children, some old people, various people with disabilities (deafness, blindness and a child presumably undergoing chemotherapy), and some Asian children, all quite stereotypically drawn. In this book, there are no frightening white Americans. Additionally, even though by the end the reader is told not to fear these people, the inclusion of them in the first place as naturally fear-provoking is privileged and likely to be remembered.

This can be contrasted with the other more positive image; the nicely dressed (albeit in a fifties frock), white girl beaming a positive smile, shining in her individuality in front of an audience. These illustrations appear to embody an American subject. The 'good' American is White, and appropriately center-stage.

The texts illustrate the conflation of America as the center of the entire world, and the further construction of America not only as the physical center but also the *moral* center of the world. *On That Day* explains that the world is "mostly good" and "pretty peaceful" (2).

On one hand, these books can be read as an innocent reassurance of children who may have felt fear that they were *not* safe after 9/11; as such the book could be seen as providing respite from perceived anxiety. And yet, of course, the world is *not* pretty peaceful for much of the world, nor was that the norm for Iraq immediately after 9/11. Hibbs refers to reassuring texts such as these as an "unreflective innocence," and a desire to return to an age which never existed in the first place, and to which we "must and cannot return."[17] The Rousseaudian belief that the world and all those within it are good at the core represents a "false universalism" that is "largely moralistic in intent and communal in character."[18]

FAMILY VALUES: HOW THE
WHITE FAMILY SERVES A COLLECTIVE PURPOSE

In addition, in these two books goodness is strongly linked to images of the White 'average' American family, working inter-textually alongside the many other ways family values have been promoted since 9/11. The illustrations in *On That Day* represent a happy nuclear family consisting of what looks like a father, a mother and two children. Readers are thus presented with a clichéd American sitcom family, an 'imaginary' family life that is closely related to the 'popular knowledge' likely familiar to the young reader of the text.[19] This is the "fantasy landscape of whiteness" as defined by Kumar[20] out in full force since 9/11. There is, of course, a precedent for the reemergence of the strengthened bond between family and national unity in times of trouble. Hall and DuGuy have historicized the political use to which this idealized nuclear family has been put, for instance in Britain during the Thatcher era when it was evoked to counter a sense of fragility in the economy.[21] It is not uncommon to use 'family values' and to imagine the nation *as though it is a family* to restore peoples' confidence in times of uncertainty. For instance, like Hall, in *his* historical linking of nationalistic discourses, West also provides information on the "fervent neonationalism, traditional cultural values" and "free market politics [which] served as the groundwork for the Reagan-Bush era."[22] Said was only one of a number of critics who saw this as intentional after 9/11, accusing George W. Bush of having consciously drawn "God and America into alignment against Islam."[23] In the two picture books, this occurs in many ways. The American child has agency in *On That Day* if s/he helps others/shares/is kind and performs 'good' acts. In other words, the child must negotiate that complicated act of both behaving as an individual, while being part of a greater family. Whilst not entirely a new paradigm, the suggestion that, after 9/11, new ways were required to prove loyalty both to family and to nation has been noted by others as well.[24]

Uncovering the ways utilized to enlist nationalism enables these two texts to be critiqued as potentially powerful examples of how the American subject is reconstituted since 9/11. It can be argued that the nuclear family is a useful image now, in the aftermath of 9/11, to restore a public faith in order and stability.

FINDING 'OUR' PLACE AFTER 9/11: HOW PRONOUNS POSITION THE READER

Judith Butler proposes that 9/11 led to a decentring of America within the international political domain.[25] Having now (in an unprecedented act) been attacked at home, America found itself having to make a choice: to admit themselves as 'global actors' (one of many nations to have enemies declaring war on them) or to reestablish themselves as safe at the center. Butler suggests that Americans lost their First World complacency after 9/11, which might be illustrated in narrative decisions made in these two books through their use of pronouns. Who are 'we' now in uncertain times? Who are 'you'? If it is so that 9/11 pushed America to ask, 'Who is with us? Who is against us?'[26] Narrative points of view thus become important semiotic signifiers in texts such as these. Both books begin by addressing the reader as 'you,' directly speaking to the implied reader and thus positioning him/her as the recipient of the healing narrative. Who, then, is this 'you' the books address?

The use of pronouns shifts throughout the text of *On That Day* in significant ways. No matter whether, from page to page, the point of view is first, second or third-person, the central faces in both of these texts are White. It seems logical, then, that the reader is imagined as White. For example, in *On That Day* an illustration of a White girl is on the page where the text reads, "You can help by sharing" (8). The book is written in second person until the page where the reader is asked the question, "Is there anything we can do to make the world right again?" (6). This 'we' as a reading position is a useful way now to generate a collective identity necessary to clarify an 'us against them' binary, though as the late Susan Sontag noted in her discussion of photography after 9/11, "No 'we' should be taken for granted. . . ."[27] The pronoun changes again two pages later, shifting the reader's position back again from the plural 'we' to the singular 'you': "You can help by sharing." Most crucially, several pages later the text reads, "There will always be good things in the world. You are one of those good things"(12). Thus two things are established in the text: the reader is part of a greater, collective (American) cause, and has an individual responsibility to uphold American goodness. The separation of 'us' from 'them' is implicit (there are indeed very bad things in the world, but you are not one of them). These are the binaries of Self and Other which Appiah claimed, 10 years prior to 9/11, were . . . "the last of the shibboleths of the modernizers that we must learn to live without."[28] It is difficult here not to recall Said's prediction, soon after 9/11, about renewed binaries in Western thought: "We have all succumbed to the promiscuous misuse of language and sense, by which everything we don't like has become terror and what we do is pure and good."[29] It can similarly be argued that the cultural politics of difference proposed by Cornell West, to "trash the monolithic and homogeneous in the name of diversity"[30] may have shifted back to the politics of sameness since 9/11.

Similarly, in *There's a Big, Beautiful World Out There!* it is the female, White child who some people look different from (which we are told might cause her fear), and it is this White child who has a big, beautiful world out there, "just waiting" for her. In this picture book (whose illustrations could come directly from a 1950's reader with their bright colors and nuclear family with a white picket fence and a tidy kitchen) the protagonist (the 'you') is a White girl of about ten, and all the images of people in authority in the book are White as well. This includes her parents, the staff at the depicted summer camp, the newsreader on TV, the faces in the newspaper her parents are reading. If these books construct community, it is clear who belongs to that community. There are people of color in this world (an imagined 'melting pot'), and it's good to befriend them, but they stand to the side, at the margins. This is a rather unevenly weighted distribution of equality, with a distinctly White subject position.[31] Indeed, it is a good example of what Haggis and Schech also call "a nostalgic return to an imagined golden age,"[32] with its sentimental representation of a White American, often Christian, family. This increased attention to apparently Christian values in children's books after 9/11 has not gone unnoticed. Christian titles headed the charts in the *Publishers Weekly* bestsellers lists for both fiction and non-fiction in 2001.[33]

It can be argued that the nuclear family is a useful image now, in the wake of 9/11, to restore public faith in order and stability. The last illustration in *On That Day* shows that same Caucasian, blue-eyed child at the center of the globe. This is the white American 'you' who illustrates a taken-for-granted Whiteness, so natural as to be unspoken, its privilege and power masked in its supposed naturalness. The 'good' family is this white, four-person unit, which "defines normality and fully inhabits it."[34]

THE FACE OF GOOD, THE FACE OF EVIL: HOW DIVERSITY IS REPRESENTED

On That Day and *There's a Big, Beautiful World Out There!* are both concerned with ways to live in the world post 9/11. This section of the paper suggests that these books *invent* the world in particular ways and in doing so privilege particular ideologies. How the world is defined in the texts is related to race and culture in ways that once again are problematic when read against familiar discourses of multiculturalism.

Prior to 9/11, discussions about multiculturalism and inclusion celebrated difference and lauded diversity. In *On That Day* in particular, the world is really America, with one value to uphold, one reading of right and wrong, and a binaried definition of goodness and badness.

In this sense, this book is a recolonization rather than a decolonization.[35] For instance, the repeated image of the globe in the illustrations offers an illusion of concern for the whole world. Under one illustration of the globe, the text says that when "the world got hurt, everyone was sad" (3). In reality, of course, the whole world didn't get hurt (not on that day, at any rate), and we may not even be able to conclude that everyone was sad. In many parts of the world, in fact, more pressing and immediate concerns of poverty and violence most likely took precedent. But this use of the word 'everyone' firmly places the text within an ethnocentric tradition, where America stands for everywhere and Americans for everyone.

The discourse of globalization also takes a step back in these two picture books. Again, despite their slender attempts to present the world as diverse and interconnected, each book is primarily concerned with constructing the unified American subject, which claims superiority. They both glorify the social mission in America that is stated on the second page of *On That Day*, "the world is very big, and really round, and pretty peaceful." The illustration on that page shows a collaged globe in green, blue, black and white. We are told at various times in the text that, "the world . . . got badly hurt" and "everyone was sad" when "the world broke" (3). This reconfiguring of America as the whole world succeeds in constituting America as heroic, and this conflation is an example of "a single culture masquerading as the originating center."[36] This is at odds with the discourse in the same text, which romanticizes a global brotherhood, implied by many of the illustrations of the globe breaking into pieces. The globe is thus a floating signifier, which has shifted in meaning since 9/11. In *On That Day*, the globe has to stand for two competing things at once: the utopic globalized multicultural world, and the redefinition of America as the center of that world. These are complex desires to bring together.[37] It is interesting to note as Voloshinov argued that the inner dialectic quality of a sign (i.e., the double-meaning of the globe in this book) often comes out fully in the open only in times of social crisis.[38] Indeed, post-colonial theorists such as Graham Huggan have suggested ways a reading of maps, globes and atlases tell us about our cultural understandings of history.[39] The pictorial representations, for instance, of America as the center of the world signifies a purposeful and political intent. In *On That Day*, the tragedy of 9/11 is illustrated as having split the entire world into pieces; America's healing would piece it together again. In this way, as Bhabha suggests, we remain safe in the Utopianism of a mythic memory of a unique collective identity.[40] We are all as one.

Similarly, in *There's a Big, Beautiful World Out There!* contradictory ideologies are present with respect to the globe. The book ends with an illustration of the American flag flying at half-mast. Despite the fact that the text says there's a big beautiful world out there, the flag at the end suggests that its not, in fact, out there in the whole world, but is found on America's soil.[41] One might not wish to venture, in fact, out into the rest of the world, which in this text barely exists in the reader's consciousness.

In the images of people in *On That Day* we also see a morphing of diverse cultures into a more homogeneous American body. As Anouar Majid has also noted, after 9/11 America began immediately to play down the distinctive traits of cultures and replaced these appreciations of diversity with the recolonized desire to protect the one, universal identity that mattered once more.[42] There is little hybrid, multicultural identity in *On That Day*. The illustrations mostly show faceless children or children with their backs to the reader.

Though their race is somewhat ambiguous (it could, I suppose, be argued that they aren't necessarily White), it is significant that they are faceless. This is no celebration of difference but an uncertain depiction of a homogeneous group, working together as one. By the end of the book the 'face,' which according to Levinas is the "very cultural means through which the paradigmatically human is established"[43] is blonde and blue-eyed, a representation which, taken up the last frame on the last page, takes priority as the face of goodness.

Although the face in the center is both 'good' and White, the text never comes out and names its position directly. The books discursive strategies, representing Whiteness as an idea, are only implicit. This 'hidden' Whiteness is an interesting phenomenon written about by Haggis and Schech amongst others. In fact, part of the 'goodness' of the post 9/11 White subject lies in its tolerant relationship to those people of color found elsewhere in the text. The acknowledgment of difference, as represented by the multicultural illustrations in the two picture books, is an imperative; it is part of what Haggis and Schech call, "Doing Good and Being White."[44] But by the time readers got to these picture books after 9/11, they already knew the raced nature of the 'face' they had to fear, and they already understood it was not white, but of 'Middle Eastern appearance.' Even one day after 9/11 the authors and readers of these texts would have understood who the enemy was, as Islam was immediately vilified[45] and so this information becomes part of the reader's dialogue with these texts.

This complicated relationship with race continues. The text of *On That Day* renders the Other largely invisible. Although the reader is told that "sometimes bad things happen because people act in mean ways and hurt each other on purpose"(5), these bad people are unnamed. These 'mean' people are central to the plot but absent in specifically explicit cultural identity. It is this Other that has done evil to America, but it has neither name nor voice in the text. In the invisibility, then, of people of Arab background in these books, their presence in fact becomes loud. These bad people behave in ways, the book suggests, that are inexplicable and irrational which is, as Fanon suggests, traditionally the way the Other has been represented.[46] As the villains of the plot are both unnamed and invisible, readers are denied the opportunity to make any critical or political analysis of the way 9/11 is narrated, and America is characterized, as it was in the media, as the victim rather than the aggressor.[47] There is only two ways to read the world as portrayed in these books: as good (as defined in particular ways) or as bad. Only the Western perspective of goodness is on offer, as though it is the only perspective there is. The voices of the Other are silenced, marginalized and decentered in this text.

In an article about multiculturalism after 9/11, Haithe Anderson goes further in this analysis. He suggests that in the prevalent post 9/11 discourse that revives the binaries of good and evil, multiculturalism was set back in crucial ways.[48] The now familiar division of nation and culture into good and evil is in itself, he claims, a rejection of multiculturalism. Anderson states: "The assertion that these adversaries are amoral is a gesture of intolerance, not impartiality, and what it reveals is a clash of cultures and not an embrace of multiculturalism."[49] In addition, he attests that "one cannot embrace a doctrine of plural judgments and advocate for the celebration of cultural differences and then turn around, when the going gets tough and claim that world-wide standards of judgments are in force and should be followed."[50] These tensions that Anderson illustrates are present in both of the children's books. In *On That Day* some of the illustrations are ambiguous and *could* be other than white. For instance in most of the illustrations people are faceless and one figure could even be imagined to be wearing something vaguely ethnic, like a long white scarf.[51] However, within the book, this is the only hint of a multicultural world. Overall, the world of *On That Day* is divided into the good 'you' and the bad 'them,' who "act in mean ways and hurt each other on purpose" (5). Similarly, in Carlson's text, 'we' may make friends with scary people but they are still the ones who make you want to "hide under your covers and never come out" (13). Fear of the Other is given final privilege over tolerance. It is the fear that 'sticks.'

A further critique of whiteness explains how the ideologies in *On That Day* are culturally framed. Dyer affirms that

> White people have power and believe that they think, feel and act like and for all people, unable to see their particularity, cannot take account of other people's; white people create the dominant images of the world and don't quite see that they thus construct their world in their own image; white people set standards of humanity by which they are bound to succeed and others bound to fail.[52]

The moral dictates of *There's a Big, Beautiful World Out There!* are that 'goodness' lies in such things as taking care of your friends, taking care of nature, being kind, laughing and playing. Although these seem like universal guidelines for children, they are still part of a culturally-bound, taken-for-granted discourse, part of a pervasive humanism noted by many[53] and which seem to have enjoyed a revival since 9/11. Despite the superficial attempts these books makes to be inclusive of other cultures, it can be argued that they do not affirm the uniqueness of cultures, and are morally certain about the ways goodness can be enacted. This leaves little room for the reader to interrogate or subvert the strongly stated notions of goodness (the result of particular conscious and rational ways of behaving as listed) and badness (inexplicable). It is not a leap to suggest that *There's a Big Beautiful World Out There!* makes use of a colonial discourse, the objective of which may be claimed to "construe the colonized as a racially degenerate population in order to justify conquest."[54] Within a picture book, however, it couches that desire in the discourse of caring and sharing.

GOOD AND EVIL: HOW RESISTANT
READINGS ARE DISCOURAGED

There are still very few available texts in English about 9/11 which offer an alternative meta-narrative to the good/bad binary.[55] Goodness is constituted discursively in its rationality, and badness in its unquestioned irrationality. Edward Said claimed that the lack of critique available after 9/11 masks the real global power struggles for land, oil and defence that were the issues behind the attacks on the World Trade Center. It is useful and convenient, then, to use 'badness' to explain away a situation of much greater complexity. The enemy is constituted in simplistic forms within both picture books. This text gives us an example of namelessness and invisibility that Cornel West labels a social and psychic erasure.

On the subject of 9/11 one cannot yet safely propose that multiple perspectives are possible, that there might be another side to the story. It seems radical and almost sacrilege to suggest it. But in the absence of such a perspective, in the narrative 'gaps,' there is political and social intent. Toni Morrison explains that it is useful and convenient to see other cultures as savages and uncivilized[56] ('bad' and 'mean' in *On That Day*). Indeed, Morrison might claim that these books fulfil another goal, in allowing the reader to believe that savagery is 'out there' rather than within the reader's own self. *There's a Big, Beautiful World Out There!* strives to convince the child that she/he is one of those 'good' things. Perhaps it was not only children who needed this reassurance. It was a major concern for America as a nation to reestablish itself as the representation of goodness and truth when, in a dramatic way, it became clear that other States and cultures might not think of them as such.

BE KIND TO OTHERS:
HOW DIDACTIC PURPOSES ARE SERVED

In the explanation in *On That Day* that "sometimes bad things happen because people act in mean ways and hurt each other on purpose" (5), the irrational act of the terrorists on 9/11 is contrasted with the counsel offered by this book to its readers. They are instructed to think rationally about what they must do to heal the world. For instance, the illustrations in the book show the globe having broken into pieces, floating around in a chaotic state after 9/11. Children may read this to understand that the world can be returned to its natural order by rational and good (American) children, like themselves, who will help this to happen. Chaos in the world returns to order, nature is restored, and the random savageness of the world is tamed and the chaotic margins, if you like, return to their orderly center. Similarly, in *There's a Big Beautiful World Out There!* readers are instructed to get out from under the blankets, face their fears, and return to the world of sunshine, flowers and happy families. Both books can be understood as expressing a strong desire to return to a more innocent, simple world where goodness is visible and the world order is clear. This desire for a 'happier ending' in children's literature was noticeable, after 9/11 in a range of online discussions about the banning of children's books with 'depressing' endings,[57] and in the many discussions that took place about whether children should be sheltered from the 'truth' or immersed in its harsh realities.[58]

The two picture books discussed above appear to herald, at least in part, a return to more nationally insular agendas illustrating a need to create a more trustworthy and unified, singular American identity (in itself an 'imaginary community' according to Benedict Anderson). They begin to back away from recent multicultural agendas, or at the least find them difficult to represent in clear-cut ways. As such, multiculturalism and diversity now pose problems for the reader who must negotiate the cultural meaning of new race relationships against a myriad of preexisting ideas about culture and race, and a barrage of texts about and since 9/11. Whereas prior to 9/11 multiculturalism had a (not uncontroversial) history as policy "directed at producing a harmonious, tolerant and therefore united national community,"[59] after 9/11 these national qualities, though still desirable, sat less comfortably.

Even seemingly simple picture books such as *On That Day* and *There's a Big, Beautiful World Out There!* highlight the complexity of cultural shifts since 9/11. Exploring the complicated ways multiculturalism and globalization emerge in these books enables a reflection on the political agendas and the construction of new subjectivities in the West; the ways in which these texts have a stake in constituting the reader as a particular kind of subject, who engages in 'helping' the world in very specific ways. And as McGillis reminds us, an examination of this sort enables us to see how children's books contribute to the social and cultural fashioning of readers.[60] These two books were published very soon after 9/11, and may consequently mark the early emergence of new versions of multiculturalism, which we might look at with great interest as new children's books about 9/11 appear.

NOTES

1. Thomas S. Hibbs, "Film and TV in Anxious Times," *The New Atlantis: A Journal of Technology and Science* (Summer 2004), 1.

2. Susan Hawthorne and Bronwyn Winter, "Introduction" in *September 11, 2001: Feminist Perspectives* (Melbourne: Spinifex, 2002), xvii–xxviii.

3. See for example: Judith Butler, *Precarious Life: The Powers of Mourning and Violence* (London: Verso, 2004); Susan Sontag, *Regarding the Pain of Others* (New York: Farrar, Straus and Giroux, 2003).

4. Andrea Patel, *On That Day: A Book of Hope for Children*. (Toronto: Tricycle Press, 2001). All page references will hereafter appear parenthetically and refer to this edition.

5. Nancy Carlson, *There's a Big, Beautiful World Out There!* (New York: Viking, 2002). All references will appear parenthetically and refer to this edition.

6. Bill Cope and Mary Kalantzis, eds., *Reconciliation, Multiculturalism, Identities: Difficult Dialogues, Sensible Solutions* (Altona, Victoria: Common Ground, 2001).

7. Bruce Bawer, "Edward W. Said, Intellectual," *The Hudson Review* 54, no. 4 (Winter 2002): 261.

8. Stuart Hall and Paul Du Gay, eds., *Questions of Cultural Identity* (London: Sage, 1996).

9. See: David Carter, "Multicultural Australia or Australian Multiculturalism?" in *Dispossession, Dreams & Diversity*, ed. David Carter (Frenchs Forest, NSW: Pearson, 2006).

10. Roderick McGillis, "The Delights of Impossibility: No Children, No Books, Only Theory," *Children's Literature Association Quarterly* 23, no. 4 (1999): 203.

11. See: Carter, "Multicultural Australia."

12. Glenn Jordan and Chris Weedon, *Cultural Politics: Class, Gender, Race and the Postmodern World* (Oxford: Blackwell, 1995).

13. See: Joel Taxel, "Multicultural Literature and the Politics of Reaction," *Teachers College Record* 98, no. 3 (1997) http://www.tcrecord.org/content.asp?contentid=9617 (accessed June 8, 2008).

14. Hibbs, "Film and TV," 2.

15. Anouar Majid, "The Failure of Postcolonial Theory After 9/11," *The Chronicle of Higher Education* 49, no. 10 (2002): B11.

16. Butler, *Precarious Life*.

17. Hibbs, "Film and TV," 3.

18. Simon During, "Introduction," in *The Cultural Studies Reader* (New York: Routledge, 1993), 15.

19. Children would be familiar with this four-member family from any number of TV shows, or more recently from Pixar films like *The Incredibles*.

20. Amitava Kumar, "Conditions of Immigration," in *Whiteness: A Critical Reader,* ed. Mike Hill (New York: New York University Press, 1997), 274.

21. Hall and Du Gay, *Questions*.

22. Cornel West, "The New Cultural Politics of Difference," in *The Cultural Studies Reader*, ed. Simon During (New York: Routledge, 1993), 209.

23. Quoted in Bawer, "Edward W. Said," 626.

24. See: Benedict Anderson, *Imaginary Communities: Reflections on the Origins and Spread of Nationalism* (London: Verso, 1983); Marilyn Gardner, "Families see a subtle, lasting shift in values," *Christian Science Monitor* 94, no. 23 (December 6, 2001); Ghassan Hage, *Against Paranoid Nationalism: Searching for Hope in a Shrinking Society* (London: The Merlin Press, 2003).

25. Butler, *Precarious Life*.

26. Butler, *Precarious Life*, 7.

27. Sontag, *Regarding Pain*, 7.

28. Kwame Appiah, "The Postcolonial and the Postmodern," in *The Post-Colonial Studies Reader*, eds. Bill Ashcroft, Gareth Griffiths and Helen Tiffin (New York: Routledge, 1995), 124.

29. Edward Said, "White Price Oslo?" *Al-Ahram On-line* 2002, http://weekly.ahram.org.eg/2002/577/op2.htm (accessed March 20, 2002), 2.

30. West, *New Cultural Politics*, 203.

31. Aileen Moreton-Robinson, "Whiteness Matters: Implications of Talkin' up to the White Woman," *Australian Feminist Studies* 21, no. 50 (July 2006).

32. Jane Haggis and Susan Schech, "Migrancy, Multiculturalism and Whiteness: Recharting Core Identities in Australia," *Communal/Plural: Journal of Transnational & Cross-Cultural Studies* 9, no. 2 (2001): 155.

33. Michael Standaert, *Skipping Towards Armageddon: The Politics and Propaganda of the Left* (New York: Soft Skull Press, 2006).

34. Richard Dyer, *White* (London: Routledge, 1997), 9.

35. See: Frantz Fanon, *Black Skin White Masks* (New York: Grove Press, 1991).

36. Bill Ashcroft, "Constitutive Graphonomy," in *The Post-Colonial Studies Reader*, 196.

37. There are also very few books about 9/11 written by authors of color. The only one I know is the short story 'Alone and All Together' (Geha, 2002) in the collection *Big City Cool*, for young adults. The author (and the protagonist) of this story is Arab.

38. Influenced by Bakhtin and cited in Pam Morris, ed., *The Bakhtin Reader: Selected Writings of Bakhtin, Medvedev, Voloshinov* (Sydney: Edward Arnold, 1997), 55.

39. Graham Huggan, "Decolonizing the Map," in *The Post-Colonial Studies Reader* (New York: Routledge, 1995), 407–12.

40. Homi Bhabha, "Cultural Diversity and Cultural Differences," in *The Post-Colonial Studies Reader* (New York, Routledge, 1995), 206–13.

41. Nearly every children's book about 9/11 contains that now ubiquitous image of the American flag.

42. Majid, "The Failure of Postcolonial Theory," B11.

43. In Butler, *Precarious Life*, 143.

44. Haggis and Schech, "Meaning Well," 388.

45. Mustapha Marrouchi, "Introduction: Colonialism, Islamism, Terrorism," *College Literature* 30, no. 1 (Winter 2003).

46. Fanon, *Black Skin White Masks*.

47. Patricia Keeton, "Reevaluating the 'Old' Cold War: A Dialectical Reading of Two 9/11 Narratives," *Cinema Journal,* 43, no. 4 (Summer 2004).

48. Haithe Anderson, "On the Limits of Liberalism and Multiculturalism," *Teachers College Record* August 12, 2002, http://www.tcrecord.org/Content .asp?ContentID=11009 (accessed August 20, 2002).

49. Anderson, "Limits of Liberalism," 3.

50. Anderson, "Limits of Liberalism," 5.

51. Patel, *On That Day*, 7.

52. Dyer, *White*, 9.

53. Such as Jordan and Weedon, *Cultural Politics*.

54. Benita Parry, "Problems in Current Theories of Colonial Discourses," in *The Post-Colonial Studies Reader,* eds. Bill Ashcroft, Gareth Griffiths and Helen Tiffin (New York: Routledge, 1995), 41.

55. It is tempting here to refer to another picture book about 9/11. In Mordicai Gerstein's *The Man Who Walked Between the Towers* (Brookfield, Connecticut: Roaring Brook Press, 2003), the tightrope image is used explicitly, retelling the story of a heroic man who once, many years ago, achieved the stunt of walking between the

North and the South Towers. The tightrope usefully signifies the fine balance between risk and security that must now be achieved. I imply here that this fine balance must also be negotiated between appreciation of racial diversity, and the national security that racializes good and evil.

56. Toni Morrison, *Playing in the Dark: Whiteness and the Literary Imagination* (Cambridge: Harvard University Press, 1992), 45.

57. Richard Lea, "Burning Children's Books Wasn't Meant to be Nazi," *The Blog: Books* October 5, 2007, http://blogs.guardian.co.uk/books/2007/10/burning _childrens_books_wasnt.html (accessed June 8, 2008).

58. Jo Lampert, "Teach Your Children Well (Or Not): Children, Media and War," in *Terrorism Media Society*, ed., Tomasz Pludowski (Torun, Poland: Cellgium Civitas, 2006).

59. Carter, "Multicultural Australia," 333.

60. McGillis, "Delights of Impossibility," 2.

Chapter Four

Consuming Pathologies: *The Australian* against Indigenous Sovereignties

Fiona Nicoll

The whole notion of separateness puts indigenous Australians into a different category and they are not. They are first Australians, *they are ours* . . . and they deserve to get the treatment that everybody else gets.[1]

—Amanda Vanstone, Minister for Immigration and Indigenous Affairs

We will do whatever is necessary . . . Its one of those occasions in public life where you feel you can strike a decisive blow to make things better for a weak and vulnerable section of the community.[2]

—John Howard, Prime Minister of Australia

What context is given to these conversations about us? Who even understands this process of colonialism, who wants to speak its truth, and who wants to own it? The line, the continuing song line of colonialism is now sung up and enlarged as the song for globalization . . . all humanity is diminished while we sit aside, failing to act, watching, and blaming the 'other,' instead of seeing and interrogating the role of the white privileged self in this 'other' Aboriginal story.[3]

—Irene Watson, 2007

Drawing on Aileen Moreton-Robinson's account of the "possessive investment in patriarchal white sovereignty" this chapter will examine how *The Australian* newspaper both fosters and reproduces white racialized understandings of the material, spiritual, cultural, political and economic property of Indigenous people as 'ours.'[4] I will use a close reading of several related storylines to argue that it effectively engage readers' possessive investments against Indigenous sovereignty claims by staging Indigenous Australia as a theater of pathology with specific roles allocated to Indigenous and non-Indigenous men and women as journalists, officials, victims and criminals.

I have chosen to focus on news stories published in hard-copy versions of *The Australian* between 2001 and 2007 for several reasons. Firstly, as the national broadsheet, it self-consciously constructs a "public idiom"[5] as the eyes, ears and voice of the nation and as the mobilizer of its collective conscience. Secondly, it provides an example of how newspapers are themselves changing in response to shifts occurring in other areas of media. Aspects of the representations to be analyzed in detail below can be related to the influence of 'reality' genres in television and popular culture more generally and are facilitated by distinctive features of the hardcopy format including: the use of photographs and cartoons, the juxtaposition of different stories on a single page and the hierarchical ordering of stories, from the all-important front-page through to the national and international news, features, and opinion and sports pages. Thirdly, the publication's aggressive promotion to young people on university campuses[6] indicates an ambition to convert a new generation to the convenient availability, portability and disposability that newspapers offer. These factors are perhaps reflected in increases in the publication's circulation[7] and suggest considerable influence on non-Indigenous readers' perceptions of Indigenous Australians, with whom most do not have everyday relationships.

Indigenous Australia clearly provides marketable content for *The Australian*. This is evident in the regularity with which it takes up valuable front-page space and forms the subject of the newspaper's opinion columns, features and editorials. Stories are often complemented by large, color photographs such as that taken of a young man sniffing petrol in the central Australian community of Mutitjulu while a coronial Inquest was being held into the deaths of three other sniffers to illustrate a feature report by Stuart Rintoul.[8] These images evoke familiarly ambivalent feelings of disgust and fascination in audiences accustomed to reality genres across a range of low and high-brow platforms from free-to-air television to highly awarded novels. And their prominence is related to a specific challenge faced by *The Australian*: to reconcile a claim to provide a responsible forum for debates of national importance with the need to attract new readers in a popular cultural context where there is an apparently insatiable appetite for extreme representations of criminal, abject and excessive behaviors that reality television and celebrity gossip outlets serve up daily. The point of what follows is not simply to demonstrate that Indigenous Australians have been misrepresented in *The Australian* but, rather, to analyze storylines run over several years as the basis on which to describe and understand a "way of seeing"[9] Indigenous Australia that is embedded in colonial power relations established from the

18th century and which remains naturalized in everyday life. I will argue that *The Australian*'s way of seeing not only interpellates[10] non-Indigenous Australians in our capacities as journalists, academics, politicians, lawyers and concerned citizens but also as subjects with what George Lipsitz describes as a "possessive investment in whiteness."[11]

To understand the ideological work performed by *The Australian* a framework of analysis and interpretation is required to which the vast literature on 'racism in the media'[12] is less well suited than critical theories of whiteness.[13] For *The Australian* and its journalists are engaged not so much in a racist campaign to demonize Indigenous Australians as they are in the everyday reproduction of commonsense understandings of the nation as a "white possession."[14] Such possessive understandings are required to sustain Australia's persistence as a 'white state' characterized by David Theo Goldberg as having "the design or effects of which are to (re)produce, manage, and sustain overall the conditions and structures across all dimensions of social, political, economic, legal and cultural life of the relative power, privilege, and properties of whites."[15] With the discrediting of 'scientific' theories of racial difference which shaped the governance of many nation-states in the 19th to late 20th centuries and with the unprecedented global flows of migration through processes of economic globalization, the claim that Australia is a white state may seem anachronistic or perverse. This research follows Goldberg and others who seek to understand the paradoxical ways in which "White privilege reigns whether the social conditions it signifies are taken to be 'non-white states' or (in some idealized, normative sense) *raceless* states."[16] In spite of disparities between white, Indigenous and other Australians racialized as non-white across social indicators such as employment, incarceration, mortality, education and housing, politicians, journalists, academics and other public representatives have consistently sought to convey an impression in both domestic and international contexts that, notwithstanding its constitution on racially discriminatory grounds in 1901, contemporary Australian society is essentially 'raceless.'

This has had at least two important implications for the way whiteness is publicly discussed in media forums like *The Australian*. The first is that the situation of Indigenous Australians has been increasingly disarticulated from questions about the role of whiteness and race in Australian history and contemporary society. This means that public criticism of Indigenous people and their rights claims are almost invariably framed in terms of 'cultural dysfunction' rather than of racial inferiority. But, in spite of carefully adhering to racially neutral speech codes, I'd suggest that media corporations' use of graphic images of individuals visibly marked as Indigenous in contexts of abject poverty and violence in newspapers and current affairs television programs evokes and perpetuates biologically essentialist discourses of racism. The second, related, effect of the official quarantining of questions of race and whiteness is that the category of 'non-Indigenous' is mobilized to 'recruit' non-white and non-Indigenous subjects into colonizing understandings of and orientations towards Indigenous people with, and to whom, they might otherwise identify and lend political support.

Within a nominally raceless state, 'non-Indigenous' functions as an indefinitely expansive category even as it is predominantly wielded by and in the interests of white Australians from Anglo-Celtic backgrounds. Contemporary expressions of whiteness are more likely to take the form of valuing the cultural inheritance of the Irish or the political and legal institutions bequeathed by Britain[17] than the violent protests against Australians of middle-Eastern appearance in the almost exclusively white enclave like Sutherland Shire in Sydney, which captured world media attention in 2004.[18] While writers such as Karen Brodkin[19] and Noel Ignatieff[20] have provided accounts of the process of 'whitening' of Jews, and Greek Italian and Irish migrants to America, Australian theorists such as George Vassiliocopoulos and Toula Nicolopoulos,[21] Ghassan Hage,[22] Jon Stratton[23] and Suvendrini Perera[24] have disaggregated the category 'non-Indigenous' to consider the different ways in which non-Anglo-Celtic and non-white migrants are positioned both in relation to Indigenous Australians and in relation to the dominant Anglo-Celtic norm. And research on recent migrants by Jane Haggis and Susanne Schech found that, although whiteness "is constantly produced in specific historical, institutional and political contexts," it is experienced as "taken-for-granted, invisible, primordial or [an] essential set of 'core Australian values.'"[25] Examples abound in everyday media news discourse, with *The Australian* informing us the typical skilled migrant is a 31-year-old accountant from Britain,[26] while the *Courier Mail* cites "failure to integrate" as a reason for a reduction in humanitarian visas for African refugees.[27] The discursive effect of the ex-nomination of 'white' in favor of 'non-Indigenous' in public forums like *The Australian* is that non-white, Anglo-Celtic, and white non-Anglo-Celtic subjects are ascribed with a shared orientation toward the nation and the position of Indigenous Australians. Thus, readers of *The Australian* are not only addressed as always already non-Indigenous but actively encouraged to identify with a set of understandings of Indigenous people shaped by historical and contemporary forms and processes of whiteness which, in turn, perpetuates a hostile orientation toward their rights claims.

In 2003, in a chapter aptly titled 'I Still Call Australia Home,' Moreton-Robinson coined the term 'post-colonising' to indicate the necessarily incomplete project of post-colonialism in Australia:

Indigenous and non-Indigenous peoples are situated in relation to (post) colonisation in radically different ways—ways that cannot be made into sameness. There may well be spaces in Australia that could be described as postcolonial but these are not spaces inhabited by Indigenous people. It may be more useful, therefore, to conceptualise the current condition not as postcolonial but as postcolonising with the association of ongoing process, which that implies.[28]

This argument highlights the paradoxical ways in which ongoing processes of colonialism against Indigenous people are sometimes conveyed in the very confidence with which public commentators announce Australia's arrival as a 'postcolonial' nation. In her subsequent critique of the High Court's Yorta Yorta decision in 2001, Moreton-Robinson identifies a major obstacle in the path of achieving a nation in which Indigenous people are able to enjoy postcoloniality. She argues that the capacity of the legal system to recognize native title claimants' grounds of rights to their country is limited by a possessive investment in "patriarchal white sovereignty" which she defines as ". . . a regime of power that derives from the illegal act of possession and is most acutely manifested in the form of the Crown and the judiciary [denying and refusing] what it does not own—the sovereignty of the Indigenous other."[29] This not only highlights the mutually constitutive relationships between race and whiteness; it also provides the basis for a reading of media texts which register the differentiated ground of subject formation, agency and investment in places where fundamental questions of sovereignty and belonging are unresolved.

To argue that Australian media representations and institutions are shaped by a "possessive investment in patriarchal white sovereignty," is *not* to argue that Indigenous subjects are not active producers and consumers of every kind of media, nor is it to suggest that in this engagement they are always or necessarily victims rather than the empowered users of it. Rather it is to emphasize the "role that Indigenous sovereignty plays in shaping the body politic through its relationship to patriarchal white sovereignty."[30] Identifying Indigenous sovereignty as a site of resistance to patriarchal white sovereignty as a key ideological matrix of social order and cultural production in Australia is necessary if we wish to move beyond quests for 'race-blind' media representations[31] and the critique of critiques of racism in the media[32] to expose 'mainstream,' 'community' and 'alternative' news publications to a new kind of scrutiny. It enables us to explain the broader processes, which can make media representations dysfunctional for Indigenous people[33] *at the same time* as they function effectively to support and perpetuate the collective interests of non-Indigenous people.

Some precedents for this research exist. For example, the unresolved matter of Indigenous sovereignty informs Jon Stratton's account of the radically disparate media coverage of the survival ordeals of white Tasmanian miners and Torres Strait Islanders in relation to historical and contemporary configurations of the nation's racialized political, geographical and psychic borders.[34] And Steve Mickler's research[35] on the media construction of an 'Aboriginal crime wave' in Perth's media in the 1990s concluded that the challenge for Australian political and media institutions was not so much media racism as the need to recognize Indigenous sovereignty as *ordinary*. The contribution of the following study is to examine how *The Australian*'s construction of Indigenous pathology as extraordinary (rather than ordinary in a context of historical dispossession and subsequent intergenerational poverty) works against representations that would acknowledge the ordinariness of Indigenous sovereignty.

Before proceeding further, *The Australian*'s coverage of Indigenous Australian affairs should be linked to a more general shift toward social conservatism and neoliberal economic reform during the Howard government's period in office. It is in this political and cultural context that the national and international activism of the Aboriginal and Torres Strait Islander Commission (ATSIC), established in 1990 to represent Indigenous people on a regional basis and to inform national Indigenous policy,[36] the High Court's recognition of native title in the Mabo (1992) and Wik (1996) decisions as well as calls for a national apology to members of the 'stolen generations' emerged as 'problems' for mainstream political institutions and as 'issues' for mainstream media institutions. To distinguish his vision for the reformation of Indigenous Australians and their communities, the Prime Minister, John Howard, consistently characterized his 'practical' approach to reconciliation against that of his predecessors which he dismisses as 'symbolic.' A point of contrast is his predecessor, Paul Keating who, in his famous 'Redfern Speech' in 1992, the Year of Indigenous Peoples, clearly linked social disadvantage to the inequalities that Indigenous Australians had endured since invasion.

In 2007, after a decade of Howard's government, the dominant political interpretation of Indigenous disadvantage could not be more different. Negative social indicators were being interpreted as the product of a dysfunctional attachment to an outdated collective rights agenda preventing Indigenous people from exercising the freedoms and exploiting the opportunities available to them as individuals and subjects of 'modern' nuclear rather than 'traditional' and extended families. At stake in this shift[37] are fundamental questions about legitimacy and governance (who should hold social power and in respect to which domains?) and property (whose claims to it count? who counts as belonging to the nation? Who can enjoy the property of citizenship without question or qualification?) *The Australian* newspaper's translation of this political shift, into the discourse of news, was achieved through the construction of Indigenous Australia as a theater[38] of pathology. Within this theater, I argue, Indigenous men were cast as unfit to govern themselves[39] and their domains while Indigenous women and children were constructed as their abused property with non-Indigenous politicians, journalists and professionals constructed as virtuous subjects capable of solving their problems.[40]

The Australian clearly placed its support behind the Howard government's extension of a vision of economic progress based on private property and enterprise underpinned by the social values of the patriarchal nuclear family to encompass the situation of the minority of Indigenous Australians who live in remote communities in public housing which governments are increasingly reluctant to fund, maintain or replace. This support is apparent in the following, randomly selected, list of headlines over the past few years: "Land Is Not Enough"; [41] "The Third World Housing that Shames our Nation"; [42] "Land Rich, Dirt Poor";[43] "Land profits 'a solution to black poverty'" and "Chance of a Home Instead of a Shed."[44] An editorial titled "Homes of Their Own: The terms of the debate on indigenous issues are changing"[45] dismissed collectively based regimes of land ownership on the basis that "transferable property rights are integral to development" and warned people in remote communities "to adapt their culture to a modern capitalist society, or risk becoming museum exhibits."

The frequent use of tropes of domesticity and domestication illustrates how intimately a sense of Australian-ness is entangled with a possessive relationship to Indigenous people. This is perhaps most obvious in the public language used to refer to Indigenous people and their affairs. Thus, the Minister for Health, Tony Abbott, urged remote Aboriginal Communities to accept greater responsibility in the fight against petrol-sniffing by describing: "Aboriginal people as '*an asset to be cherished.*'"[46] The contingent of non-Indigenous police and health workers sent by the Federal government into Northern Territory Indigenous communities in June 2007, on the pretext of protecting children from sexual abuse, overriding existing authorities and local service providers, underscores the coercive paternalism of this discourse of domesticity. The military style of this intervention and the government's declaration of a 'state of emergency' seemed designed to send a strong message to international bodies such as the United Nations and Oxfam which have agitated for social justice as well as health improvements that Indigenous issues were unequivocally the 'domestic' business of the Australian nation.[47]

An understanding of Indigenous people as domestic rather than sovereign subjects with legitimate claims to self-determination and political representation has been evident for some time in *The Australian*'s reportage on the Aboriginal and Torres Strait Islander Commission. A front page story on ATSIC's first national policy conference published in 2002 was illustrated with photos of Geoff Clark, the commission's head, and Professor Marcia Langton under the headlines: "Black Graft Endemic, ATSIC told." While these words and images clearly suggested a terminal failure of Indigenous governance, the story actually referred to Langton's concern that much dedicated Aboriginal funding never reached its destination but was instead being taken out of communities via transient *non-Indigenous staff*.[48] Of all the threats to John Howard's preferred vision of a nation that is relaxed and comfortable about its past, present and future, Geoff Clark's election as ATSIC chairman in 1999 arguably loomed largest. A long term rights activist and member of the Aboriginal Provisional Government, Clark kept the unresolved issues of Indigenous sovereignty and a treaty alive both nationally and internationally while 'history wars' declared by conservative intellectuals and journalists determined to stem what they perceived as a rising tide of 'political correctness,' promoted Keith Windshuttle's book, *The Fabrication of Aboriginal History*,[49] a denial of organized Indigenous resistance to invasion in the State of Tasmania.

On April 16, 2004, *The Australian*'s front-page announced the government's decision to dismantle ATSIC and to 'mainstream' Indigenous services with the assistance of an Advisory group to be selected by the Minister for Indigenous Affairs, Amanda Vanstone. Under the headline: "Indigenous representation 'a failed experiment': Howard buries ATSIC" were pictures of the suspended Clark and acting Chief Lionel Quartermaine. An entire page four spread was also devoted to the story. This included a timeline charting the rise and fall of ATSIC and significant milestones along the way; photographs of and statements by past leaders; a huge photograph of deputy ATSIC Chair, "Sugar" Ray Robinson (the subject of corruption allegations) as well as photographs and commentary on the composition of the prospective Advisory group (now the National Indigenous Council). The overwhelmingly negative responses to the proposed Advisory group by past and current Indigenous leaders were also published along with Clark's parting shot: "We will keep fighting. We will fight by whichever means necessary to get [ATSIC] back."[50]

The following day, in the face of Clark's defiance, Vanstone strenuously asserted the possessive prerogative of whiteness: "They are first Australians, *they are ours* . . . and they deserve to get the treatment that everybody else gets."[51] Her response clearly precluded any initiatives to make ATSIC a more effective and representative body. The persistence of an elected Indigenous voice would only create a stronger base of resistance to the assimilationist agenda encapsulated in Vanstone's possessive claim: "they are ours." With knowledge of the appalling treatment given to asylum seekers in a context where Vanstone was Minister for Immigration *and* Indigenous affairs, her promise to give Indigenous people the "treatment that everybody else gets" carried distinctly sinister overtones.

However the important question raised here is: how was the dismantling of ATSIC able to be presented in *The Australian* as the inevitable finale of a failed experiment in Aboriginal self-determination rather than as an outrageous attack on Indigenous rights? Part of the answer to this question lies in the publication of allegations printed in *The Australian*'s competition, the Fairfax publications, the *Age* and the *Sydney Morning Herald* in 2001 that Clark had sexually assaulted non-Indigenous and Indigenous women in the 1970s and 1980s. In spite of *The Australian*'s self-appointed role as agenda-setter on Indigenous issues, the 'scoop' belonged to a Fairfax journalist, Andrew Rule, whose story won the 2001 Gold Walkley Award for journalism.[52] The extent to which the breaking of this story enabled a broadly bipartisan opposition to Indigenous political representation to be formulated can be appreciated with reference to former Labor Party leader, Mark Latham's, support for the abolition of ATSIC on the basis of Clark's alleged misbehavior: "The current model has not delivered sufficient gains to Indigenous communities. It's been very much damaged by Geoff Clark."[53] Latham's conflation of a model of self-governance with the behavior of an individual office bearer is symptomatic of the way in which Indigenous rights issues were managed during the Howard era.

In June of the year that the allegations against Clark were publicized, *The Australian*'s 'Weekend Inquirer' announced a 'landmark series' of Opinion pieces titled "What Matters Most" promising to "open the nation's eyes to the harsh reality of Aboriginal life"[54] with articles by Paul Toohey who went on to win the 2002 Magazine Feature Writing Award for his piece "Highly Inflammable" an article on petrol sniffing in central Australia. The final of the *Weekend Inquirer* articles included pictures of the two previous articles with the following anchoring text: "Provoking: How *Inquirer* brought the debate on Aboriginal Australia to the fore." At the same time, *The Australian*'s weekly 'Media' lift out section featured a cover story by Stuart Rintoul asking whether "Fairfax press [was] right to print allegations that Geoff Clark raped four women?" This was answered affirmatively in an interview with *Australian* editor Michael Stutchbury who said "definitely I would have published . . . one, it's a matter of public interest. The media has a right and a duty to investigate and report on matters such as this, two it's a cracking good story."[55] Here the broadsheet explicitly stakes a claim to representing the nation's interests while simultaneously constructing Indigenous Australia as a theater in which compelling narratives unfold, replete with its heroes and villains and victories and defeats.

The Australian's coverage of the allegations against Clark and of violence in Indigenous communities more generally highlights another feature of the paper's theatrical construction of Indigenous Australia: the implicit choices it seems to force between readers' feminist and anti-racist allegiances.[56] The interplay between silence and speech in media reports of violence in Indigenous communities thus deserves closer examination. Rule's story was praised in the Walkley Awards for "bringing about a *frank examination* of hidden violence in indigenous communities" while Paul Toohey was congratulated for having "*laid bare* the levels of violence against women in Northern Territory Aboriginal communities" in his *Weekend Inquirer* feature "Sticks and Stones: With White law Impotent and Tribal Law Convenient, Too Many Aboriginal Men Rape with Impunity. Now Paul Toohey Reports, Some Black Women are Speaking Out."[57] A year after Rule's scoop, the *Sydney Morning Herald*'s 'Spectrum' magazine promised to investigate "*the silence* surrounding Geoff Clarke and those rape allegations."[58] And, five years later, Northern Territory Prosecutor, Nannette Rogers, was being lauded in *The Australian* for having the courage to "*expose*" violence in Aboriginal communities.[59] Most recently the newspaper continued its crusade to "open the nation's eyes to the harsh reality of Aboriginal life," with the following headings and subheadings about a report on child abuse in remote Aboriginal communities "Report not for the faint-hearted, Nation's child sex shame uncovered" and "Aboriginal abuse 'should shock all.'" This is notwithstanding the following quotation by Patricia Anderson, one of the report's co-authors: "We know it all. We know what needs to be done. There's no reason [for the situation] except lack of political will."[60]

Vindicating Michel Foucault's critique of the repression hypothesis,[61] *The Australian*'s continually repeated promises to break the silence on domestic violence and sexual abuse fly in the face of the sheer volume of academic scholarship[62] and journalism—especially in the pages of *The Australian*— dealing with dysfunction in remote Aboriginal communities. This type of reportage not only makes dysfunction and Aboriginal masculinity seem inextricable; it also has the ideological effect of *extricating* non-Indigenous Australian men from violence against women both past and present. The publication of two different photographs of journalist, Nicholas Rothwell, on *both pages* of a recent story about the release of the report into child abuse in remote communities discussed above suggests that there is a particularly heroic ethos attached to journalists reporting on Indigenous issues. This can also be observed in the enthusiasm with which an editorial in *The Australian* editorial defended Paul Toohey's unauthorized entry to the Northern Territory Community of Wadeye in 2002 to cover a funeral. Following the refusal of a permit to a different journalist from *The Australian* and taking aim at all Aboriginal communities which insist on seeing copy prior to publication, the editorial raged threateningly: "This is completely unacceptable. The job of newspapers is to report fearlessly in the public interest. The use of the permit system to block the public gaze from the disastrous direction of Aboriginal communities can no longer be tolerated."[63] What remains unsaid in this high-minded defense of press freedom is that *The Australian* was *selectively* excluded from covering a story in a community that *allowed* access both to The Australian Broadcasting Corporation and one of *The Australian*'s competition broadsheets, the Melbourne based *Age*.

These examples highlight *The Australian*'s role in 'Aboriginalizing' the worst social pathologies by condemning as 'politically correct' any analyses which linked them to past experiences of dispossession, child removal and unequal or stolen wages.[64] Its racialized and gendered constructions of the national interest not only make white male journalists who venture into remote communities to bring the nation 'the awful truth' about Aboriginal men seem to be constitutionally incapable of violence against women of any race. They also serve to legitimate government violence against organizations and institutions developed by previous governments in conjunction with Indigenous stakeholders. Thus John Howard rationalized his military style intervention to protect children from sexual abuse in Indigenous communities as "strik[ing] a decisive blow to make things better for a weak and vulnerable section of the community."[65] Moreover, as we will see, the support for key aspects of the government's practical reconciliation program[66] from a prominent Indigenous spokesman enabled *The Australian* to maintain the fiction of a raceless society even as it presented Indigenous male violence in particular as both systemic and spectacular.

The Australian's revelations about violence within Indigenous communities were coupled with a failure to address the systemic and excessive character of violence against Indigenous people both past and present. The spectacle of Aboriginal dysfunction and promotion of the solutions being developed to 'fix' it has sometimes quite literally overshadowed news about violence against Indigenous people where non-Indigenous men or women are the perpetrators. Thus, it was shortly after revelations of racist abuse in The Australian Defence Forces following a leaked photograph of Indigenous recruits sitting in front of other soldiers with white pillowcases over their heads in the style of the Klu Klux Klan, that *The Australian* featured a report on joint projects between Indigenous communities and the private sector designed to "get

Indigenous Australians away from welfare dependency" by participating in the "real economy." Such initiatives were strongly backed by the Howard government as exemplifying 'practical reconciliation' and the article ended with a quote from retail giant, Woolworths' chief executive officer Robert Corbett, one of the partners in an initiative with the Fred Hollows Foundation and the Jawoyn Association: "The Aboriginal communities are absolutely superb in the way they want to take pride in their own future and are working to control the negatives in their societies . . . if we can help in that process, well then Woolworths welcomes the opportunity to be able to do so."[67] In retrospect, the lack of journalistic attention to Woolworth's own interests in the economic situation of remote Indigenous communities is striking. When the quarantining of welfare payments of Indigenous residents in remote NT communities was implemented, Woolworths organized direct distribution of its vouchers for groceries and other 'essential' items through Centrelink (Australia's federal welfare service).[68]

In spite of the fact that neither of the examples of corporate and local community partnerships reported in the above issue of *The Australian* were in Cape York, or even in the State of Queensland, this story was illustrated by a large photograph (by David Sproule) under the headline: "Hope in land of dreams" of Noel Pearson. The lawyer, public intellectual and head of the Cape York Institute as well as the winner of *The Australian*'s 2004 'Australian of the Year' competition and regular columnist, is shown sitting in front of a fire apparently waiting for his billy to boil anchored by the text: "On the right track: Pearson heads an educational facility that aims to get indigenous Australians off welfare dependency."[69]

On page four of the same issue, a narrow column continuing previous reports on racism against Indigenous army recruits in Townsville was overwhelmed by a picture of the interior of an overcrowded house in Arnhem Land. The following day, on Saturday, the *Weekend Australian Magazine* published its feature story about Noel Pearson (with more photos by David Sproule) titled "Out on a Limb" discussing the leader's vision and philosophy that "Any advancement program for Indigenous Australians cannot be based on a cultural relativism that denies the obvious fact that indigenous Australians must fully engage with the English language, the European social and political institutions, science, modern economic behavior, national and global economic integration and geographic mobility."[70] Photographed cooking over an open fire and informally attired in t-shirt, Moleskins and Blundstones, Pearson explained his controversial analysis of problems in Indigenous communities as symptoms of a collectively addicted people in denial and all too willing to project responsibility onto historical dispossession and racism.

A clear pattern is discernible, with *The Australian* presenting appalling conditions and pathology in remote Indigenous communities in different parts of Australia—on one hand—and the promotion of Noel Pearson as the hero—on the other hand—*regardless of his connection or lack thereof to the particular community in question.*[71] The extent of *The Australian*'s active promotion of Pearson's solutions to Indigenous disadvantage can be gauged by disparaging comments about a report on child abuse by journalist Nicolas Rothwell on the basis of its failure (or refusal) to reiterate "The agenda of personal responsibility sketched out by Noel Pearson of Cape York and editorially supported by this newspaper."[72] What is concerning about this and other presentations of Pearson as the man with the answers for Indigenous Australia is the lack of articulation between abstractly satisfying solutions—such as "practical reconciliation," "corporate partnerships" or "breaking cycles of addiction, violence and welfare"—and the specifically *political* dimensions of the concrete challenges faced by particular communities in Australia including rights to native title or cultural heritage protection for example.[73] While ATSIC was an attempt to represent the diverse range of views across Indigenous communities all over the country, after its abolition the government-appointed National Indigenous Council (NIC) was given the task of developing and defending one-size-fits-all solutions to a range of problems from school attendance and domestic violence to substance abuse and low self-esteem.

While the reaching of an 'accord' in Canberra in October 2005 between 'the new guard' of Indigenous leadership represented by Pearson and Pat Dodson (sometimes referred to as the 'father' of the rights-based reconciliation movement) and his brother Mick Dodson (former Human Rights and Equal Opportunity Commission head and co-author of the *Bringing Them Home* report on the removal of Aboriginal and Torres Strait Islander children from their families) who was editorially relegated to being an "*iconic* figure in the rights based movement for Aboriginal progress"[74] was given the front page treatment by *The Australian*,[75] stories concerning ongoing issues including complaints about police negligence on Palm Island in Queensland ("Police 'on holiday' as Island anger simmered") and the racist assault with a noose of an Indigenous teenager caught trespassing on a property at Goondawindi ("Noose Victim's fear and shame") were relegated to page 10. Also striking in view of the newspaper's celebration of corporate contributions to Indigenous community prosperity was a short article published days after the feature stories on Woolworths and Pearson's Cape York Institute reporting a draft environmental impact statement on the construction of a gas pipeline across the Northern Territory under the headline: "Aboriginal sexual jealousy 'may affect pipeline.'" Among other issues, including claims that some Aboriginal communities had "an unrealistic expectation of benefits" from the project, such as free gas and "enough royalty money to buy vehicles and build up homelands," was a concern that the project could trigger Aboriginal sexual jealousy leading to violent reactions and the vandalization of property. The article concluded with a positive evaluation of the consultation process by a representative of Alcan, the Canadian multinational behind the pipeline proposal "we are confident we can work through those issues."[76]

If this piece at first sight appears to be a bizarre addition to *The Australian*'s wrap up of a heavy week of Indigenous affairs, it begins to make sense considered in conjunction with the previous Tuesday's story on the relationships corporations are building with Indigenous communities and the final exclusion of Indigenous sovereignty from the sphere of public ideas circulating in the newspaper. For what is being made clear is that traditional owners should not expect any *capital* benefits flowing to them from the pipeline and—in return—the company will ensure it conducts the project in a 'civilized' manner, minimizing the environmental impacts and increasing the number of female construction employees. The assumption of heterosexuality aside, the subtext of patriarchal white sovereignty echoes resoundingly: non-Indigenous men are irresistible to Indigenous women; Indigenous men are possessive, violent and greedy, attributes which are not in the interests of the nation which stands to gain 98 million dollars from the pipeline. What is never considered is Indigenous sovereignty, which in this context would entail the right to refuse or to profit from the pipeline; instead, the project's impact on Indigenous people is reduced to its possible exacerbation of sexual and violent pathologies.

As with the media coverage of allegations against Geoff Clark, what seems to go without saying in the headline "Aboriginal sexual jealousy 'may affect pipeline,'" is that, considered as a collective within the body politic, Indigenous men lack the self-control required for self-determination and that Indigenous women are always already their property and potential victims of their violence. This constantly reiterated story of dysfunctional gender-relations in Indigenous communities imposes a historical amnesia and selective blindness with respect to the prominent political role of Indigenous women such as former ATSIC chief, Lowitja O Donahue, Reconciliation Australia co-chair, Jackie Huggins, academic Marcia Langton, Magistrate Pat O'Shane and NSW Labor MP, Linda Burney (to name only a few). In *The Australian*'s theater of Indigenous affairs, the key interventions of such women seem to have been consigned to a 'politically correct' era of the Indigenous rights agenda that is implicitly contrasted to the 'tough love' approach to Indigenous issues taken by those predominantly male leaders such as Noel Pearson and ALP President, Warren Mundine, who were apparently prepared to play 'hard-ball' in the Prime Minister's court.

On the bottom of the same page reporting on "Aboriginal Sexual Jealousy," another short article reported: "In Melbourne, outgoing ATSIC chairman, Geoff Clark, no longer regarded as a credible voice in Indigenous affairs, gate-crashed a meeting of Indigenous affairs ministers where he was cold-shouldered by federal Indigenous Affairs Minister Amanda Vanstone." In this sentence, over two centuries of Indigenous resistance to colonization and the positive achievements of elected ATSIC representatives all over the country are simultaneously relegated to invisibility through the metonymic attachment of the 'rights agenda' to an individual who is allegedly a rapist and bar room brawler. This underscores the impression that Indigenous Australians lack qualities of self-governing subjects which, in turn, makes their sovereignty unthinkable, except in terms of the separatism and savagery imagined by Keith Windschuttle in his attack on Indigenous rights claims anxiously titled "The Break Up of Australia" and published in the conservative journal *Quadrant*.[77] In a neoliberal political environment where "Indigenous rights" became a metonym for "sexual abuse, alcoholism, drug abuse and violence" and "Indigenous responsibilities" brought connotations of "mortgages, health, individual success and empowerment," it seemed that the only way to maintain a credible public voice was to insist as Patrick Dodson did in an article published in *The Australian* that "responsibilities" are also recognized as having roots in Indigenous traditions.[78]

Almost six months since the election of the Labour government under Prime Minister Kevin Rudd, the attack on Indigenous rights persists. While Rudd delivered a moving and overdue apology to stolen generations of Indigenous Australians in February 2008, he also took federal compensation to individuals and families affected by policies and practices of child removal off the government's agenda.[79] In April 2008, with several other Indigenous leaders, Patrick Dodson succeeded in placing a treaty recognizing Indigenous sovereignty at the center of discussions at the new government's 2020 Summit to generate a vision for Australia. In spite of this, a treaty was apparently relegated to a minor point in the final report of the Indigenous group's recommendations. *The Australian* covered the 2020 summit in its 'Inquirer' section the following weekend. In an article on constitutional issues by Natasha Robinson titled "A Country for all of us" canvassed a number of Indigenous and non-Indigenous legal views, writing dismissively that "Dodson's return to the old language of treaty was not the answer."[80] Noel Pearson's opinion piece in an article on the same page titled "No progress without wide support" reinforced a sense that "treaty" was a "dead horse" and suggested that its contemporary advocates needed to examine why "concepts such as constitutional reform and treaties failed to gain traction in the past."[81] Such constructions of Indigenous rights as a primarily 'symbolic' issue with minority appeal for non-Indigenous constituencies are indicative of the extent to which Rudd's approach to Indigenous affairs is broadly consistent with that of his conservative political predecessors.

Apart from Rudd's acknowledgement of the legitimacy of the grounds on which members of the stolen generations and their supporters have demanded an apology since 1996, there is another point to distinguish the current government's approach to Indigenous Australia, which is likely to have effects on *The Australian*'s coverage as well as on media representations more broadly. The government's intention to extend elements of the Northern Territory intervention (such as welfare quarantining) to non-Indigenous Australians who are unemployed, alcohol or substance-addicted or identified as delinquent parents, will address criticisms about the racially discriminatory basis of the intervention.[82] The question is to what extent to which this will counter the "Aboriginalisation of pathology" identified in my research on *The Australian* over the period of the Howard government? And to what extent have the publication's readers become 'addicted' to the parade of abject images and intra-Indigenous conflicts staged in domestic and political spheres?

We have seen that the theatrical production of Indigenous affairs offered by *The Australian* requires Indigenous agents to constantly adjust their performances to those of non-Indigenous political agents as well as to other Indigenous agents. But the question I want to conclude with is: what about the readers to which the national broadsheet directs its theater of pathology? As audiences, what do we do with this 'news'? Are we content to be mute consumers of a spectacle that—like reality television—relies on our voyeuristic fascination to reproduce itself? Or are we obliged to respond to this theater by establishing and supporting alternative media forums as well as producing vigorous critiques of the show being staged for our benefit? I think that the important challenge for non-Indigenous readers is to extricate our understandings of 'rights' and 'responsibilities' from our own possessive investments in patriarchal white sovereignty and to find the courage to explicitly refuse any vision of the future that asks or expects Indigenous Australians to surrender their sovereignty in return for equal access to health, housing, employment and education and the opportunities for physical and social mobility these bring.

This is no easy task. As we have seen, a powerful effect of *The Australian*'s continuous stream of 'revelations' about violence in Indigenous communities over the past decade is that they are profoundly pacifying. Those who may be otherwise positively disposed to Indigenous rights become afraid to speak up lest we be seen to be condoning violence against Indigenous women and children. As readers of *The Australian* and other news sources covering the issue, it was easier to allow ourselves to become mesmerized by the spectacular representations of Geoff Clark, the alleged sexual abuser, than to voice our objections as non-Indigenous citizens to the abolition of ATSIC. It was as though Clark's alleged violence against women cancelled out—if not explicitly legitimized—the political violence of the government in abolishing a representative body elected by Indigenous citizens. The question this raises is what does it mean for people respectively racialized as white and non-white through the aggregate category 'non-Indigenous' *not* to speak about major political decisions in Australia which effect Indigenous people? The Howard government's militaristic intervention in the Northern Territory highlights disturbingly performative dimensions of our silence.

As long as the ongoing issues raised by the failure to recognize Indigenous sovereignty remain quarantined from public discussion of race relations, Australian media consumers will continue to be positioned as unmoved and immovable spectators of *The Australian*'s unfolding theatre of Indigenous affairs. And this will prevent us from asking questions like: how did the alleged wrongdoings of one man come to discredit an entire Indigenous rights agenda? And what was the role of the media in bringing down a representative apparatus, which entailed the termination of so many other elected leaders regardless of their own characters and records of performance? In this context, Moreton-Robinson's work on the "possessive investment in patriarchal white sovereignty" is a reminder not only of the challenge that faces those who would become involved in the task of 'post-colonizing' Australia; it also suggests that when we contribute to media representations and political and academic debates that fail to address this challenge—as the current political moves to reverse Indigenous rights gains attest—we lend our implicit support to the persistent being of a colonizing regime.

To unsettle this regime we need to do more than to boycott the theatres of Aboriginal representation with which we disagree in order to patronize alternative venues such as are offered by Indigenous community and 'Indy' publications such as *The Koori Mail* and the *National Indigenous Times*. As non-Indigenous men and women and as academics and journalists who would recognize Indigenous sovereignty in this place against the possessive claims of whiteness, critical readings of media texts with which we might vehemently disagree are not simply a necessary part of any serious refusal to 'buy' into *The Australian*'s ideological construction of Indigenous Australia. My closing suggestion is that everyday engagement with such texts might make it possible for our residual and continuing attachments to the white racialized sovereignty that makes of Aboriginality an object of theatrical representation to be better understood and slowly undone one day at a time.

NOTES

1. *Australian*, 17–18/4/04.

2. John Howard, in Paul Toohey, "Hard Law: Hard Love," *Bulletin*, July 3, 2007, front page and 25.

3. Irene Watson, "Settled and Unsettled Spaces: Are We Free to Roam?" in Aileen Moreton-Robinson's "Writing Off Indigenous Sovereignty: The Discourse of Security and Patriarchal White Sovereignty," *Sovereign Subjects: Indigenous Sovereignty Matters* ed. Aileen Moreton-Robinson (Sydney: Allen&Unwin, 2007).

4. I am extremely grateful to Aileen Moreton-Robinson and Maryrose Casey for their suggestions and always constructively critical comments on several versions of this paper. Thanks are also due to Tanja Dreher, Clare McCarthy and Maureen Burns for generously taking time to read and give feedback on this research.

5. Stuart Hall et al., "The Social Production of News," in *Policing the Crisis: Mugging, the State, and Law and Order* (London: Palgrave Macmillan, 1978), 77.

6. For example, on the university campus where I work, a special offer has been available aimed at university students. For around $15.00 they can pick up a free copy of the paper at the university news agency everyday and have the weekend paper delivered free to their home address.

7. "The Australian newspaper was selling 133,000 copies Monday to Friday, an increase of 2.3 per cent, or 3,000 copies, over the same period last year while The Weekend Australian's circulation was up 1.2 per cent to 292,000 copies, an increase of 3,500 copies," in 'Papers Still Dominate Media,' *Sydney Morning Herald*, October 15, 2004, http://www.smh.com.au/articles/2004/10/15/1097784016870.html (accessed June 7, 2006).

8. *The Australian,* October 11, 2005.

9. For a detailed analysis of the ideological role of vision in Western society see John Berger, *Ways of Seeing* (1972).

10. See Louis Althusser, "Ideological State Apparatuses," in *Mapping Ideology,* ed. Slavoj Žižek (London: Verso, 1994).

11. George Lipsitz, *The Possessive Investment in Whiteness: How White People Profit from Identity Politics* (Philadelphia: Temple University Press, 1998).

12. See for example: John Downing and Charles Husband, *Representing "Race": Racisms, Ethnicities and Media* (London: Sage, 2005).

13. Further elaboration of the relationship between whiteness, subjectivity and possession can be found elsewhere. In the U.S. context, Cheryl Harris, "Whiteness as Property," in *Harvard Law Review* 106, no. 8 (June, 1993): 1707, and George Lipsitz, *The Possessive Investment in Whiteness.* In the Australian context, Toula Nicolacopoulos and George Vassilacopoulos,' "Racism, Foreigner Communities and the Onto-pathology of White Australian Subjectivity," in *Whitening Race: Essays in*

Social and Cultural Criticism, ed. Aileen Moreton-Robinson (Canberra: Aboriginal Studies Press, 2004), 75–89.

14. See: Ghassan Hage, *White Nation: Fantasies of White Supremacy in a Multicultural Society* (Sydney: Pluto Press, 1998).

15. David Theo Goldberg, *The Racial State* (Malden, MA: Blackwell Press, 2002), 196.

16. Goldberg, *The Racial State,* 196.

17. See: Aileen Moreton-Robinson, "The House that Jack Built: Britishness and White Possession," *Journal of the Australian Critical Race and Whiteness Studies Association* 1 (2005): 21–29.

18. See: Aileen Moreton-Robinson and Fiona Nicoll, "'We Will Fight Them on the Beaches': Protesting Cultures of White Possession," *Journal of Australian Studies* no. 89 (2006); Suvendrini Perera, "Race, Terror, Sydney, December 2005," *Borderlands E-journal* 5, no. 1 http://www.borderlandsejournal.adelaide.edu.au, 2006 (accessed May 26, 2008).

19. Karen Brodkin, *How Jews Became White Folk* (New Brunswick, NJ and London: Rutgers, 1999).

20. Noel Ignatiev, *How the Irish Became White* (New York: Routledge, 1995).

21. Nicolacopoulos and Vassiliacopoulos, "Racism, Foreigner Communities."

22. Ghassan Hage, *Against Paranoid Nationalism* (Sydney: Pluto Press, 2003).

23. Jon Stratton, "Before Holocaust Memory: Making Sense of Trauma Between Post Memory and Cultural Memory," *Journal of Australian Critical Race and Whiteness Studies Association* 1, no. 1 (2005).

24. Suvendrini Perera, "Who will I become? The Multiple Formations of Australian Whiteness," *Journal of Australian Critical Race and Whiteness Studies Association* 1, no. 1 (2005).

25. Jane Haggis and Susanne Schech, "Incoherence and Whiteness," *Unmasking Whiteness: Race Relations and Reconciliation* (Nathan, QLD: Griffith University, 1999).

26. *Australian*, August 17, 2007, 7(N).

27. *Courier Mail* August 18–19, 2007, 6(N).

28. Aileen Moreton-Robinson, "I Still Call Australia Home: Indigenous Belonging and Place in a White Postcolonizing Society," *Uprootings/Regroundings: Questions of Home and Migration*, eds., Sara Ahmed et al. (Oxford: Berg, 2003), 30.

29. Aileen Moreton-Robinson, "The Possessive Logic of Patriarchal White Sovereignty: The High Court and the Yorta Yorta Decision," *Borderlands E-Journal* 3, no. 2 (October 2004), http://www.borderlands.net.au/vol3no2_2004/moreton _possessive.htm (accessed June 10, 2008).

30. Aileen Moreton-Robinson, "Writing Off Indigenous Sovereignty: The Discourse of Security and Patriarchal White Sovereignty," *Sovereign Subjects* (Sydney: Allen & Unwin, 2007), 87.

31. For an excellent introduction to the cultural politics of challenging racist representation see Stuart Hall's "The Spectacle of the Other," *Cultural Representations and Signifying Practices* (London: Sage, 1997).

32. John Hartley exemplifies this critique of critiques of racism when he writes for example: "the media may in fact constitute the public sphere for modern/postmodern societies, and that the notion of a mediated 'Aboriginal public sphere' may be useful to understand how coverage of indigenous issues can be rethought in this context. If there is an 'Aboriginal public sphere' within a larger 'mediasphere,' then the question for researchers is not 'Are media racist?' but 'Who has sovereignty in the Aboriginal public sphere?'" in John Hartley, "An Aboriginal Public Sphere in the Era of Media Citizenship," *Cultural Policy* 8, no. 2 (1997): 43.

33. See for example comparative content analysis by Michael Meadows of news coverage in Australian papers of the High Court's Wik decision and the Canadian news coverage of the Nisga'a treaty which demonstrated that Indigenous sources were used only 20% of the time in Australia and 22% in Canada. (1999) This represented a decrease in usage of Indigenous sources in Australia from around 33% twenty years previously.

34. Jon Stratton, "Two Rescues, One History: Everyday Racism in Australia," *Social Identities* 12, no. 6 (November 2005).

35. Steve Mickler, *The Myth of Privilege: Aboriginal Status, Media Visions, Public ideas* (Perth: Freemantle University Press, 1998).

36. See Moreton-Robinson's "Writing off Indigenous Sovereignty," 100.

37. *Australian*'s journalism is both representative and exemplary of more general tendencies shaped by socially conservative political agendas and media industrial factors over the past decade. The academy has not been exempt from these tendencies. As Maryrose Casey shows in this volume, a prominent Australian academic historian recently deployed Elaine Showalter's psychoanalytic account of hysteria to reframe the stories of members of the 'stolen generations' of Indigenous children from evidence-based calls for social justice to a model of the social contagion generated by pathological individuals in search of a common cause to justify their suffering.

38. For another discussion of the theatrical framing of Indigenous-non-Indigenous relationships in Australia see Maryrose Casey, "After Mabo: What's at Stake?" *Australian Screen Education* 32 (Spring 2003): 107–11.

39. I am not arguing that there are never opposing views presented in the pages of this newspaper but what I am saying is that these tend to operate as a sideshow to complement the main event staged by the headlines anchoring captions and editorials. An unfortunately all too rare example of a balanced approached to the Aboriginal rights debate in *The Australian* is when Albrechtsen's opinion piece "Sorry's Just Not Enough" was juxtaposed with a piece by William Jonas, HREOC Social Justice Commissioner, titled "Native Title the Key to Real Equality: Yes, a rights approach to indigenous issues can improve Aboriginal life, says William Jonas," May 22, 2002, 11(N). And immediately following ATSIC's dismantlement, Deputy Chief, Ray Robinson was given space to voice his objections, "Folly of Abolishing Peak Aboriginal Body," *Australian*, April 16, 2004, 13(N). Such balanced representation of the rights agenda has become increasingly rare.

40. It should be noted that, while the use of reality genres to further neoliberal political goals is a relatively recent phenomenon, the circulation of representations of Australian Indigenous people as abject and violent has been used to discredit their

sovereignty claims from the origins of British settlement in Sydney Cove. Far from being the product of Cold War propagandists, as *The Australian*'s neoconservative opinion authors frequently claim, debates over Indigenous rights can be traced to the early 19th century. Nor are suggestions of inherent Indigenous dysfunction new; they formed the ground of policies and practices of Indigenous re-settlement and child removal in the 19th and 20th centuries. In this context, current proposals to withhold welfare benefits and to make infrastructural improvements contingent on remote community members entering into mutual obligation agreements are consistent with earlier regimes of governance which held back payment to Indigenous workers in their 'own best interests.'

41. *Australian*, June 1–2, 2002, 19 (N), Weekend Inquirer feature.

42. *Australian*, November 19, 2004 (illustrated cover story).

43. *Australian*, October 29–30, 2005, 23(N).

44. *Australian*, October 6, 2005 (cover story).

45. *Australian*, October 26, 2005, 6 and 17(N).

46. *Australian*, September 24, 2005, 6 (N).

47. See Gideon Polya, "Body Count: the Awful Truth," *National Indigenous Times*, June 14, 2007, <http://www.nit.com.au/news/story.aspx?id=11552> (accessed June 8, 2007).

48. *Australian*, March 27, 2002 (front page).

49. Keith Windschuttle, *The Fabrication of Aboriginal History Volume One, Van Diemen's Land 1803–1847* (Sydney: MacLeay Press, 2002).

50. *Australian*, April 16, 2004, 4(N).

51. *Australian*, April 17, 2004.

52. "Some important stories are controversial, though not all controversial stories are important. This story was both, casting light on the character of an elected official running a budget of $1 billion a year. The revelation that the current ATSIC chairman had allegedly raped several women in the past, opened fault lines in the political and social landscape. Rule's story took three months, tracing victims and witnesses in four States, and was important for bringing about a frank examination of hidden violence in indigenous communities," <http://www.walkleys.com/2001> (accessed December 3, 2004).

53. *Australian*, April 1, 2004, 11(N).

54. *Australian*, May 6–7, 2001.

55. *Australian*, June 21–27, 2001.

56. The terms of this choice are critically analyzed by Moreton-Robinson in her book *Talking' Up to the White Woman*, with reference to a debate which saw Dianne Bell, a white feminist anthropologist, 'speak out' against rape in Indigenous communities in an international academic journal and in this process silence the voices of Indigenous women who were already working to address the problem in different ways and on numerous fronts.

57. *Australian*, April 14–15, 2001.

58. *Australian*, June 8–9, 2002.

59. *Australian*, January 1, 2007, 2(N), my italics.

60. *Australian*, June 16–17, 2007.

61. See Michel Foucault's introduction to *History of Sexuality, Vol. 1* (London: Penguin Books, 1998) in which he discusses the paradoxical point that the Victorian age within which sexuality is regarded as having been most strictly repressed gave rise to an unprecedented flood of discourse about the subject of sex, and its uses and abuses.

62. White anthropologist, Peter Sutton, is an example of an academic taken up by the media to make 'expert' pronouncements on violence in Aboriginal communities. See "The Politics of Suffering: Indigenous Policy in Australia since the 1970s," *Anthropological Forum* 11, no. 2 (November, 2001).

63. *Australian*, May 23, 2006, 4 and 13(N).

64. For a detailed account of wages withheld from Indigenous workers in Queensland see: Rosaline Kidd, *The Way We Civilize* (Brisbane: University of Queensland Press, 1997).

65. John Howard, "Hard Law: Hard Love," 25.

66. The violence of this intervention can pass without serious criticism only in the absence of meaningful comparative data about rates of child sexual abuse and health problems in non-Indigenous communities, particularly those as impoverished and under-policed as those given sustained and spectacular journalistic treatment in *The Australian*.

67. *Australian*, November 16, 2004, 25(N).

68. See: "Government Needs to Consider Human Rights in Territory Intervention," *The 7.30 Report*, March 31, 2008, http://www.abc.net.au/7.30/content/2007/s2203948.htm (accessed May 3, 2008).

69. *Australian*, November 16, 2004, 25(N).

70. *Weekend Australian Magazine*, November 20–21, 2004, 24(N).

71. This might be less concerning if the argument that Indigenous Australia is too heterogeneous to command a single solution were not routinely used against pan-Aboriginal political aspirations (expressed by the Aboriginal Provisional Government for example).

72. *Australian*, June 16–17, 2007, 3(N).

73. Consider the headlines promoting an article on September 17–18, 2005 by David McKnight, author of *Beyond Right and Left*: "This is progress: Final victory in the culture war may just lie with the approach taken by Noel Pearson." In this piece, Pearson is presented as an Australian intellectual by the academic author of, who is rethinking "the frozen positions of Left and Right on indigenous issues," 27.

74. *Australian*, October 26, 2005, 17(N).

75. *Australian*, December 4–5, 2004 (cover story and editorial).

76. *Australian*, December 4, 2005, 10(N).

77. Keith Windschuttle, "The Break Up of Australia," *Quadrant* 44, no. 9 (September 2000).

78. *Australian*, December 7, 2004.

79. Stephen Lunn, "Apology to the Stolen, but no Fund," *Australian*, January 8, 2008, http://www.theaustralian.news.com.au/story/0,,23020566-2702,00.html?from=public_rss (accessed January 14, 2008).

80. Natasha Robinson, "A Country for all of us," *Australian*, April 26–27, 2008, 24(N).

81. Noel Pearson, "No Progress Without Wide Support," *Australian*, April 26–27, 2008, 24(N).

82. Policies such as welfare quarantining are already being extended to 'delinquent' non-Indigenous parents. See Imre Salusinsky, "PM gets tough to protect children," *Australian* 26–27 April 26–27, 2008, 1(N).

Chapter Five

Writing off Treaties:
White Possession in the United States
Critical Whiteness Studies Literature

Aileen Moreton-Robinson

Whiteness studies proliferated in the United States during the 1990s in response to overt acts of racist violence reported in the press and the need to reconsider the persistence of racism in light of the proposition that race was socially constructed and not biologically determined. Whiteness studies scholars share in common their commitment to racial justice, anti-racism and a more humane society. In most of the literature, prescriptive politics assumes a central role; many writers are committed to the abolition of whiteness through naming it, deconstructing it, resisting it and betraying it. Their scholarship is informed by a variety of disciplines such as literary studies, cultural studies, anthropology, feminism, postcolonialism, sociology and history while their research methods include textual analysis, ethnography, interviews, surveys and the archival. Whiteness studies has entered Canada and crossed both the Pacific and Atlantic providing a new history of race and modernity in 'settler' colonies.[1] However, the United States of America remains one of the most productive sites for whiteness studies.[2] A field of studies that is full of contradictions and ambivalences as well as sympathetic critics.

Mike Hill argues that "the contradictions surrounding whiteness studies remain one of its most salient and worthwhile features . . . the study of whiteness was never—and with hard enough work will never be—an unproblematically unified institutional force."[3] Debates about the epistemological assumptions and approaches to whiteness within the field continue to abound. Robyn Wiegman surmises that the contradictory nature of white power has been underplayed by Dyer and other white studies scholars through claiming its invisibility and universality as the source of its power. Wiegman argues that the universal serves to work in the interests of white particularity. This particularity simultaneously distances itself from white supremacy and denies the benefits of white power creating a disassociation that takes the form of

81

"liberal whiteness, a colour blind moral sameness."[4] Peter Kolchin critiques whiteness studies for its lack of historical specificity and the claim that whiteness is everything or nothing leads him to question whether it is a useful tool of enquiry and explanation. He argues that "underlying the new interest in white power, privilege and identity there is evident an intense discouragement over the persistence of racism, the unexpected renewal of nationalism, and the collapse of progressive movements for social change."[5] While Stephen Knadler cautions whiteness studies scholars against "an increasing linguistic slippage from the fiction of race into the fiction of racism."[6] The pliable morphology of whiteness, its utilization of the universal, the lack of historical specificity and the linguistic slippage that fictionalizes racism as problems have shaped this paper's consideration of the relationship of this field of study to Indigenous sovereignties.

The field of Whiteness studies is not a uniquely white enterprise, African Americans have commented on and written about whiteness since the early 1800s.[7] African American scholarship has been influential, particularly the work of W. E. B. Du Bois and more recently Toni Morrison whose seminal text *Playing in the Dark: Whiteness and the Literary Imagination* challenged the naturalized whiteness of American literature by illuminating how the omnipresence of African Americans has historically shaped it.[8] She exposes the embedded racial assumptions that enable whiteness to characterize itself in the literary imagination in powerful and important ways. In her analysis of Hemmingway's *To Have and to Have Not*, Morrison illustrates how black men and women were positioned as inferiors within his texts to prop up white masculinity.[9] Morrison further suggests in "Black Matters" that the African American presence has also "shaped the body politic, the Constitution, and the entire history of the [USA] culture."[10] Indigenous peoples are outside the scope of Morrison's analysis. Through the centering of the African American presence, Native American texts that have challenged, resisted and affected the American literary imagination, politics, history and the Constitution remain invisible. This silence is an interesting discursive move considering that the best-selling novels within the USA in the late eighteenth century were captivity narratives. And as Native American legal scholar Raymond Williams argues it was the positioning of Indians as incommensurable savages within the Declaration of Independence that enabled "'the Founders' vision of America's growth and potentiality as a new form of expansionary white racial dictatorship in the world."[11] The most valuable contribution of Morrison's work for my purposes is her thesis that "blackness," whether real or imagined, services the social construction and application of whiteness in its myriad forms. In this way it is utilized as a white epistemological possession. Her work opens up a space for considering how this possessiveness operates within the whiteness studies literature to displace Indigenous sovereignties and render them invisible.

WHITE POSSESSIVENESS

Most historians mark 1492 as the year when imperialism began to construct the old world order by taking possession of other people, their lands and resources. The possessive nature of this enterprise informed the development of a racial stratification process on a global scale that became solidified during modernity. Taking possession of Indigenous people's lands was a quintessential act of colonization and was tied to the transition from the Enlightenment to modernity, which precipitated the emergence of a new subject into history within Europe. Major social, legal, economic and political reforms had taken place changing the feudal nature of the relationship between persons and property in the 16th and 18th centuries. "These changes centered upon the rise of 'possessive individualism,' that is, upon an increasing consciousness of the distinctness of each self-owning human entity as the primary social and political value."[12] Private ownership of property both tangible and intangible operated through mechanisms of the new nation state in its regulation of the population and especially through the law. By the late 1700s people could legally enter into different kinds of contractual arrangements whereby they could own land, sell their labor and possess their identities all of which were formed through their relationship to capital and the state. A new white property owning subject emerged into history and possessiveness became embedded in everyday discourse as "a firm belief that the best in life was the expansion of self through property and property began and ended with possession of one's body."[13] Within the realm of intra-subjectivity possession can mean control over one's being, ideas, one's mind, one's feelings and one's body or within inter-subjectivity it can mean the act or fact of possessing something that is beyond the subject and in other contexts it can refer to a state of being possessed by another. Within the law possession can refer to holding or occupying territory with or without actual ownership or a thing possessed such as property or wealth and it can also refer to territorial domination of a state. At an ontological level the structure of subjective possession occurs through the imposition of one's will-to-be on the thing which is perceived to lack will, thus it is open to being possessed. This enables the formally free subject to make the thing its own. Ascribing one's own subjective will onto the thing is required to make it one's property as "willful possession of what was previously a will-less thing constitutes our primary form of embodiment; it is invoked whenever we assert: this is mine."[14] To be able to assert 'this is mine' requires a subject to internalize the idea that one has proprietary rights that are part of normative behavior, rules of interaction and social engagement. Thus possession that forms part of the ontological structure of white subjectivity is reinforced by its sociodiscursive functioning.

WHITE WRITING

A number of texts have been written historicizing the acquisition of white identity and the privileges conferred by its status through a trope of migration, which is based on the assumption that all those who came after the white people had taken possession are the immigrants. White possession of the nation works discursively within these texts to displace Native American sovereignties by disavowing that everyone else within the USA are immigrants whether they came in chains or by choice. The only displacement that is theorized is in relation to African Americans. Theodore Allen's work on how the Irish became white in America illustrates that the transformation of their former status as the blacks of Europe relied on their displacement by African Americans in the new country.[15] David Roediger discusses how the wages of whiteness operated to prevent class alliances between working class whites and African Americans.[16] Karen Brodkin's excellent book on how Jews became white demonstrates that the lower status of African American workers enabled Jewish class mobility.[17] Jacobsen illustrates that European migrants were able to become white through ideological and political means that operated to distinguish them from African American blackness.[18] The black/white binary permeates these analyses enabling tropes of migration and slavery to work covertly in these texts erasing the continuing history of colonization and the Native American sovereign presence. Blackness becomes an epistemological possession that Allen, Roediger, Brodkin and Jacobsen deploy in analyzing whiteness and race, which forecloses the possibility that the dispossession of Native Americans was tied to migration and the establishment of slavery driven by the logic of capital. Slaves were brought to America as the property of white people to work the land that was appropriated from Native America tribes. Subsequently, migration became a means to enhance capitalist development within the USA. Migration, slavery and the dispossession of Native Americans were integral to the project of nation building. Thus the question of how anyone came to be white or black in the United States of America is inextricably tied to the dispossession of the original owners and the assumption of white possession. The various assumptions of sovereignty beginning with British 'settlers' the formation of individual states and subsequently the United States of America all came into existence through the blood-stained taking of Native American land. The USA as a white nation state cannot exist without land and clearly defined borders, it is the legally defined and asserted territorial sovereignty that provides the context for national identifications of whiteness. In this way I argue Native American dispossession indelibly marks configurations of white national identity.

Ruth Frankenberg acknowledges in the introduction to her edited collection *Displaying Whiteness* that whiteness traveled culturally and physically, impacting on the formation of nationhood, class and empire sustained by imperialism and global capitalism. She wrote that notions of race were tied "to ideas about legitimate 'ownership' of the nation, with 'whiteness' and 'Americanness' linked tightly together" and that this history was repressed. After making this statement she then moves on to discuss immigration and its effects.[19] Her acknowledgement did not progress into critical analysis that centered Native American dispossession, instead Frankenberg represses that which she acknowledges is repressed. Repression operates as a defense mechanism to protect one's perception of self and reality from an overwhelming trauma that may threaten in order to maintain one's self image. Repressing the history of Native American dispossession works to protect the possessive white self from ontological disturbance. It is far easier to extricate oneself from the history of slavery if there were no direct family and material ties to its institution and reproduction. However, it is not as easy to distance one's self from a history of Indigenous dispossession when one benefits everyday from being tied to a nation that has and continues to constitute itself as a white possession.

Within the whiteness studies literature whiteness has been defined in multiple ways. It is usually perceived as unnamed, unmarked and invisible, and often as culturally empty operating only by appropriation and absence.[20] It is a location of structural privilege, a subject position and cultural praxis.[21] Whiteness constitutes the norm operating within various institutions influencing decision making and defining itself by what it is not.[22] It is socially constructed and is a form of property that one possesses, invests in and profits from.[23] Whiteness as a social identity works discursively becoming ubiquitous, fluid and dynamic[24] operating invisibly through pedagogy.[25] What these different definitions of whiteness expose is that it is something that can be possessed and it is tied to power and dominance despite being fluid, vacuous and invisible to white people. However, these different conceptualizations of whiteness, which use blackness as an epistemological possession to service what it is not, obscure the more complex way that white possession functions sociodiscursively through subjectivity and knowledge production. As something that can be possessed by subjects it must have ontological and epistemological anchors in order to function through power. As a means of controlling differently racialized populations enclosed within the borders of a given society, white subjects are disciplined, though to different degrees, to invest in the nation as a white possession that imbues them with a sense of belonging and ownership. This sense of belonging is derived from ownership as understood within the logic of capital and citizenship. In its self-legitimacy, white possession operates discursively through narratives of the home of the brave and the land of the free and through white male signifiers of the nation such as the Founding Fathers, the 'pioneer' and the 'war hero.' Against this stands the Indigenous sense of belonging, home and place in its sovereign incommensurable difference.

BLACK WRITING

Within the African American scholarship whiteness is theorized as a form of power, as supremacy, as hegemony, as ideology and ontology, rarely in the theoretical focus is the social construction of white identity and whiteness not invisible, unnamed or unmarked. As Knadler states "in contrast to whites who have traditionally located racism in 'colour consciousness and find its absence in colour blindness' peoples of colour have emphasized more how racism involves 'institutionalized systems of power' and racialized practices that are part of everyday experience."[26] bell hooks argues that whiteness in the everyday is connected to "the mysterious, the strange, and the terrible" and while African Americans may imitate whites, they are still suspicious and afraid of them.[27] Charles W. Mills evaluates whiteness according to a white supremacy paradigm because he argues we are dealing with systematic white domination. He notes "the idea of white supremacy is intended, in part, to capture the crucial reality that the normal workings of the social system continue to disadvantage blacks in large measure *independently* of racist feeling."[28] George Yancy examines the social ontology of whiteness arguing that a central component is the reluctance of whites to discuss their investments in whiteness and its connection to white supremacy and racism, which are perceived as anomalies.[29] Valerie Babb illuminates how the ideology of whiteness supports and reinforces systemic privilege and informs the way it is represented in American literature and culture.[30] She argues "by ascribing common qualities to a select racial group, the ideology of whiteness could accomplish exclusion without explicit rationales of racial superiority."[31] One of the few scholars to connect the formation of whiteness to the appropriation of Indigenous lands is Cheryl Harris.[32] She argues that whiteness became a form of property originally through the appropriation of Indigenous peoples' lands and subsequent enslavement of African Americans. However, the center of Harris's theory is how 'blackness' enabled whiteness as a form of property. What circulates discursively within this literature is the idea that African Americans were possessions that could be bought and sold and the basis of this status was premised on their being perceived as inferior beings and that freedom from slavery did not bring racial equality.

The theoretical focus on the structural and systematic nature of white supremacy within this literature indicates that the nation is perceived to be a white possession that confers propriety on whites through the racial contract between the state and its citizens. African American scholar C. W. Mills argues that it is the racial contract that stipulates who can count as full moral and political persons setting the boundaries for those who can 'contract' in to the freedom and equality that it promises and those who must be kept out. White possession operates sociodiscursively producing the racial contract as a regulatory ideal, which enables, constrains and disciplines subjects in various ways. The possessiveness of white subjectivity is thus regulated through its relationship with the nation state. African Americans have limited access to this proprietaryness because the possessive claim to be truly human and a full citizen is marked by whiteness.

Within the United States of America the sovereignty claims of Native American and Pacific Island nations under its jurisdiction are not configured through citizenship rights. They are different from other minority rights at the center of the struggle for racial equality because they are not "based on equality of treatment under the Constitution and the general civil rights laws."[33] Their sovereignty is not epistemologically and ontologically grounded in the citizenship of the white liberal subject of modernity. The coexistence of these different and competing sovereignties complicates white possession and the way in which it shapes knowledge production. The historical amnesia about Indigenous sovereignty occurring in the whiteness literature is tied to a political and epistemological commitment to the idea of the universal white liberal subject. Freedom, liberty and equality operate discursively marking critique scoped through the black/white binary in ways that require the exclusion of Native American sovereignties. The relationship between the nation state, Native Americans and other Indigenous peoples colonized by it, is an outcome of colonization, the establishment of 'democracy' and its universal white liberal subject. Indigenous peoples' sovereignty claims are outside the individualized rights framework accorded to this subject. Indigenous rights are collective rights based on an ownership of land that is not configured through the logic of capital.

INDIGENOUS WRITING

Few Native American scholars engage theoretically with the whiteness studies literature. One exception is Frances V. Rains who argues that "white race privilege is the corollary to racism" because the unearned benefits whites gain are derived from a system based on racial inequality and stolen land.[34] However, 'race' is embedded in the work of Native American scholars. Robert Williams and Vine Deloria Jr.[35] have written extensively on the continuing colonization and exploitation of Native Americans by white America and Devon A. Mihesuah[36] has challenged and demystified racialized stereotypes of Native Americans while illuminating the continuing racism in American society. Within the Native American literature the racialization of their sovereignty struggles, in its many forms, is denoted by the concept 'white man' which is operationalized extensively as a metaphor for the nation state and American culture. The hegemony of white possession is exposed but not explicitly theorized as such.

When reading the Native American legal history literature the starting point is the invasion of their lands by 'settlers' who were the subjects of other countries and treaty making. Deloria and Lytle argue, "treaty making became the basis for defining both the legal and political relationships between Indians and European colonists. And when the young colonies finally became the United States, the treaty-making powers that earlier had been exercised by the European nations were assumed by the Americans with their independence."[37] However, not all Native Americans have treaties with the Unites States government and those that seek to reclaim their status as a tribe must do so under criteria formulated by the nation state. In this way tribes become constituted as an epistemological possession of the nation state.

Many Indigenous people have written about their sovereignty struggles in different ways.[38] As Robert Warrior, writing about the work of Native American scholars John Joseph Mathews and Vine Deloria Jr., and others, argues:

> Both writers point to the process through which the U.S. government abrogated the sovereign-sovereign relationship with the Natives as a major turning point in the history of that conflict. The multifaceted battle to appropriate Native land, supplant Native religion, and undermine Native traditional social structures is the mise-en-scene of American Indian intellectual work of the past one hundred years.[39]

Other Indigenous peoples whose lands are also occupied and possessed by the United States, such as Samoa, Hawaii and Guam are invisible in the whiteness literature. However, within the academy analyses of their sovereignty struggles and resistances are being written. In her groundbreaking book *Aloha Betrayed* Noenoe Silva has excavated the hidden history of *Kanaka Maoli* resistance to the invasion of Hawaii by the United States of America.[40] Silva's work successfully erases the myth of Hawaiian passivity by revealing their resistance to colonialism and imperialism through examining historical newspaper reports written by Hawaiians in their own language. America's origin story of possession through annexation no longer holds sway; the Hawaiian Queen and her people did not ask for 'help' from the USA. Instead it was a group of white capitalists and whites who positioned themselves as 'native' born Hawaiians who wanted 'help' to secure possession of Hawaii. They lobbied the US government to invade and secure their interests by extending its sovereignty beyond its borders. Despite its illegality under international law the USA complied with their demands. Taking possession of Hawaii was in the best interest of the USA and her white citizens. Kehulani Kauanui argues that Hawaiian identity is also appropriated by white people as a way of indigenizing their presence within the Hawaiian landscape free from the history of colonial occupation by the United States of America. Their claims to Hawaiian identity are articulated through a discourse of equality and anti-Hawaiian sovereignty as was evidenced in the formation of a group naming themselves 'Aloha for All.' This white group supported a number of lawsuits against Native Hawaiians receipt of government funds. They stated "it is not in keeping with the spirit of Aloha for the government to give one racial group land or money or special privileges or preferences from which all other racial groups in Hawaii are excluded."[41] In this statement the Aloha for All group makes a possessive claim on the nation state by asserting how government funds can or cannot be used. The nation as a white possession confers privileges on whites living in Hawaii which remain invisible to its recipients while they simultaneously exercise power.

The white American claim to Indigeneity to substantiate their possession is not new for Indigenous people of the Americas. Philip Deloria argues that one of the key origin stories for national identity within the United States of America is the Boston Tea party. He asks "why of all the possible stories of rebellion and re-creation, has the notion of disguised Indians dumping tea in Boston harbor had such a powerful hold on American's imaginations?"[42] Articulating the paradox of white Americans playing Indian he concludes:

> The self-defining pairing of American truth with American freedom rests on the ability to wield power against Indians—social, military, economic, and political—while simultaneously drawing power from them. Indianness may have existed primarily as a cultural artifact in American society, but it has helped create these other forms of power, which have then been turned back on native people. The dispossessing of Indians exists in tension with being

aboriginally true. . . . And so while Indian people have lived out a collection of historical nightmares in the material world, they have also haunted a long night of American dreams. As many native people have observed, to be American is to be unfinished. And although that state is powerful and creative, it carries with it nightmares all its own.[43]

The numerous texts produced within the academy by Indigenous peoples particularly since the 1980s raises the question of why their work does not surface more within the writing of whiteness studies scholars within the United States. Similarly much of the Native American literature does not engage with whiteness studies. Perhaps this is because Native American scholarship, like Indigenous scholarship elsewhere, has sought to produce its own epistemological boundaries and knowledges to critique white possession in its multiple forms.

OUTSIDE WHITENESS AND RACE?

Despite the colonial history of the United States and racializing Native Americans in popular culture, as the embodiment of 'redness,' the whiteness literature makes a racial demarcation between African Americans and Native Americans. That is by making blackness synonymous with 'race' African Americans are placed in a reified position within the literature. This binary understanding of 'race' places the literature in one sense out of colonial history. That is the theorizing about whiteness does not begin with nor center the appropriation of Indigenous peoples' lands and the continuing sovereignty struggles with the US nation state. They are, but they are marginalized within the theories of race and whiteness offered by whiteness studies despite its political commitment to and epistemological engagement with white race privilege and power. The conceptual links between the privileges and benefits that flow from American citizenship to Native American dispossession remains invisible. Instead slavery, war and migration are the narratives by which the historically contingent positionality of whiteness unfolds. This reflects a failure to address the sociodiscursive way that white possession functions to produce racism.

The racism attending the sociodiscursive nature of white possession informed the establishment of the Advisory Board of Race in 1997. President Clinton established this Board to counsel and inform him about race and racial reconciliation couching the terms of reference within a civil rights framework.[44] No Native American representative was appointed to the Board even though they are the only racial group required to carry a blood quantum card as proof of tribal membership.[45] This exclusion was the catalyst for numerous protests by different Native American groups. They stated that while Native Americans shared with other racial groups the need for improving their socioeconomic and legal conditions, there were other conditions not shared. They argued that their position within the USA was unique because of their sovereignties and treating with the Nation State. The racism that they experience is predicated on this relationship. Native American sovereignty is constantly under threat by the Nation State and its various mechanisms of governance such as the Plenary Powers of the United States Congress. Within their daily lives they experience the effects of broken treaties, loss of land and cultural rights, genocide and breaches of fiduciary duty. They are confronted by the constant battle with Congressmen and State Governors who wish to diminish their rights by framing "the economic and political empowerment of Indigenous tribes as evidence of a threatening tribal movement to transgress the temporal and spatial boundaries of colonial rule, consume American property and colonise the American political system."[46] Resisting and diminishing Native American sovereignties also includes tactics such as positioning their claims outside racism which serves to protect and reinscribe possessive investments in the nation as a white possession.

Some twelve months after its establishment, President Clinton was invited to discuss his Race Advisory Board with a panel of eight people on a PBS broadcast. One member of the panel was Native American Sherman Alexie. The panel discussed with Clinton a number of race issues including affirmative action. During the show Clinton did not address Native American sovereignty claims but tried to connect with Alexie by informing him that his grandmother was one-quarter Cherokee. Later in the program Alexie was asked if he was often engaged by others in discussions about race to which he replied that a dialogue often takes place when he is approached by people who "tell me they're Cherokee."[47] In other words people do not talk about racism to Alexie unless they claim some form of Indigeneity. Alexie's comment serves to illustrate how Clinton tries to capitalize on a Native American ancestry by staking a possessive claim to a subject position that is not purely white in order to connect with his native brother while having excluded Native Americans from the Race Committee. Clinton can stake a possessive claim to Cherokee descent because there is no threat to his investment in his white identity, which carries a great deal of cultural capital enabling him to make the claim on biological grounds outside of Cherokee sovereignty. What Clinton was also signifying to the audience was that race does not matter: even a person of Cherokee descent can be President of the United States because this is the land of freedom, liberty and equality. A similar rhetorical strategy was also deployed in March 2008 by Barack Obama in his speech on race in Philadelphia, which was framed by the black/white binary operationalizing narratives of slavery and migration. Obama declared that slavery was the original sin in the making of the nation and it is the African American experience that dominates his speech though he acknowledges Latinos, Hispanics and refers to Native Americans once. His narrative on migration is reserved for white working and middle class people who he says feel they have not been privileged by their race, they have worked hard to build their dream but are now victims of globalization. Obama stakes a possessive claim to whiteness throughout this speech by discursively operationalizing an American dream which is beyond race. He stages this through an appeal to Christian principles, civil rights, patriotism, citizenship, liberty, freedom and equality noting that the Declaration of Independence was developed by men who "travelled across an ocean to escape tyranny and persecution."[48] The tyranny and persecution inflicted upon Native Americans and slaves by white male possessors who framed the constitution is disavowed by Obama, who epitomizes them as the bearers of freedom and liberty.

Clinton's executive and personal actions and Obama's speech serve to negate Native American claims that race and racism were operating, when Indigenous peoples were dispossessed, and they continue to mark their everyday lives and sovereignty claims. The genealogy of racism toward Native Americans can be traced back to "Greek and Roman myths of warlike, barbarian tribes and biblical accounts of wild men cursed by God" which informed renaissance-era travel narratives describing them as the embodiment of primitive human savagery.[49] Enlightenment theorists such as Locke and Hobbes developed their ideas of the state of nature utilizing the American Indian as the quintessential example of "humanity living in its pure, unadulterated savage state."[50] These ideas operated discursively to inform theories about the rights of man within the context of the rise of democracy relegating Indigenous people to a state of nature without any sovereign rights. They continue to circulate preventing Indigenous sovereignties from gaining recognition as relevant and alternative visions of differently constituted modernities and global futures. The exclusion of Native Americans from the Race Committee correlates with their invisibility within the whiteness literature. Native Americans are located outside 'racism' because United States' status as a former colony and its current mode of colonization is separated from its historical narrative as being the land of liberty, freedom and equality.

CONCLUSION

I have shown that white possession operates discursively within the whiteness literature shaping analyses about its social construction and morphology which are divorced from its colonial history and colonizing present. Tropes of migration and slavery become the dominant narratives that inform analyses. The historical amnesia within the literature is tied to what white possession promises—migrants can become white and blacks can achieve racial equality. The selective historical amnesia mitigates the fear of opening oneself up epistemologically and ontologically to being a disoriented, displaced and diasporic racialized subject whose existence within the nation state is predicated on the continuing divestment of Indigenous people's sovereign rights. Instead it is the black/white binary that becomes the parameter for the constitution of whiteness by operationalizing blackness as an epistemological possession.

Indigenous sovereignties within the USA are excluded from the whiteness literature because analyses of 'race' and 'whiteness' are sociodiscursively constituted by the racial contract and white possession which enable, constrain and discipline subjects in various ways within and outside the academy. White possession sets the limits of knowledge about the black/white binary disappearing beyond or behind the invention of this knowledge mediated through the racial contract. These practices of knowledge production work to deny Indigenous sovereignties as they reinforce the power, control and authority of the nation as a white possession. The work produced in the field of whiteness studies within the United States of America is written on and yet over the sovereign ground of Native Americans and Indigenous people from its other territories. While this literature does produce knowledge about whiteness and racism, there are powerful vested interests in not knowing Indigenous sovereignties and continuing to know Indigeneity in ways that confine it to a specialist domain of ethnographic expertise. The failure of this literature to address the explicit colonial and continuing imperialism of the nation state results in the writing off of Indigenous sovereignties in the service of white possession. This servicing produces a particular way of being racialized within the United States of America and is fundamental both to its establishment and to its continued existence.

NOTES

1. See: Warwick Anderson, *The Cultivation of Whiteness: Science, Health and Racial Identity in Australia* (Melbourne: Melbourne University Press, 2002); Ghassan Hage, *White Nation* (Annadale: Pluto Press, 2000); Cynthia Levine-Rasky, ed., *Working Through Whiteness: International Perspectives* (Albany: State University of New York Press, 2002); Aileeen Moreton-Robinson, ed., *Whitening Race: Essays in Social and Cultural Criticism* (Canberra: Aboriginal Studies Press, 2004) and Fiona Nicoll, "Reconciliation in and out of Perspective: White Knowing, Seeing, Curating and Being at Home in and Against Indigenous Sovereignty," in *Whitening Race:*

Essays in Social and Cultural Criticism, ed., Aileen Moreton-Robinson (Canberra: Aboriginal Studies Press, 2004).

2. See: Maurice Berger, *Whiteness and Race in Contemporary Art*, Center for Art and Visual Culture (Baltimore: University of Maryland, 2004); Kimberle Crenshaw, et al., *Critical Race Theory: The Key Writings that Formed the Movement* (New York: The New Press, 1995); Chris Cuomo and Kim Hall, eds., *Whiteness: Feminist Philosophical Reflections* (Lanham, MD: Rowman & Littlefield, 1999); Jessie Daniels, *White Lies: Race, Class, Gender and Sexuality in White Supremacist Discourse* (London: Routledge, 1997); Richard Delgado and Jean Stefancic, eds., *Critical Whiteness Studies: Looking Behind the Mirror* (Philadelphia: Temple University Press, 1997); Ashley Doane and Eduardo Bonilla-Silva, eds., *White Out: the Continuing Significance of Racism* (New York and London: Routledge, 2003); Mike Hill, ed., *Whiteness: A Critical Reader* (New York: New York University Press, 1997); Birgit Rasmussen, et al., *The Making and Unmaking of Whiteness* (Durnham: Duke University Press, 2001); and David Roediger, *Working Toward Whiteness: How America's Immigrants Became White* (New York: Basic Books, 2005).

3. Mike Hill, *After Whiteness: Unmaking an American Majority* (New York: New York University Press, 2004), 16.

4. R. Wiegman, "Whiteness Studies and the Paradox of Particularity," *Boundary* 2, no. 28 (3) (1999), 121.

5. Peter Kolchin, "Whiteness Studies: the New History of Race in America," *Journal of American History* 89, no.1 (June 2002): paragraph 30.

6. Stephen P. Knadler, *The Fugitive Race: Minority Writers Resisting Whiteness* (Jackson: University Press of Mississippi, 2002), 205.

7. Mia Bay, *The White Image in the Black Mind* (New York: Oxford University Press, 2000).

8. Toni Morrison, *Playing in the Dark: Whiteness and the Literary Imagination* (Cambridge: Harvard University Press, 1992).

9. Morrison, *Playing in the Dark*, 76.

10. Toni Morrison, "Black Matters," in *Race Critical Theories: Text and Context*, ed. Philomina Essed and David Theo Goldberg (Massachusetts: Blackwell Publishers, 2002), 266.

11. Raymond Williams, *Like a Loaded Weapon: the Rehnquist Court, Indian Rights and the Legal History of Racism in America* (Minneapolis: University of Minnesota Press, 2005), 35–37.

12. Margaret Davies and Ngaire Naffine, *Are Persons Property? Legal Debates about Property and Personality* (Aldershot, Dartmouth Publishing, 2001), 32–33.

13. Thomas K. Nakayama and Judith N. Martin, eds., *Whiteness: The Communication of Social Identity* (Thousand Oaks: Sage, 1999), 16.

14. Toula Nicolacopoulos and George Vassilacopoulos, "Racism, Foreigner Communities and the Onto-pathology of White Australian Subjectivity," in *Whitening Race: Essays in Social and Cultural Criticism*, ed. Aileen Moreton-Robinson (Canberra: Aboriginal Studies Press, 2004), 16.

15. Theodore Allen, *The Invention of the White Race: Volume One, Racial Oppression and Social Control* (London: Verso, 1994).

16. David Roediger, *Towards the Abolition of Whiteness* (London: Verso, 1994).

17. Karen Brodkin, *How Jews Became White Folk* (New Brunswick: Rutgers University Press, 1999).

18. Matthew F. Jacobson, *Whiteness of a Different Color: European Immigrants and the Alchemy of Race* (Cambridge: Harvard University Press, 1998).

19. Ruth Frankenberg, ed., *Displacing Whiteness: Essays in Social and Cultural Criticism* (London: Duke University Press, 1997), 6.

20. Richard Dyer, *White* (London: Routledge, 1997).

21. Ruth Frankenberg, *White Women Race Matters: The Social Construction of Whiteness* (London: Routledge, 1993).

22. See: Barbara Flagg, *Was Blind but Now I See: White Race Consciousness and the Law* (New York: New York University Press, 1998); Ian Haney-Lopez, *White by Law: The Legal Construction of Race* (New York: New York University Press, 1996).

23. George Lipsitz, *The Possessive Investment in Whiteness: How White People Profit from Identity Politics* (Philadelphia: Temple University Press, 1998).

24. Nakayama and Martin, *Whiteness.*

25. See: Michelle Fine, et al., *Off White; Readings on Race, Power and Society* (New York: Routledge, 1997); and Joe L. Kincheloe, et al. *White Reign: Deploying Whiteness in America* (New York: St. Martin's Griffin, 2000).

26. Knadler, *The Fugitive Race*, 204.

27. bell hooks, *Black Looks: Race and Representation* (Boston: South End Press, 1992), 166.

28. Charles W. Mills, "Racial Exploitation and the Wages of Whiteness," in *What White Looks Like: African American Philosophers on the Whiteness Question*, ed. George Yancy (New York: Routledge, 2004), 32.

29. George Yancy, ed., *What White Looks Like: African American Philosophers on the Whiteness Question* (New York and London: Routledge, 2004), 1–7.

30. Valerie Babb, *Whiteness Visible: The Meaning of Whiteness in American Literature and Culture* (New York: New York University Press, 1998).

31. Babb, *Whiteness Visible*, 170.

32. Cheryl Harris, "Whiteness as Property," in *Critical Race Theory: The Key Writings that Formed the Movement*, ed., Kimberle Crenshaw et al. (New York: The New Press, 1995), 276–91.

33. Williams, *Like a Loaded Weapon*, xxxv.

34. Francis V. Rains, "Is the Benign Really Harmless?: Deconstructing Some 'Benign' Manifestations of Operationalised White Privilege," in *White Reign: Deploying Whiteness in America*, ed., Joe L. Kincheloe, Shirley Steinberg, Nelson M. Rodriguez and Ronald Chennault (New York: St. Martin's Griffin, 2000), 80.

35. See: Vine Deloria Jr., *Custer Died for Your Sins: An Indian Manifesto* (Oklahoma: University of Oklahoma Press, 1988) and also by the same author, *Red Earth, White Lies: Native Americans and the Myth of Scientific Fact* (New York: Scibner, 1995).

36. Devon A. Mihesuah, *American Indians: Stereotypes and Realities* (Atlanta: Clarity Press, 1996).

37. Vine Deloria Jr., and Clifford Lytle, *American Indians: American Justice* (Austin: University of Texas Press, 1983), 3.

38. See: Richard A. Grounds, et al., *Native Voices: American Indian Identity and Resistance* (Kansas, University Press of Kansas, 2003); Joanne Barker, *Sovereignty Matters: Locations of Contestation and Possibility in Indigenous Struggles for Self-Determination* (Lincoln: University of Nebraska Press, 2005).

39. Robert Warrior, "Tribal Secrets: Recovering American Indian Intellectual Traditions" (Minnesota: University of Minnesota Press, 1995), 87.

40. Noenoe Silva, *Aloha Betrayed: Native Hawaiian Resistance to American Colonialism*, 4th printing (Durham: Duke University Press, 2006).

41. Kehulani Kauanui, "Diasporic Deracination and 'Off-Island' Hawaiians," *The Contemporary Pacific* 19, no. 1 (2007): 137–60.

42. Phillip Deloria, *Playing Indian* (Michigan: Yale University Press, 1998), 3.

43. Deloria, *Playing Indian*, 191.

44. President's Advisory Board on Race, "Executive Order 13050," *The Multiracial Activist* June 13, 1997, http://www.multiracial.com/government/whitehouse-eo13050 .html (accessed March 7, 2008).

45. Sonja Keohane, "Continuing thoughts on 'A Presidential Sham,'" *We The People*, 2001, http://www.dickshovel.com/sonsham.html (accessed March 9, 2008).

46. Kevin Bruyneel, *The Third Space of Sovereignty, the Postcolonial Politics of US—Indigenous Relations* (Minneapolis: University of Minnesota Press, 2007), 215.

47. Elizabeth Shogren, "Clinton Calls for New Approach to 'Affirmative Action,'" *AAD Project*, 1998, http://aad.english.ucsb.edu/docs/PBS-july98.html (accessed March 9, 2008).

48. Transcript: "Barack Obama's Speech on Race," *New York Times* (March 18 2008) http://www.nytimes.com/2008/03/18/us/politics/18text-obama.html?ei=5070 &en=eeb9fd47e9f2bd55 (accessed March 25, 2008).

49. Williams, *Like a Loaded Weapon*, 33.

50. Williams, *Like a Loaded Weapon*, 33.

Part II

GENDERING WHITENESS

Chapter Six

White Man's Burden:
Whiteness in Rudyard Kipling's *Kim*
and Rabidranath Tagore's *Gora*

Urbashi Barat

Whiteness and race are undoubtedly constructs of imperialism and colonialism, but they are also profoundly gendered concepts. Whiteness in colonial discourse is usually essentialized as male, powerful, victorious, moral, rational; darkness as feminine, mysterious, amoral, always available for conquest and possession. Concomitantly, the dark male is unnatural, effeminate or evil, and represents the threat to white/European hegemony over the colonized land. The relationship of power between white and black is almost invariably expressed through gendered imagery: in Rudyard Kipling's *Naulakha*, for instance, the colonizing project is seen in terms of a white sexual assault on a dark woman's body,[1] while the colonial fear of the unknown and unknowable (and therefore 'dark') colony is articulated through the continuing images of miscegenation or of rape of white women by black men, so that Shakespeare's *Othello* replicates itself in British narratives of India's "Sepoy Mutiny" of 1857, E. M. Forster's *Passage to India*[2] and Paul Scott's *Jewel in the Crown*.[3] The binaries between white and black, male and female, were reinforced by the mid-nineteenth-century anthropometric analogies between race and gender: thus white females were 'blacker' than white men because they belonged to an inferior 'race': "lower [i.e., darker] races represent the 'female' type of the human species, and females the 'lower race of gender.'"[4]

This colonialist/imperialist identification between color/race and gender undoubtedly grew out of the traditional identification of the feminine/female as 'dark'[5] and the equally traditional feminization and maternalization of the land, home and language (as evident, for example, in terms like *Mother Earth*, *motherland*, *mother country*, *mother tongue*) in most patriarchal/ patrilineal societies.[6] Colonial encounters in Asia inevitably led, moreover, to the (white, male) European's growing obsession with his dark and feminized

Other;[7] in South Asia it was accompanied by the dark Indian's corresponding fascination for white masculinity, one which he himself, he came to believe, he had lost and needed to regain.[8] The results of this gendering of color/ race and the coloring/'race'ing of gender are very obvious in indigenous Australian women's life-writing and Black American women's texts, which constantly underscore the ways in which the private and personal world of women, both white and black, are impacted upon and formed by social relationships in a public world inhabited and dominated by (white/racialized) males. In South Asia, whiteness-as-masculinity and the nation-as-mother became inextricably linked from the time that British colonization took root in the region, for the white man's relationships with the black and with white females highlighted the lacks and the absences in Indian gender relationships, and led to a continuing interrogation of Indian identity itself.[9]

But there is something more about whiteness that has not always been noted. In the gendered world of whiteness, where privilege and superiority are almost invariably associated with males, the binaries between public and private, between whiteness and color, can become a burden that debilitates and diminishes the white man at least as much it does the woman. A reading of two early twentieth-century novels makes this clear: Rudyard Kipling's English *Kim*[10] (now the *locus classicus* of imperial/colonial discourse) and Rabindranath Tagore's Bengali *Gora*,[11] written shortly after Kipling's novel and perhaps influenced by it. The novels are almost invariably conflated with each other by Indian postcolonial critics, for both novels begin with a young white boy orphaned during the 1857 War of Independence (formerly known as the Sepoy Mutiny), and brought up as an Indian in India; both interrogate, in similar stories but in different ways, the idea of India and Indianness. What does not seem to have been noted earlier, however, is the fact that both do so through competing notions of whiteness, masculinity and femininity. Both end with their discovery and their acceptance of their rightful place in India. But these places are different in each novel. Kipling is the ardent advocate of empire; consequently, Kim's whiteness sucks him into the mire of empire and removes him from the dark feminine world that India stands for. Tagore, on the other hand, is the critic and opponent of empire and nationalism alike; Gora's whiteness, accordingly, joins with and ultimately reinforces the power of the dark and feminine India.[12]

Whiteness in India has not operated in quite the same way as in the United States, Africa or Australia, where the contrast and the conflict between white and black is much more strongly marked; racial identity and/or privilege has not been constructed for Indians only or primarily in terms of skin color, for the hot Indian sun blackens the whitest skin and smudges the distinction between white and black.[13] India has continually been conquered and colonized by paler-skinned peoples, from the Aryans in ancient times to the Europeans in the modern one; it has even been suggested that Indians are in fact degenerate Europeans, and therefore 'whites' who have lost their 'whiteness' in this "continent of Circe."[14] Color here has always been a marker of race,[15] a lighter skin the indicator of descent from a conquering or colonizing race of white males. But these males rarely brought along their women with them; the foremothers of most Indians were dark, and their descendants, accordingly, are no longer 'white' but, rather, 'brown' as distinct from 'dark.'[16] Even the Portuguese,[17] the French and the Dutch, who colonized India during the last four centuries, became so completely absorbed into its already hybrid society that the skin coloring of their descendants is like that of all Indians, which varies from a 'Caucasian' paleness through shades of 'Mongolian' yellow to ebony, sometimes within the same linguistic or ethnic community.

Not surprisingly, therefore, there is considerable ambiguity about whiteness in India. A fair skin is prized, especially in females, for, as Nirad Chaudhuri puts it:

> The Hindu civilization was created by a people who were acutely conscious of their fair complexion in contrast to the dark skin of the autochthons, and their greatest preoccupation was how to maintain the pristine purity of the blood-stream which carried this colour. . . .This faith in the sanctity of *Varna*, colour, or caste endures and abides in Hindu society. . . . The Hindu regards himself as heir to the oldest conscious tradition of superior and as the carrier of the purest and most exclusive stream of blood which created that colour.[18]

But the early encounters between European colonizers and Indian society did not always or necessarily confirm or establish white civilizational or cultural superiority, though they certainly did prove the masculinity of whiteness to the Indian. In an overwhelmingly patrilineal society maleness is undoubtedly highly valued, but that does not automatically make whiteness its highest attribute. Whiteness itself, indeed, is frequently conflated with disease (vitiligo, albinism, leprosy)[19] and mourning (wearing white, rather than black, is a sign of grief), with the white man often being regarded in the past as a *mleccha*, outcast, and even, in an ironic reversal of colonial attitudes, a monster (Chaudhuri recalls being told as a child that the unnatural color of "the English race" was due to the fact that they "were of a she-monkey by a demon born").[20] Two popular Hindu gods, Rama and Krishna, are dark, the Indian Earth Goddesses are certainly not white-skinned, and the two most beautiful women in Indian mythology, Sita in the *Ramayana* and Draupadi in the *Mahabharata*, are dark. No wonder, then, that South Asians cannot identify either with the white Anglo-Saxon settlers or with the black indigenous people in Africa or Australia. Yasmine Gooneratne's Navaranjini/Jean in *A Change of Skies* encapsulates the South Asian attitude to whiteness: she believes the Australian "WAP" (in which the yen-powered Japanese are bestowed the honor of "honorary whiteness") was formulated because "Australians are afraid of the dark," but the color of her own brown skin, quite unlike the "unappetizing" Australian whiteness, is so beautiful that she is beyond white racism:

> racism's unknown in India and Sri Lanka. [. . . .] Our people aren't racist about colour, they just honour a very ancient and holy tradition that has clear rules about what's beautiful and what's not. The marriage ads at home rate complexions according to that tradition, and I've always been pleased that my own complexion happens to be the exact shade they rate highest. I notice that manufacturers of suntan creams here call it Natural Tan, and Australian women seem to kill themselves every summer trying to acquire it.[21]

It was when racial hegemony became an integral part of the colonial program that the gendering of white and black became obvious in India. In the early years of the British presence in India the white man had frequently taken on dark Indian women as wives, mistresses, concubines, and harem slaves, often with official encouragement, and the dichotomy between white and black became part of the multicolored mosaic of Indian society.[22] Once, however, he had established himself more firmly in India, and brought over white women to join him,[23] and white missionaries to succor him and to evangelize the heathen around him,[24] the ambiguities of the White Mughal's position were replaced by a sharper definition of the roles of white and black and a much more problematic and confrontational relationship between whiteness and darkness. Now the white male desire for the dark Other was sublimated through the Englishman's representation of himself taking over the dark unknown feminine/effeminate India, notably in his role in preventing *sati* (as Spivak so famously puts it in another context, "White men are saving brown women from brown men").[25]

The social and cultural consequences of the masculinization of the white and feminization of the dark is the major theme of *Kim* and *Gora*. The titles of the novels, named as they are after their respective protagonists, might suggest that they are the usual stories of development, Bildungsromans; instead, they are about the relationship between whiteness, gender and power. Kim may be white, but his androgynous name, coupled with his tanned skin, clearly indicates the two opposing directions in which the young boy is pulled: the male world of his white soldier father, whose profession makes him part of the colonizing force in India, and the female/maternal and colonized world of India, where the orphan feels he belongs more truly rather than in the white world.[26] Gora's name is as ambiguous and suggestive. It is a common Bengali name for an unusually fair male, and a popular North Indian nickname for a white soldier; furthermore, it is also, paradoxically enough, one of the epithets of Krishna, the dark androgynous God, the friend and lover of women and female beauty, who embodies the love and the beauty of the full moon. Tagore's protagonist, like Kipling's, is white, the son of a soldier; he embodies those qualities of whiteness conventionally attributed to both masculinity and the colonizer—aggressiveness, power, competition—qualities, however, he ultimately rejects when he grows beyond the constricting whiteness of his European heritage and turns to embrace the power and the humanity of the dark and the androgynous/feminine world of Krishna and his (foster) mother Anandamoyi. Both Kim and Gora have Indian foster-mothers; but where Gora, Krishna-like, is devoted to his, Kim's whiteness deadens him to any emotional attachment toward all the maternal figures he encounters. He never shows any interest in his dead mother, who may have been Eurasian like the "half-caste" woman who claimed to be her sister and who has fostered him from birth (7), and whom he easily leaves behind and forgets, perhaps because he shares the traditional contempt that both white and dark have for people of mixed blood (159). But neither do the more 'authentic,' dark, Indian mother-figures, like Huneefa the prostitute in chapter X or the Sahiba at the end of the novel, mean much to him. They may provide him food, shelter and care when he needs it, but he does not let them affect his life and personal growth, because what he is in search of is not a mother, but a (white) father from whom alone he can derive his identity. He may exploit the interest women obviously have in him, whether sexual or maternal, but he himself remains unmoved by them. This may be because Kipling was incapable of bringing to life an Indian woman as subject or agent,[27] but it is also true that whiteness leaves no space for the feminine, which, in both colonial discourse and Indian tradition and mythography, is dark. Not surprisingly, therefore, there are no white women in the novel at all.[28] *Kim*, then, is above all a "male novel."[29] The meaning of *Gora*, however, would remain incomplete without its women.

Interestingly, Kim and Gora are both of Irish origin. In colonial India real whiteness was reserved only for the Anglo-Saxon, not for the white-skinned but racially inferior Celtic;[30] the Irish have always been liminal and sympathetic figures for Indians, as fellow participators in anti-colonial and anti-Anglo-Saxon feeling. Besides, the Irish in India were overwhelmingly Catholics: in Indian experience, Roman Catholicism was not the religion of empire except in the Portuguese colony of Goa, and unlike other Christian sects it has always been more open to the cultural styles and the traditional religious beliefs of Indians. This is a point which Kipling's novel certainly

makes, as, for instance, in the contrast between the Church of England Padre
and Father Victor in the fifth and sixth chapters. Tagore's novel makes no
reference to differences between Christian sects in their attitudes to India
and its 'darkness' as *Kim* does, but its protagonist was modeled on an Indian
Catholic who later turned a Vedantist without renouncing Christianity,
Brahmabandhab Upadhayay.[31] He was an ardent nationalist whose mission
was "*firingijaivrata*, literally 'the rite of conquering the whites,'" and who,
like other nationalists in India at the time, particularly disliked 'liberated'
white women.[32]

Kim's liminality, like Gora's whiteness, is, paradoxically, what makes
him feel he belongs to India, an India that Europe had constructed in its
imagination and Britain in its administration. Indeed, India as a political unit
had never existed before colonization; it was, rather, the site of an emotional
and spiritual sense of belonging, which the Indian traditionally associates
with his ties to his mother. Unlike the nation, a political and 'white' concept,
maternity cannot be quantified or contained. But the nation demands
definition; its primary marker is its border, which is what the white man set
out to establish in India. Perhaps that is why the most important characters in
Kim are its liminal male figures, who map out its borders: the geographically
liminal, like the Lama, a Buddhist who comes from India's northern frontier,
Tibet, and the Pathan Mahbub Ali, who belongs to Kabul and Peshawar; the
socially and intellectually liminal, the effete "mimic man" Hurree Babu; and
the racially and emotionally liminal Kim himself, who may be born white,
but whose whiteness remains ambiguous until he learns how to make himself
a member of the ruling race by following the rules of manhood.

At the center of the colonial construct of India was the imperial project
of knowing it, through travel to and along its margins, through reading
about India, through intelligence agencies, through institutions like the
Archeological and Geographical Surveys of India, and above all through
ordering and classifying this knowledge and putting it to use to assert their
domination over the colony. The year of the first census in India was the year
Kim was published (1901); both census, which counted and classified the
people, of India, and novel, which explores the process of learning about dark
and how to overcome it, indicate the methods by which only a few thousand
white men could exercise power over millions of dark "natives." The novel,
therefore, confidently reaffirms the validity of British knowledge; it shows
how the British managed to control India by domesticating what might have
seemed unknowable, the alarming Otherness of enormous masses of unruly
and unmanageable people who could not be fitted comfortably into known,
rational or logical compartments. Thus the Ethnological Survey collects and
collates information about India's roads, rivers, plants, stones and customs and

makes available to the British Government the information and understanding that enables it to exercise power over India. The simple-hearted Tibetan lama learns the newest discoveries about his own religion and culture from the English curator of the Lahore museum, and accepts a pair of spectacles from him that empowers him to see better (18) (much like Gooneratne's Bharat discarding his spectacles for contact lenses when he decides to become the Australian Barry);[33] this gives him the knowledge that sets him, and with him Kim, on their respective journeys toward self-discovery, the lama toward transcendence and Kim toward whiteness.

Kim finally learns and decides to be white after he finds his way into the secrets of India and puts this knowledge at the disposal of a benevolent Raj. That is, he exploits his knowledge of the dark world of India to destroy resistance to the white colonizer, even though, in doing so, he betrays the dark and his own emotional ties with it. Kim's constant shifts in identity between white and black, with his final rejection of the black and its women, then, are an ironic echo of the 'going native' of earlier Englishmen, who wished to remain in India with their dark women; they parallel the frequent changes of disguise and skin color that Sir Richard Burton used to discover India with. To quote Benita Parry, "because Kipling's India is reified under western [white] eyes as a frieze or pageant, and romanticized as an object of sensuous and voluptuous pleasure to be enjoyed by Europe, it is an invention which colonizes the space of India's own significations with western fantasies."[34]

Kim enjoys playing the Great Game, which is for him at first just one of the street games of his boyhood, with himself as Little-Friend-of-all the-World, a bearer of the white man's burden, epitomized in the way the novel opens with the young boy sitting on an old gun, the phallic symbol of empire. Despite his dark skin, his poverty, and his orphaned status, his supremacy over his dark playmates and other acquaintances is unquestioned everywhere, for he is white, and he knows it. He slips effortlessly between his two identities, becoming black or white as his situation demands; but the more he plays the dark boy in the Great Game, the more he becomes the white man. His uncertain positioning between whiteness and darkness might be very important to the Great Game, which requires an effortless de-whitening at certain moments. Nevertheless, he is clearly more at home, and happier, as a part of various and variegated India than as a white man excluded from its dark teeming millions in the glory of his whiteness. Kim, without quite knowing what it is that pulls him away from the whiteness he is in search of, frequently tries to escape the white man's world, jumping from white carriages or over white walls to the Indian and the lama's world of love and commitment, and continually declares that whatever he is, he is not and will never be a Sahib, that repository of supreme whiteness. The constant alternation between his two selves forces him continually to question his own identity and to face a sense of loss whenever he has to be white. When Kim asks Mahbub Ali whether Lurgan Sahib is "by chance one of us," Mahbub, who has known Kim as an Indian street boy for years, answers immediately:

> "What talk is this of *us*, Sahib?" Mahbub Ali returned, in the tone he used towards Europeans. "I am a Pathan; thou art a Sahib and the son of a Sahib." (162)

The distance between white and dark is made clear: if Kim is white he must accept the burden of whiteness as much as he enjoys its privileges, and cannot participate in the human qualities and values of India that were once a part of his dark self. Because the white man, whether Creighton or Lurgan, schoolmaster or clergyman, knows only how to use others for his own ends, the dichotomy between white and dark has become an instrument in the power struggles of the colony, not a mark of the multiple identities of eternally accepting India.

It is a painful choice for him finally to repudiate his emotional ties to the dark for the rationality and impersonality of whiteness. Indeed, when he first encounters the white man's world in the army camp, it is a traumatic experience; but as he becomes more and more white, and is further co-opted into in the Great Game, he turns from being Friend-of-all-the-World to the Friend-of-the-Stars, one who participates in imperial power through the mental strength and discipline that whiteness has taught him, and attempts to escape no longer. His victory over the European spies, the enemies of the British Empire whose values he has decided to uphold, confirms his own whiteness to himself, even if he can never be as white as the soldiers in his father's army but only as white as other "native-born" white men like Creighton. Significantly, Kim's dark self dies as the lama's mystical search ends, and the results of his choice of whiteness remain ambiguous: "'I am Kim. I am Kim. And what is Kim?' His soul repeated it again and again." (305)

Through the white boy who thinks in Hindi, the street urchin who is also a white man, Kipling foregrounds the mimicry and the hybridity of the colony; Kim represents the desire of/for the Other by both colonizer and colonized. Even the potentially threatening 'minority discourse' of the natives is appropriated by the positioning of 'hybridity' in Kim's identity. Kim's double in the novel, the Bengali Hurree Chunder Mookerjee, underlines this; both are mimic men symbolizing the deracination and deculturation of the colony, the white man playing at darkness and the black playing at whiteness. Like Kim, Mookerjee has received an 'English' education (he is an MA in English from Calcutta University); like Kim he has been ensnared in the Great Game by his

English masters; like Kim he is a superb actor. But because he is not white, he becomes a pathetic travesty of East and West. Angry and confused because Creighton has not permitted him to poison the Russian spies, he declares: "It is all *your* beastly English pride. [. . .] It is *our* British pride" (242; emphasis added). The Russians and the French may be Europeans, but they cannot be as white as the English: "By Jove, they are not *black* people. . . . They are Russians, and highly unscrupulous people" (243; emphasis added). For the Russians Hurree Babu "represents in little India in transition—the monstrous hybridism of East and West," which has made him lose "his own country" without acquiring another, a man who at once admires and has "a most complete hatred of his conquerors." (259) It is significant that Kim's dark double should be a Bengali, a 'race' which epitomized the effeminacy of the black man the colonizers despised but which had also begun to represent the black threat to the white empire: at the time the novel was written, Bengalis were leading the earliest middle-class struggles against white power, both intellectual and physical, including terrorist attacks against white colonial officials.

It is, ultimately, not the color of Kim's skin but his choice of whiteness itself, his decision to take up the white man's burden that finally alienates him from his Indian self and the eternal feminine principle embodied in Mother Earth and Mother India. *Kim*, in fact, is not so much an apology for imperialism as a nostalgic attempt on Kipling's part to represent what the darkness of India meant for the white Englishman; to a large extent, indeed, the novel is a fictionalized version of his poem, "To the Native-Born,"[35] dedicated to the white man in India who, like Kim, is torn between his white male origin in England and his feminized presence in India, for whom England is the father whom he hardly knows and India the mother who loves and nurtures him. Kipling's "native-born," like Kim, is incomprehensible to his "English brother" (3); he has been taught to "call old England 'home'" (12), to read about the English skylark and the English spring (13–14), but it is India which is his "native soil" (24), with its "dear dark foster-mothers" and "the heathen songs they sung," the women who taught white boys "the heathen speech we babbled/Ere we came to the white man's tongue" (83–86). India is the dark Other for the white man, a feminine Other invariably linked with motherhood; it is the lost object of desire which must be relinquished for the sake of entry into the patriarchal law.

This was something that the first nationalists in India were acutely aware of; they sought to provide the Indian woman the education and the domestic virtues of cleanliness and discipline they associated with Englishwomen, but they also expected her to remain the repository of whatever could be called uniquely and completely Indian. India could be free only if Indian men would take up the white man's burden themselves, only if they could infuse the white man's masculinity into a debilitated, ailing and feminized nation that had lost its selfhood. To save Mother India was the duty of every Indian son. For the revolutionary-turned-ascetic Sri Aurobindo, India was Shakti, the female source of all power, now enslaved by whiteness, who had to be liberated by the blood of her sons: "I know my country as Mother. I offer her my devotions, my worship."[36] In place of the *Ardhanarishwar*, the androgynous deity of ancient India who symbolized the union between *Prakriti/shakti* (Nature, power, femininity) and *Purusha/shiva* (knowledge, masculinity), the nationalist saw the necessity only for the *purusha* they associated the white man with; womanliness, femininity, *naritva*, could lead only to *klibatva*, the neutered and the impotent.[37] For Tagore, however, the nation and nationalism were by-products of whiteness and of the enforced homogeneity and masculinity it stood for; real Indianness lay in the traditional femininity of a diverse and plural Indian society. In a series of essays in *Nationalism* he pointed out that nationalism was merely a lust for ownership, a thrust for power and domination, not the power of the female principle of *Shakti*, which was the core of Indian identity. It is this that he underscores in *Gora*.

Gora, like Kim, is an Irish orphan, brought up as an Indian. But the resemblance ends here. Gora is not left to struggle on the streets but is part of a warm and affectionate family in which he is devoted to his mother, Anandamoyi. Kim always knows he is white, with a white father, and therefore never quite Indian; but Gora learns of his 'true' identity much later, although the reader is informed of his history early in the novel. He regards himself as a passionate Indian, and has become virulently Hindu in the belief that the humiliation of colonization can be overcome only by a return to the what he believes is the indigenous life of India, which he identifies with the most 'fundamentalist' form of Hinduism, even though it may be caste-ridden, superstitious and backward-looking. Anandamoyi herself, however, does not agree with this idea of India: she has been raised by her grandfather, a Brahmin priest at Varanasi,[38] and is, accordingly, deeply rooted in Indian/Hindu tradition; she knows, therefore, that Mother India, whom she represents, is always at peace with cultural differences and dissent. This conviction has been reinforced ever since she, a childless woman, was given a white man's baby to love and nurture as her own; India is the eternal maternal principle for whom love and diversity are the core of identity. So *as* a traditional Indian woman—rather than *in spite of* being one—she wears chemises under her saris (even though it was a European import adopted only by the 'Westernized' Bengali woman), and accepts the services of her Christian maid Lachhmia.

Gora, however, strongly disapproves of this. If he is a true Indian he must live up to the demands of his Brahmin ancestry: he must uphold the values of racial and social purity, and reject the outsider, and the outsider's ways. Lachhmia was his nursemaid, and adores him; but his Indianizing zeal sees her as merely a Christian, a *mleccha* whose touch would defile him (the irony, and the Indian inclusiveness, of a Christian named after a Hindu goddess escapes Gora). From the beginning of the novel, accordingly, Gora's whiteness is contrasted with Anandamoyi's maternal darkness. When he is first introduced, the novelist remarks that the whiteness of his coloring is "*ugra*," aggressive, without a touch of the dark to soften its harshness, and his strongly marked features are sharply severe (8). Anandamoyi, however, is dark (12), and full of love, not only for her own son but also for all the sons of India.

The events in the novel continuously interrogate and undermine Gora's ideas of nationalism and self-definition. It begins with Binoy, his best friend, accidentally meeting a reformist Brahmo family, and his subsequent attraction for Pareshbabu, the father, Lolita, his spirited daughter, and Sucharita, his friend's daughter, whom he has brought up as his own. The Brahmos, who attempted to return to the core of the Vedic religion from which modern Hinduism has developed, believed they were modern and Westernized because they had discarded the superstitions and the irrational social practices of contemporary Hindus that were not sanctioned in the ancient religion; Tagore's grandfather was one of the founders of the Brahmo sect, and the poet-novelist and his family had been Brahmos for three generations. Like most Hindus of the time, who rejected the Brahmo turn to the West and its alienation from conventional society, Gora resents the influence Pareshbabu's family exerts on Binoy. He feels it is taking his friend away from the social exclusiveness without which Indianness cannot be retained, and resents 'liberated' ways of the Brahmo girls in that family as unIndian. The two friends gradually begin to drift apart as Binoy begins to accept the fact that their visions of Indianness are as opposed to each other's as Gora's and Anandamoyi's are. Gora leaves Calcutta in search of the true, Hindu, India which is supposed to live in its villages, in an ironic of retelling of the white man's travels to discover and know India which Kim, too, had undertaken.

Then Lolita precipitates a crisis that forces Binoy to marry her, a crisis in which Gora unknowingly plays a central role. She and her family, and Binoy, are visiting their family home in the country, when her mother, Baradasundari, the stereotyped, almost caricature-like Brahmo woman for whom the white man is the symbol of enlightenment, organizes a play to be performed by her family in honor of a white official who had imprisoned Gora a few days earlier for championing the cause of oppressed villagers. Lolita refuses to act in front of the white man who so dishonors the brown man in his own land. She runs away to Calcutta to her father, only to discover on the journey that Binoy, too, is going back there. Their travelling together like this without a chaperone causes a major scandal among Hindus and Brahmos alike, which can be set right only if they get married; they decide to do so, for they realize they are in love. But only Pareshbabu and Sucharita among the Brahmos accept the match, for Binoy refuses to convert to their faith, and only Anandamoyi among the Hindus welcomes it, for Lolita remains a Brahmo. As mother, the one thing that matters to Anandamoyi is that it is love, the supreme Indian value that binds the young couple together. Anandamoyi the foster mother is thus Tagore's own vision of Mother India, against which he juxtaposes two other models: the unthinking mimic modernity of the Brahmo woman, Barasundari, adoptive mother to Sucharita, and the equally unthinking traditional woman who clings to a meaningless and inhuman orthodoxy, Sucharita's Hindu aunt, who tries desperately to reconvert her niece to Hindu ways by exerting her authority as a mother-substitute. Both these women are failed mothers, for they are exclusivist and unloving, propagating an Indianness that is not dark but white.

Gora himself rejects Binoy, as he does Anandamoyi. They have betrayed his ideals, and he refuses to acknowledge that they may have different ones that may be equally valid. But his ideas about India have been severely shaken by his experiences in rural Bengal, by the resistance of Muslim villagers to his fundamentalist Hindu ideas and by the kind of Hinduism practiced by the village barber, who has adopted a Muslim boy whose family has been devastated by the British indigo planters. He discovers that his nationalism, his idea that India is a single homogenous nation, is a borrowed 'white' one that has no cultural roots, that Mother India never was nor shall be culturally exclusivist. He also finds himself falling in love with Sucharita. There was a time when Gora had never considered the fact that there were women in India; his India was a male one. Now he discovers India through Sucharita, who becomes for him the representation of Indian womanhood itself. He realizes that women do not merely *symbolize* the motherland: they *are* the motherland, and that it is the indifference to the humiliation of women-as-mother-and-motherland that has led to the Indian male insecurity about his loss of masculinity.

It is at this point that Gora suddenly discovers the truth about his own origin. He has been preparing for undergoing the rituals of penance after his imprisonment, where he had not been able to maintain the standards of purity demanded of the Brahmin, but his father refuses him permission to do so. Just as Gora is beginning to question whether the burden of purity, of Indianness, that he was carrying was indeed natural or justified, Krishnadayal, who is dying, sends for him and tells him that he has no religious rights as his son, because he was the child of white parents, not of Indian ones. Gora now finds himself suddenly reduced from a Brahmin, purest of the pure of all Indians, to a white man, and therefore an untouchable and a non-Indian: he had no mother, no father, no country, no race, no name, no family or clan, no god; his whole existence was only a negative (346). When the white doctor comes in to examine Krishnadayal, Gora, who had always turned away from white men, wonders whether it is the white man who is his kin, his own, and not the Indian with whom he had always identified himself. It is now that Gora discovers that the boundaries between India and not-India, between the indigenous and the exogenous, between white and non-white, are indeterminate; the concept of Indianness as indigenousness he had so far upheld, he sees, is in fact white, nonindigenous, and violates the fundamental principles of an inclusive and feminized Indianness. All these years, unbeknownst to himself, he was simply carrying the white man's burden in trying to gain India; now that burden has gone from him. Gora the white man becomes most truly Indian because he has chosen to be so. Unlike Kim's acceptance of his whiteness, his realization of his Indianness is embedded in a discourse of woman: above all in his identification of India with his (foster) mother, who represents in her womanliness, her rejection of caste and religion, the spirit of India more genuinely than his own masculine and white version (349). Now he can drink water from the hitherto spurned Lachhmia, and acknowledge the love of the emancipated Brahmo woman Sucharita.

Kim and Gora are both outsiders who become insiders to India. What marginalizes Kim in British India is what makes him belong to the real India: a white boy, he can merge into the darkness of India effortlessly. Gora's role, however, is to expose the hypocrisies and contradictions in India through his obtrusive whiteness and maleness. He is Tagore's mythical white man who was sent by Fate "to burst through our rickety door and enter into the very interior of our house."[39] That is why, though he may be brought up as an Indian, he remains a white man physically and psychologically: he is tall, "roars" when he speaks, is always assertive, and lives in a black-and-white world in which there are no shades of grey. But when the white man repudiates the white man's burden he is saved from a narrow white nationalism by returning to his mother and, by implication, motherland. He achieves a self-definition by including his white self in a larger philosophy of life. At the very moment that he realizes that he is neither white nor dark he is reborn; the narrowness of contemporary Indian nationalism may exclude him, but he is reborn into Indianness and the feminine. Kim, however, narrows down his self-definition to become a member of the security services of empire; he has to become an outsider to his own cultural self.

The differences between Kipling's *Kim* and Tagore's *Gora* are, then, not simply a matter of being on opposing sides of the colonial divide but, rather, of different interpretations of masculinity, nationhood and society. Kim must leave the India of his emotions, which might emasculate him, to become a "white man," a member of the colonizing race, while Gora consciously chooses to reject the male notions of nation and selfhood derived, ironically, from the male colonizer, which he had hitherto embraced, and identify himself with the feminine India, symbolized in his mother. Gora, in spite of his name, discards both whiteness and maleness for the power of a female India that includes all colors in its social, cultural and political being, an identity that is based on the female belief in inclusiveness rather than on the male insistence on Otherness.

NOTES

1. Rudyard Kipling, *The Naulahka: a Story of West and East,* 2nd ed. (London: W. Heinemann, 1892).

2. Edward Morgan, *A Passage to India* (London: Dent, 1961).

3. Paul Scott, *The Jewel in the Crown* (London: Heinemann, 1966).

4. Nancy Leys Stepan, "Race and Gender: The Role of Analogy in Science" in *The Anatomy of Racism,* ed. D. T. Goldberg (Minneapolis: University of Minnesota Press, 1990), 40–43.

5. See, for instance, George Demetra, *Mysteries of the Dark Moon: The Healing Power of the Dark Goddess* (San Francisco: HarperSanFrancisco, 1992), 8–20, 27–29; and Julia Kristeva's reading of Lacan in "Stabat Mater" and "Women's Time," in *The Kristeva Reader,* ed. Toril Moi (New York: Columbia University Press, 1986), 225–47, 188–213.

6. See, for instance: Elaine Lindsay, *Spirituality in Australian Women's Fiction* (Amsterdam: Rodopi, 2000), 20–31.

7. In "Supplementing the Orientalist Lack: European Ladies in the Harem" Meyda Yeğenoğlu points out "the metonymic association established between the Orient and its women. . . . The Orient, seen as the embodiment of sensuality, is always understood in feminine terms and accordingly its place in the Western imagery has been construed through the simultaneous gesture of racialization and feminization." *Colonial Fantasies: Towards a Feminist Reading of Orientalism.* (Cambridge: Cambridge University Press, 1998), 72–73.

8. See: Ashis Nandy, *The Intimate Enemy: Loss and Recovery of Self Under Colonialism* (Delhi: Oxford University Press, 1999).

9. Partha Chatterjee, *The Nation and Its Fragments: Colonial and Postcolonial Histories* (Delhi: Oxford University Press, 1995).

10. Rudyard Kipling, *Kim* (New Delhi: Rupa & Co, 2004). All textual references will hereafter appear parenthetically and refer to this edition.

11. Rabindranath Tagore, *Gora. Rabindra-Rachanabali,* Centenary Edition (Calcutta: West Bengal Government, Bengali year 1368 [1961]). Vol. 9—Novels. 1–350. All textual references will appear parenthetically and refer to this edition.

12. The prominence of the theme and motif of whiteness in *Kim* has been frequently noticed, as in Parama Roy's *Indian Traffic: Identities in Question in Colonial and Postcolonial India* (Berkeley: University of California Press, 1998), or D. K. Barua's "Kipling's *Kim*: A Parable of Imperial Hope," *Rabindra Bharati Patrika* (2000–2001): 8–18. Surprisingly enough, however, the issue of whiteness in *Gora*, in spite of its title ("white male") has not received due attention.

13. Lisa Suhair Majaj points out in "Arab-Americans and the Meanings of Race" that the Naturalization Act of 1790 in the U.S. had granted the right of citizenship only to "free white persons," a much contested category in the case of Arabs or Indians who sought naturalization because of competing and contradictory definitions of "whiteness." Their "darker complexions set them at odds with popular perceptions of whiteness" even though they "were scientifically identified as Caucasian" in *Postcolonial Theory and the United States: Race, Ethnicty, and Literature*, ed., Amritjit Singh and Peter Schmidt (Jackson: University Press of Mississipi, 2000), 322.

14. Nirad C. Chaudhuri, *The Continent of Circe: Being an Essay on the Peoples of India* (Mumbai: Jaico, 2000).

15. The terms *varna*, color, and *jati*, tribe, caste, race, are more or less synonymous in popular usage, and *varna* is used interchangeably for color and caste.

16. Chaudhuri, *Continent of Circe*, 30.

17. Ania Loomba points out that the Portuguese in India and elsewhere in Asia were actually encouraged by church and state to marry fairer upper-caste Indian women but discard darker-skinned wives and concubines. See: *Colonialism/Postcolonialism* (London: Routledge, 1999. New Critical Idion Series), 110–11.

18. Nirad C. Chaudhuri, *The Autobiography of an Unknown Indian* (Bombay: Jaico Publishing House, 1991), 129.

19. As a young man in Calcutta Chaudhuri heard a Hindi poet sing a song about Mother India's body all over which "the Whites are spread . . . as a disfiguring skin-disease," in Chaudhuri's *Autobiography*, 125.

20. Chaudhuri, *Autobiography*, 119.

21. Yasmine Gooneratne, *A Change of Skies* (New Delhi: Penguin, 1992), 19, 119–20. Most Indians, like most South Asians, believe that they can never be guilty of chromatism and racism; racism is what white people do. The recent popular indignation in India over the Australian allegation of racism levelled against an Indian cricketer arose from the Indian perception that Indians, being 'brown' themselves, can never be the perpetrators of racism, even though they might privilege 'fairness.'

22. See: Kenneth Ballhatchet, *Race, Sex and Class under the Raj* (London: Weidenfeld and Nicholson, 1980); William Dalrymple, *White Mughals: Love and Betrayal in Eighteenth-Century India* (New Delhi: Penguin, 2002).

23. The Englishwomen who came over to India were usually much more racist and exclusive than their men, probably because, suggests Ashis Nandy in *The Intimate Enemy*, "they unconsciously saw themselves as the sexual competitors of Indian men, with whom their men had established an unconscious homo-erotic bonding," 10.

24. In the early colonial period in British India missionary activity was banned, and the British Indian Army attempted to show a modicum of respect to Indian religions.

25. Gayatri Chakravorty Spivak, "Can the Subaltern Speak?" in *Marxism and the Interpretation of Culture*, ed. C. Nelson and L. Grossberg (Basinstoke: Macmillan Education, 1988), 296.

26. The epigraph to chapter VIII of *Kim*, from "The Two-Sided Man," points to the opposing pulls in Kim's psyche: "Something I owe to the soil that grew—/More to the life that fed—/But most to Allah Who gave me two/Separate sides to my head," 145.

27. See: Gayatri Chakravorty Spivak, "The Burden of English," in *The Lie of the Land: English Literary Studies in India*, ed. Rajeswari Sunder Rajan (Delhi: Oxford University Press, 1993), 275–99.

28. Patrick Williams in "Kim and Orientalism," explains the absence of white women from the novel as the novelist's way of confining condemnation of women's 'darkness,' their sexuality, to the 'dark' race itself: "Racial superiority was, by the end of the century, one of the few remaining justifications for British rule, and the perceived threat from uncontrolled female sexuality (here rendered as uncontrolled Indian female sexuality, the truth [of white women's desire for Indian males] being literally unspeakable), was a grave one indeed, " in *Kipling Reconsidered*, ed. Phillip Mallett (London: Macmillan, 1989), 49.

29. Edward Said's comments in his Introduction to *Kim* (Harmondsworth: Penguin, 1987) are well known: "The women in the novel are remarkably few in number by comparison, and all are somehow debased or unsuitable for male attention: . . . to be always pestered by women, Kim believes, is to be hindered in playing the Great Game, which is best played by men alone. So not only are we in a masculine world dominated by travel, trade, adventure and intrigue, we are in a celibate world, in which the common romance of fiction and the enduring institution of marriage have been circumvented, avoided, all but ignored," 27.

30. Noel Ignatiev's *How the Irish Became White* (New York: Routledge, 1995), points out how Irish immigrants to the U.S., victims of English colonial power back home, were subjected to the same racial discrimination at the hands of the American Anglo-Saxon upper classes until social/class mobility gradually gave them the privilege of being considered as "white" as British immigrants.

31. Ashis Nandy, *The Illegitimacy of Nationalism: Rabindranath Tagore and the Politics of Self* (New Delhi: Oxford University Press, 1994), 67.

32. Quoted in Nandy, *Illegitmacy of Nationalism*, 64.

33. Gooneratne, *A Change of Skies*, 125.

34. Benita Parry, "The Contents and Discontents of Kipling's Imperialism," in *Postcolonial Studies: A Materialist Critique* (London: Routledge, 2005), 124.

35. Rudyard Kipling, "To the Native-Born," *DayPoems*, http://www.daypoems.net/poems/1836.html (accessed September 5, 2005).

36. Quoted in Nandy, *The Intimate Enemy*, 92. The ancient saying *Janani janmabhoomishcha svargadapi gariyashi*, "mother and motherland are greater than heaven," part of a Sanskrit *shloka* attributed to the epic hero and Hindu god Rama, was adapted by the freedom movement in India to identify the nation. This maternalization of the idea of India grew out of the traditional association of home and homeland with the family, in which the mother is supreme nourisher and nurturer,

for whom all her sons—regardless of class, creed, color, caste—are very dear. The image of Mother India thus epitomizes the idea of a harmonious plural homeland that poets, philosophers, nationalists and political thinkers envisaged.

37. See Nandy, *The Intimate Enemy*, 7–8.

38. Varanasi, or Benaras, is the holiest city of the Hindus, and one of the oldest living cities of the world. By referring to Varanasi, Tagore underscores the fact that liberality, humanity, all-inclusiveness and love are the most ancient bases of Indian identity.

39. Quoted in Nandy, *Nationalism*, 45.

Chapter Seven

Fictions and Truths of Racial Production in Hannah Crafts'
The Bondwoman's Narrative

Suzanne Lynch

Until recently, the name Hannah Crafts meant little or nothing to many scholars of American literature. It was not until Henry Louis Gates Jr. purchased the auctioned manuscript *The Bondwoman's Narrative* in 2001 from Swann Galleries and in 2002 introduced it to the reading public that Hannah Crafts' name began to play a pivotal role in the reading of early American texts.

Crafts' narrative, written circa 1853 to 1860,[1] documents the story of a young mixed-race slave, whose combination of wit, vision, and honesty eventually earns her the final rewards of community and family. Written as an autobiography, Hannah Crafts tale narrates the journey of a young girl from slavey to freedom. During her escape, she is hunted and recaptured, jailed with the eccentric Mrs. Wright, sold to the benevolent Mrs. Henry, and resold to the cruel Mrs. Wheeler. As a slave narrative, however, Crafts' tale deviates from conventional form. Among other scholars, Jean Fagan Yelling has noted "Hannah does not follow the stereotypical pattern. . . . Nor does *Bondwoman's Narrative* present her as a pathetic 'mixed-race' protagonist whose 'black blood' prevents her from the 'white' life to which she aspires."[2] Although Crafts' tale begins with the traditional disclosure of the lack of parentage and continues with the expected documentations of escape and descriptions of the cruel masters and overseers, her narrative, unlike the slave narratives of many of her contemporaries, reads more poignantly as a statement about the contradictions of racial codes and beliefs than it does about the condemnation of the unjust treatment and condition of the slave, that comes as a result of a capricious slaveocracy. Whereas narratives such as *Incidents in the Life of a Slave Girl*, by Harriet Jacobs, focus on the silent fear of the protagonist and her effort to gain empowerment and reclaim her voice despite the machinations of her master to sexually exploit her and reduce her to insult,[3] Crafts' narrative bestows its protagonist with an empowerment from the beginning of Hannah's tale through a voice of confident knowing that provides the young slave girl with an understanding of herself as a racially and socially complex individual: "I was not a slave with these pictured memorials of the past. They could not enforce drudgery, or condemn me on account of my color to a life of servitude. As their companion I could think and speculate,"[4] Hannah tells her reader in the first chapter of her narrative. With these words she introduces us to a young girl intent on completing a journey toward self empowerment—one which she qualifies with the belief that "sorrow and affliction and death make us all equal" (45). Instead of the powerlessness commonly ascribed to slave women through sexual and instructive oppression, Hannah seems to experience of a sense of authority derived from the knowledge that her legal station in life is "the result of that false system which bestows on position, wealth, or power the consideration only due to a man" (205). In a world that seems to say "you are nothing because you are a slave," Hannah seems to say "I am equal, if not superior," to those who insist on reducing her to ignorance.

Hannah Crafts' narrative may be therefore read as a different kind of slave narrative. It asks that we expand our understanding of its literary tradition and rather than viewing this narrative as a movement that patterns the chronological phases of innocence, realization, resigned resolution, and freedom obtained designed to describe the process of transformation from slave to human,[5] we might also see this narrative as one that resists convention by assuming from the start a given self-evident humanity. In addition to its traditional function that documents the process from slavery to freedom, Crafts' narrative demonstrates an oral and intellectual activism that pronounces her subject a complex compound of identities whose legacy cannot be reduced to a singular racial or social experience.

As Henry Louis Gates, Jr. and Hollis Robbins state in their introduction to *In Search of Hannah Crafts*, the essays examining Crafts' text set out to explore and answer the following questions: "What kind of text is *The Bondwoman's Narrative*? Is it biographical or entirely fictional? Is it internally consistent? Did the author accomplish what she set out to do? Was she seeking to produce a work of a particular literary genre or to challenge that genre? As a writer, is Hannah Crafts as sophisticated as she appears to be? What is the extent of her class or race consciousness?"[6] In addition to the discussion that these questions generate, I am interested in furthering the argument of how Hannah Crafts' narrative expands the horizon of race thinking at a time when particular race knowledge operated as the norm. To this end I ask the question, how does the author's deviation from and juxtaposing of otherwise standard techniques and forms contribute to her understanding and depiction of identity consciousness, concluding that Hannah's reversal of norms becomes the point of an articulated self-empowerment that provides Crafts the means to materialize the woman imagined within the space of what she describes as "undeviating happiness" (246).

Crafts begins her story by telling the reader that "[Hannah][7] was not brought up by anybody in particular" and that "of [her] relatives [she] knew nothing" (5). With these words Crafts introduces the moral and philosophical issues associated with permanent bondage. The lack of information concerning her birth and parentage speaks clearly to the evils of a systematic dehumanization, as many critics have already noted; but more importantly, these evils and the contradictions associated with them that come as a result of Hannah's thoughtful scrutiny, provide Crafts with the material necessary to actively rewrite herself (and her character). Out of the often-incongruent mixture of subjective experience and cultural and historical constructions of identity, she fashions a new Hannah who neither submits to confinements of race nor to the simplicity that the concept of race (from a layman's agenda) seems to convey. In short, *The Bondwoman's Narrative* establishes the creation of a metaracial self that eats away at the seams of slavery, a system that Leonard Cassuto observes "uneasily forced [slaves] into the category of 'thing.'"[8] This easy paring of categories is the one that Crafts addresses through a bleeding of borders between the reality of experiential knowledge and the fictions designed to separate the human from the thing. Crafts' narrative consequently invites readers to participate in naming the inconsistencies associated with the idea of a fixed racial self and warns against those who attempt to reduce her novel to a singular and predictable reading of a racial agenda. Her narrative may therefore be viewed as part of a reformist discourse, much in the same vein as one may classify the colonialist narratives of Lydia Maria Child, which argue for an appreciation of the complexities of race and privilege the identity of human over that of race.

From the beginning of her narrative Hannah fashions her identity through the shedding of assigned tags, and although she presents herself as a parentless slave, she quickly rescripts this sociopolitical label without neglecting the influence it incurs and presents herself as a child, albeit a slave child, who is surrounded with "much love and confidence" (12). The clear disharmony that exists between the concepts of slave and confidence places the two characteristics at extreme and incompatible ends. Crafts' slave child who lives in the midst of love and confidence defies the representation of the slave as inhuman and powerless. Never referring to herself as property despite the understanding by others (principally the inscrutable Mr. Trappe) of her as "marketable" (109), Hannah Crafts represents herself as a girl of intelligence whose ability to "interpret" (7) the looks and attitudes of others humanizes her to the point of superiority over those who see her as less than human.

After meeting Aunt Hetty, an aged woman whom Hannah had previously seen at her master's house once or twice, Hannah *"interpreted"* the "looks and actions" (emphasis added; 7) of the older woman, concluding that "this woman would become my teacher" (7). Hannah's ability to read Aunt Hetty at the level of interpretation illustrates more than just her humanness commonly ascribed to those able to participate in the act of reading. Hannah's interpretative reading, which she demonstrates on numerous occasions, contradicts the claim of others that she is "dull and stupid" (5) and establishes an imaginative sense that subverts the expected scripts of slave behavior and opportunity. Her reading of Aunt Hetty as her future teacher allows her to visualize a future where "a new world with all its mysteries and marvels was opening" (8) and to imagine the none-too-complicated normalcy of the reconstructed slave family in "undeviating happiness" (246).

Hannah's readings, which take the form of an intricate mixture of imaginative endeavors and practical analysis, becomes her strength of agency. Midway through the text, when Hannah again meets Mr Trappe, the infamous slave trader, after having been hunted and caught by him, she reads him with the intensity of a calculated reason: "He looked calmly, though searchingly towards us and I detected an expression in his face at once complacent and self-satisfied. . . . He was sedately pleased and looked just as one may be supposed to look when some great work is accomplished" (99). Her reading of Mr. Trappe both acknowledges her own social positionality and gives commentary on the idea of one ignorant of his own ignorance. Unable to tell the difference between some "great work" and the work of a monstrous viciousness, Mr. Trappe is rendered the essence of ignorance. Hannah reads his satisfied look—one mimicking those who produce great achievements—with sardonic irony, for to her, this fusing of accomplishment with the ownership of others bears more than just a passing resemblance to the absurd. It therefore follows that because Mr. Trappe resides in a state of ignorant unknowing, believing unconditionally that "[the trapping of others into slavery] is nothing so bad after all," he thus exhibits the characteristics of one who is truly "dull and stupid" (101).

Contrary to Trappe, Hannah exhibits the ability to see beyond her own positionality, to reason logically and to understand the historically dichotomized relationship between property and owner. As she meditates on the ignorance mapped onto the body of a slave, she illustrates the necessity to know concretely and to act on one's knowledge through a demonstration of one's wisdom:

> Ignorance, forsooth. Can imagination quench the immortal mind or prevent its feeling at times the indications of its heavenly origin? Can it destroy that deep abiding appreciation of the beautiful that seems inherent to the human soul? Can

it seal up the foundations of truth and all intuitive perception of life, death, and eternity? I think not. Those to whom man . . . teaches little, nature like a wise and prudent mother teaches much. (18)

The above quote reveals the narrator's ability to reason profoundly. Hannah's soliloquy, given after she has been sent by one of the housekeepers, Mrs. Bry, to close the windows to the upstairs gallery before her master, the newly married Mr. De Vincent, returns home with his new bride, identifies the culture of both resistance that actively gives birth to the concept of Hannah as a product of her own creative *interbeing* and to her understanding of herself as a superior individual whose intuitive abilities are the result of a natural-given talent. Her soliloquy demonstrates a strategy that repositions the hierarchy of slaves and humans. It employs the performance of language to separate the myths of racial fictions from the reality of evidential truth. Hannah's poetic and reasoned attention to ignorance alerts us to the subtle complexities of language and culture in which language functions as an agent of change, able to establish its own discourse: to signify, to negate, to initiate knowledge, to dispense subjectivity. The language commonly attributed to the master, spoken by Hannah, identifies ignorance as a perception used to actively construct the "Other" in the political imagination of whites, such as Mr. Trappe, who insists on the maintenance of this perception as a means of reinforcing their own power. However, what masters and slave traders do not acknowledge is the ability of the "Other" to reason and to transcend the stagnant impressions of the dominant party and to form alternative perceptions of ignorance in which the oppressor becomes the ideal of ignorance if he fails to understand the "wisdom and prudence of nature" that provides his subject with a pragmatic view of possibilities for liberation.

When the reader is first introduced to Mr. Trappe, he is engaged in the process of reminding Mr. De Vincent's young bride of his knowledge that she belongs to a slave woman who was sold to a Georgia man and that her fortune in having grown up in luxury and whiteness comes as the result of a shrewd and timely exchange of children following the death of her father's legitimate child, at which point "the dead was exchanged for the living" (46). In sharing this information, he attempts to strip the young bride of her dignity by stripping her of her humanness. Luckily for Mrs. De Vincent, Hannah is fortuitously seated behind the curtain during this exchange and overhears information that she ultimately uses to defuse the primacy of Mr. Trappe's knowledge. She convinces her mistress to flee the De Vincent household, and in turn her mistress convinces Hannah to accompany her on her flight. The two escape leaving Mr. Trappe with an empty knowledge that serves him little use. The knowledge, appropriated by Hannah, underscores the difference between her benevolence and Mr. Trappe's cruelty, for she does not as Rudolph Byrd rightly states, "use her 'private knowledge' to entrap and exploit others."[9] Instead Hannah uses this knowledge to make herself and her mistress inaccessible to the culture that would otherwise see them as objects ripe for exploitation. In this way Hannah establishes herself as a woman of reason and authority who now becomes the bearer of the secret and one of the only people able to upset Mr. Trappe's ability to dominate through the threat of exposure. Because the secret no longer has a primary holder, its potential to disrupt decreases and Mr. Trappe's ability to manipulate his subject enters a stage of compromise with Hannah as a pivotal player in the game of unfolding secrecy.

Hannah's new knowledge foregrounds the importance of ownership in the text and attests to the precariousness of a racial economy based predominantly on the ability to subjugate others physically and ideologically. Put another way, Crafts' narrative not only establishes Hannah as a woman whose very being disrupts the agenda of race ideology, but it also demystifies the power of whiteness by illustrating the contradictions and instabilities of an apparently stable and consistent racial economy.

The scene of exposure in which Mrs. De Vincent is reraced by Mr. Trappe's knowledge therefore becomes particularly significant as an indication of the precariousness of the fixities of race and specifically the meaning of whiteness, which Richard Dyer defines as a space of "invisibility."[10] Crafts' narrative effectively contests this space as well as the assumptions that "whites are people whereas other colors are something else." In effect, Crafts does the work Dyer attests is necessary to achieve "where we want to get to."[11] Not only does the baseness of Trappe call attention to the idea that whiteness demands questioning, but by Trappe's own admission, he is no different from the slaves that he traps. In his own words he tells us that "we are all slaves to something or somebody," concluding as he goes on to say, "Freedom and slavery are only names attached surreptitiously and often improperly to certain conditions" (101). Trappe's statement is interesting in that it presents another narrative paradox as it aligns whites with slavery, and as Robert Levine notes, "raise[s] the question of whether there are any 'whites' to be found in the South."[12]

In his 1999 publication of *The Wages of Whiteness*, David Roediger writes "Republicanism had long emphasized that strength, virtue and resolve of a people guarded them from enslavement."[13] He goes on to state that America was founded on the principle of independence and developed through the system of capitalism. This begins the scheme of separation in which whites participated in a movement toward freedom and independence and later invisibility through work and ownership of that work, while blacks became slaves because they were unable to won their work. Roediger speculates, "Republicanism also suggested that long acceptance of slavery betokened weakness, degradation and unfitness for freedom."[14] Roediger's account of Republican development becomes particularly relevant to my discussion of Hannah because in arguing that neither Hannah nor Trappe submits to the rules that apparently govern their citizenship (or lack of it), I also argue for the appreciation of a space that allows for conceptual deviations from the traditional route toward claiming an Americanism and an American family. Trappe is a worker who owns nothing stable and is himself, by his own admission, enslaved by his constant labor of deception. Hannah too, who does not capitulate to the Republican ideology of weakness, defies her place as a black slave. Once she learns of her Mistress's plight, she immediately begins working to own her own situation. The two women flee to the woods, representing themselves as "poor women who have become accidentally lost" (58), which they regard as "no more than truth" (58). This truth propels them through a journey that brings them to the moral and intellectual reality that freedom and ownership of one's body is an ideal achievable to those who are open and willing to destroy, replace, and expand existing borders and limitations. Unfortunately, however, Hannah and her mistress are soon discovered in their escape and their resistance to cultural conformity is quelled. They are taken to a jail where they meet Mrs. Wright, a woman who has been imprisoned so long that she comes to believe that her prison is her palace. The woman confides in Hannah that her crime was "hat[ing] slavery . . . [,] and see[ing] no beauty in the system" (86), she assisted a slave girl in her escape.

Through Mrs. Wright, Crafts reinforces the paradoxical structure that organizes her narrative, depicting morality and reason in one of the only characters who ostensibly represents a lack of reason, logic, and sanity. Mrs. Wright personifies all that is good and possible in a culture unwilling to broaden the understanding and ownership of knowledge. Her goodness is stifled, and she is ostracized from functioning society. Interestingly, Mrs. Wright, despite her seeming madness, never loses her lucid understanding of the dichotomous world in which she can no longer participate because she "[has] learned what all who live in a land of slavery must learn sooner or later; that it is to profess approbation where you cannot feel; to be hard when most inclined to melt; and to say that all is right and good; and true when you know that nothing could be more wrong" (87).

That Crafts attributes this kind of discourse to a mad woman is telling because it dramatizes the distinction between the voice of resistance that seemingly speaks from madness and the voice of domination that seemingly speaks from sanity. Here again, through the paradox of reason and madness, Crafts provokes the reader into questioning basic beliefs about ideas commonly seen as true and stable. Her text exposes the various layers and subtexts of a brutal slave system, elaborating on her critique that truth cannot exist in a slave economy, that fiction becomes the norm of a disciplinary power, and that there is no place to go to live truthfully. As a result of all this, one must rely on creating one's own reality, and only in this reality can truth exist.

This concept places Hannah in the difficult and almost impossible position of attempting to exist outside the fictions of others that define her, and only in her constant movement can she begin to live by her own experiential and conceptual reality. In understanding and identifying herself as "a poor woman" (58), and as a "rational being" (18) within an economy that "enforce[s] drudgery [. . . and] condemn[s] [her] on account of [her] color to a life of servitude" (18), Hannah once again pushes the limits of boundaries between fiction and reality and exposes the paradox of lies inherent in a slave system. This, I argue she does, contrary to the reasoning of John Stauffer, who reads Hannah as a woman restrained in humanitarian bondage.[15] With each decision, Hannah makes a reasoned choice delivered as an assertion of her humanity and a declaration of her right to reason herself into being: she decides to leave the De Vincent household after her careful consideration of the unjust treatment directed towards her kind white mistress who must now, through the actions of an unscrupulous lawyer and an unjust law, struggle with the pains of an assigned blackness; she decides to reveal her slave status to Mrs. Henry, her new mistress, which illustrates Hannah's need to live truthfully beyond the veil of concealment; she decides not to run away with Charlotte, her slave friend, at the expense of her own "freedom," in a willing consent to a bondage, which she defines and accepts on her own terms; she decides to leave the Wheeler household, her last house of bondage, thus demonstrating her need to live as a human being with the dignity of one who claims the ability to assert her social, physical, and intellectual rights.

Truth for Hannah, a proposition inextricably intertwined with freedom, comes as a precarious and dangerous indulgence, but one necessary if she is to challenge the deep-rooted fictions and generalizations of a slave system. Her challenge demands she confront what she understands as the difference between her reasoned understanding of herself and the imposed fiction to which she is held. At this point, the text seems to suggest that each decision and confrontation that Hannah makes and encounters illustrates a type of reversal of myth. In other words, her decisions and confrontations might appropriately be read as a narrative strategy to challenge, disrupt, and rewrite racial fictions.

When Hannah reveals her slave status to the kind Mrs. Henry, who gives her sanctuary after being left for nearly dead, she makes the conscious choice not to "pass" and to represent herself as nothing other than what she imagines herself to be—a slave by social and political condition and a woman by her own private understanding of her virtue and humanity. Mrs. Henry, a polished woman of Christian politeness who has taken Hannah into her home after finding her lying almost dead following a disastrous accident, does not immediately question Hannah's race upon their first meeting and instead assumes whiteness onto the young woman. When Hannah finally regains consciousness and finds herself comfortably cared for in the Henry household, her "scene [had] changed, and [she] almost doubted her identity" (118), leaving her to wonder if she should "perpetuate that delusion" (120) of representing an unfortunate white woman who has suffered a tragic loss. This is a turning point in Hannah's discovery and consciousness, for deciding to continue in Mrs. Henry's fantasy of assisting an unfortunate white woman is as much an indulgence in a lie as it is to surrender to the labels of race and their associations. Hannah does not linger in deciding against the delusion, admitting to the ignorant Mrs. Henry that she is a slave, "one of that miserable class" (120). This admission, of course, is a relative truth and consequently makes clear the distinction between the understanding of the self and the imaginative image imposed on that self. Hannah willingly admits, through qualification, that her identification is not her own, but rather is the judgment of those who insist on her stationary and inferior position. The fiction that controls her life will continue to do so, for the power that defines Hannah operates on a reiterative practice and a blind truth reinforced by generalizations that require neither proof nor logic. In this way, Hannah's truth can only remain in her soul, separate from the body that will ultimately fall prey to the systems of disciplinary fiction. Her whiteness will never be seen as equal to the whiteness of those able to claim white purity because her whiteness is defined and qualified by a power beyond her reach as a mixed-race woman. For this reason, Hannah's only choice for self respect is to submit to an internal truth of knowing her own humanness and to the public rendering of herself as bonded property.

This idea, with its dual emphasis on the public and the private, lays bare a national portrait of self-absorption, which preserves and reproduces definitions of slavery and "otherness." When it is discovered that Hannah is alive and well and living in the Henry household, Mr. Trappe, her former nemesis, comes to reclaim his property. Hannah pleads with her kind mistress not to give her over to the vile Mr. Trappe who will once again sell her to the highest bidder. Mrs. Henry, however, cannot submit to this pleading because, as she tells Hannah, she has made a promise to her father on his deathbed, who was himself a trafficker in flesh, that she would "never on any occasion buy or sell a servant" (131). Accordingly, Mrs. Henry cannot grant Hannah her wish to remain in the Henry household and tries instead to appease her by offering her the opportunity of being "given" to a distant family relative.

This exchange, occurring at the very center of the text, highlights the pervasiveness of moral failure that operates in a system built on power and privilege. In the course of introducing Mrs. Henry, Crafts offers up an immediately benevolent character, full of morality and integrity. Mrs. Henry makes promises and does not waver in their delivery. She assists a slave woman with kindness and hospitality much like the characters of Mrs. Delano in Child's *Romance of the Republic*,[16] or Mrs. Bird and the Senator from Harriet Beecher Stowe's *Uncle Tom's Cabin.*[17] This image of Mrs. Henry's benevolence is, however, fleeting and the differences between the character of Mrs. Henry and that of Mrs. Delano or Mrs. Bird are striking. Mrs. Henry never puts herself in jeopardy in her assistance of Hannah nor does she extend herself beyond what is politically convenient. The point that Crafts makes here is clear. There is little morality in Mrs. Henry and even less so in her demonstration of truth and integrity. And although some might argue that Mrs. Henry "[reveals . . .] a real moral blind spot so far as her understanding of slavery is concerned."[18] I believe Mrs. Henry's actions exhibit far more than the unintentional often associated with a blind spot. Her refusal to grant Hannah sanctuary in her home implies a deliberate decision to claim silence where voice and action are most needed. Instead of action, Mrs. Henry passively exercises the privilege of her whiteness by saying and doing nothing. In this regard, she identifies with those in power, claiming herself as one of those of power, yet masking her choice through her perceived efforts of kindness.

Stephanie Wildman and Adrienne Davis define white privilege, a right Mrs. Henry certainly asserts, as an unconscious act in that "privilege is not visible to its holder; it is merely there, a part of the world a very way of life, simply the way things are."[19] Mrs. Henry's lack of action then becomes a natural outcome of a system that conflates race and economics as a means of maintaining privilege. Indeed, Mrs. Henry's actions reveal a general failure to relinquish privilege in order to make room for the humanity of those created out of the imagination of those in power. While Mrs. Henry provides insight into the thoughts of the fiction makers, so too do the dominated who know that "those who view slavery only as it relates to physical suffering or the wants of nature, can have no conception of its greatest evils" (134). Hannah speaks the last word of the chapter and drives home an understanding of culture and race that goes far deeper than any understanding Mrs. Henry could wish to own. With this appreciation she begins to take charge of her own truth, knowing that if she is to shed the limiting proscriptions of slavery, she must do so with an unquestionable defiance.

Crafts' (fictional) autobiography, which takes its liberties with the slave narrative form, becomes especially valuable not just for its documentation of experience, but also for the way it links the experience of racial instability and a monetary economy invested in the stability of racial markers to defy cultural conventions. In the last third of the narrative, when Hannah is given to Mrs. Wheeler, Crafts points out the alliance between race and economics through a painful discussion of recalled experience emphasizing the necessity of one as a means of maintaining the other.

The scene, which begins with a discussion of beauty, tells the reader that "Mrs. Wheeler conceived her beauty to be on the wane" (164). Because of this, she purchases a newly invented Italian powder specifically designed to enhance the beauty of the skin. What Mrs. Wheeler had not realized and what Hannah knows is that when mixed with smelling salts, the powder turns the skin black. As it happens, at the same time that Mrs. Wheeler experiments with her new face powder, Mr. Wheeler, an ousted member of Congress, propositions her with a scheme to use her beauty to assist him in securing an important office, which had recently become available. Mrs. Wheeler concedes, believing that her recently purchased beauty powder will secure her the influence she requires to seal the deal. However, just before leaving on her mission, she takes a bit of smelling salts, which unknown to her turns her skin black before she arrives at the house of Congress.

This scene, set apart from other more understated scenes of racial resistance, emphasizes the otherwise subtle paradoxes the author has elsewhere illustrated throughout the text. In turning Mrs. Wheeler's skin black, Crafts reveals, in no uncertain terms, the privilege of whiteness, its constructedness, and the systematic disenfranchisement of all who fall outside the definition of white purity. Mrs. Wheeler's insistence on acquiring beauty results in the explosive situation of her movement from the privilege of whiteness to that of the nonprivilege of blackness. But particularly ironic is the information regarding this purchase, which comes from "an antiquated lady, with a large mouth filled with false teeth, a head covered with false hair, and a thin scrawny neck, beneath which swelled out a false bust" (162). Once again, Crafts express her intent on demonstrating the constructedness (in this case of beauty) of an exterior reality. She exposes the fiction of identity by turning its constructions inside out. She displays the hypocrisy of the calculated performance and the lengths to which one must go in order to maintain this fiction, a process of narrative structure, which begins to shape her broader critique of capitalism, patriarchy, and the exploitation that results from such a fiction.

When Mrs. Wheeler reaches the congressman's office to ask for the position, she is told "it is not customary to bestow offices on colored people" (173). When she pursues the issue, relying, of course, on her beauty, which, according to her husband, "no gentleman would think of opposing" (169), she is firmly told that if either she or her husband "had possessed a particle of common sense, [neither one] would have asked for [the position]" (174). This reply points to what Crafts sees as the inseparable nature of race and economics. In the move from whiteness to blackness, Mrs. Wheeler loses her ability to negotiate, to claim her freedom, to determine her life. In short, the temporary loss of Mrs. Wheeler's whiteness results in a temporary loss of her ability to participate in American democracy. Doors do not open for her magically, nor does she, at this moment, have access to the doors. Instead, she is left with a blatant denial of opportunity and humanity based on an empty signifier. Crafts reversal of roles here, where the once haughty Mrs. Wheeler becomes a member of the despised race, points to the emptiness of race and/or color as a meaningful signifier and goes one step further to imply an interchangeability between the races. Mrs. Wheeler's representation of blackness and its acceptance by others functions to confuse the categories of race and culture, for it is not one's physical attributes that render one black or white, but rather it is perception and ideology that render identity readable. Mrs. Wheeler, by American racial standards, is no more black in the congressman's office than she was when she left her home, nor might Mrs. Wheeler have experienced the life of blackness had she not been requesting a position of influence. Through Mrs. Wheeler, Crafts underscores the idea that color has no basis in reality and functions only as the visible marker to social scripting. That Mrs. Wheeler finds herself a member of the Negro race reads significantly, because just in case the reader missed the criticism of the constructed polarity between black and white, Crafts once again makes clear it is rhetoric that forms difference, it is ideology that breeds differentiation, and it is greed that anchors the false idea of inescapable differences between black and white. Crafts' narrative seems to dramatize that blackness and whiteness cannot exist as positive or negative characteristics in and of themselves, but rather are based on a consistently reproduced fiction that insists on the economic and democratic oppression of the racial "other." Mrs. Wheeler's blackness causes the curt and undeniable response she receives, and it is her greed for power that foregrounds the difference between the privileged and nonprivileged.

One could argue that Crafts' text was specifically intended to expose the wrongs of bondage, as Buell argues, or that it articulates the "diverse range of social ills" in a racialized society as Stauffer has similarly argued.[20] One might also argue, as I have attempted to do, that it exposes the absurdities of logic inherent in a system that is socially and politically motivated to maintain dominance at all costs. However, it is important to note that Crafts' text functions on a number of levels, and in its criticism of racial oppression it also demands a revisioning of the dualisms of racial classification. She documents this idea when Hannah, after escaping from the Wheeler household, reunites with her dear Aunt Hetty who initially taught her to read and who once again secures her with love and a temporary home. This penultimate scene sets the stage for the final ending where Hannah becomes complete through a joyous reunion with her mother whom she has never known except in infancy. Crafts' depiction of freedom and humanity, however, does not end with the meeting of a mother and a daughter. In a small town in New Jersey, Hannah becomes part of a community where her close friends (former slaves of Mrs. Henry), Charlotte and William, reside. In this community she meets her husband, a Methodist preacher, and lives happily teaching children and "listening to the words of Gospel truth" (246).

It is an ending that reeks of fantasy, as William Andrews has already suggested, for it defies all claims to fugitive autobiography and establishes a world of almost practical impossibility. But this again signals the extent to which Crafts envisioned a self-governing authority created out of a willful knowledge of the self. Crafts' imagined community that closes her narrative illustrates a space of cultural possibilities, marked by the culture of a reclaimed marginality. Knowing that her identity satisfies neither the cultural need to represent similarity nor familiarity, Hannah resolves to establish her own community where its members redefine the concept of family by distancing themselves from its biological and sociohistorical meaning. In its stead, Crafts seems to recognize "common impulses and strivings,"[21] as the foundation for a new conceptualization of 'race' and family, structured from imaginative possibilities far outweigh rigid expectations.

Crafts ends her narrative with an explosion of the paradox with which she began. Her young slave girl, owned and prohibited from learning, who consistently defines the protocol of blackness, achieves the absolute American ideal. Her end is the ultimate paradox in that Hannah becomes fully humanized because, as Crafts suggests, it is not race that grants humanity, but rather the willingness to see oneself as human. With this idea Crafts disrupts the concept of race as a stable and definite signifier and demonstrates the fundamental contradiction in all racial definition. Thus, William Andrews understanding of Crafts' ending, in which he states that "Hannah's story was specifically intended to articulate what ought to happen to a woman of color"[22] can only be partially true, for Hannah is no longer a "woman of color." She has transcended color in that she has achieved what a woman of color was never intended or capable of achieving. She has become a woman endowed with the full rights of humanity to love and to belong to family and friends. Thus to say that the "novel's end challenge[s] the notion that an African-American woman had no business expecting or even hoping for such fulfillment,"[23] is to read the text only in part and to negate the voice of contradiction that strenuously argues throughout the text for a revisioning of racial ideology based on an either/or system. That Crafts' text ends in fiction seems consistent with its agenda in that it is fiction created by the author rather than fiction created for her. In this respect Crafts' text articulately takes control of itself through and with a voice whose authenticity can be none other than the author herself.

The *Bondwoman* is a complex analysis of language, culture, and racial myths. It is a text begging for someone to see through the veil of fictional identity and color into the consciousness of racial mixture. Hannah Crafts' novel is, as Nina Baym defines it, "a find of unprecedented importance."[24] Cutting across ideas of particularities by exposing cultural and racial contradictions that force us to rethink our range of understanding and our part in the creation of fictions and realities with which we live, Crafts' narrative is an important story of the American experience of the process of rearticulating culturalisms, and of addressing the possibilities that racial resistance offers toward creating dignity born out of an honest Americanism.

NOTES

1. In his pursuit of the authentication of Crafts' narrative, Henry Louis gates Jr. relied on the expertise of examiners who used historical and scientific methods such as paper and ink dating to arrive at an approximate date of Crafts' narrative.

2. Jean Fagan Yellin, *"The Bondwoman's Narrative and Uncle Tom's Cabin"* in *In Search of Hannah Crafts: Critical Essays on The Bondwoman's Narrative*, ed. Henry Louis Gates, Jr. and Hollis Robbins (Cambridge, MA: BasicCivitas, 2004), 106–16.

3. Harriet Jacobs, *Incidents in the Life of a Slave Girl* (Boston: Published for the Author, 1861).

4. Hannah Crafts, *The Bondwoman's Narrative*, ed. Henry Louis Gates Jr. (New York: Time Warner, 2002), 17. All subsequent page references refer will appear parenthetically in the text and will refer to this edition.

5. Frances Smith Foster, *Witnessing Slavery* (Westport: Greenwood Press, 1976), 85.

6. Henry Louis Gates, Jr, and Hollis Robbins, introduction to *In Search of Hannah Crafts* (New York: Basic Civitas Books), xi. This collection of critical essays focuses solely on the study of Hannah Crafts.

7. I will use the name Hannah to refer to the character and Crafts to refer to the author, for although I read this narrative as an autobiography, I am cognizant of the overlapping identities of author and character.

8. Leonard Cassuto, *The Inhuman Race: The Racial Grotesque in American Literature and Culture* (New York: Columbia University Press, 1997), 76.

9. Roudolph Byrd, "The Outsider Within: The Acquisition and Application of Forms of Oppositional Knowledge in Hannah Crafts's *The Bondwoman's Narrative*" in *In Search of Hannah Crafts*, eds. Gates and Robbins, 339.

10. Richard Dyer, "The Matter of Whiteness," in *White Privilege: Essential Readings on the other Side of Racism*, ed. Paula Rothenberg (New York: Worth Publishers, 2002), 10.

11. Dyer, "Whiteness," 12.

12. Robert Levine, "Trappe(d): Race and Genealogical Haunting in *The Bondwoman's Narrative*" in *In Search of Hannah Crafts*, eds. Gates and Robbins, 287.

13. David Roediger, *The Wages of Whiteness: Race and the Making of The American Working Class* (New York: Verso, 1999), 35.

14. Roediger, *The Wages of Whiteness*, 66.

15. John Stauffer. "The problem of Freedom in The Bondswoman's Narrative," in *In Search of Hannah Crafts*, eds. Gates and Robbins, 62–63.

16. Child's *Romance of the Republic* (Boston: Ticknor and Fields, 1867).

17. Harriet Beecher Stowe, *Uncle Tom's Cabin* (London: Blackie, 1979).

18. Dickson Bruce Jr, "Mrs. Henry's 'Solomon Promise,'" in *In Search of Hannah Crafts*, eds. Gates and Robbins, 131.

19. Stephanie Wildman M. and Adrienne D. Davis. "Making Systems of Privilege Visible," in *White Privilege: Essential Readings on the Other Side of Racism*, ed. Paula Rothenberg (New York: Worth Publishers, 2002), 94.

20. Stauffer, "The Problem of Freedom," 53.

21. Anothony Appiah, "The Uncompleted Argument: Du Bois and the Illusion of Race," in *"Race," Writing and Difference*, ed. Henry Louis Gates, Jr. (Chicago: University of Chicago Press, 1985), 27.

22. Williams Andrews, "Crafts's Dense of Ending," in *In Search of Hannah Crafts*, eds. Gates and Robbins, 39.

23. Andrews, "Ending," 40.

24. Nina Baym. "The Case for Hannah Vincent," in *In Search of Hannah Crafts*, eds. Gates and Robbins, 316.

Chapter Eight

Constructing Whiteness in the Australian Adventure Story, 1875–1920

Martin Crotty

WHITENESS AND COLONIAL MASCULINITY

It has been suggested, by Aileen Moreton-Robinson and others, that whiteness studies differs from previous ways of looking at racial 'constructions' in that it focuses on the dominant (white) understanding of self, not the white understanding of 'other.' Moreton-Robinson argues that it has usually been Indigenous people and non-white migrants who have been 'raced,' while whiteness has remained as the assumed starting point, the racial "centre."[1, 2] Interrogating whiteness in Australia has been inspired by work in the United States and Britain where scholars of constructions of race identified whiteness "as the invisible norm against which other races are judged in the construction of identity, representation, subjectivity, nationalism and the law."[3]

In this way whiteness studies has pertinent intersections with the considerable body of work on masculinity, which has proceeded from similar intellectual starting points. Historians of gender have worked from the basis that gender is not biologically determined but instead is a social and cultural constriction that is, in the words of Joan Scott, "imposed on a sexed body."[4] The culturally defined differences between genders do not flow from biology, but appeal to and exploit physical difference as a way of legitimating power relations. Physical difference is rendered into social and cultural difference, but does not create it.[5] The same applies to race, where the different colors of skin are used to denote a range of 'racial' characteristics that are then used to justify and legitimate power relations between, most pertinently in the Australian case, the colonizers and the colonized.

Moreover, just as whiteness studies seeks to interrogate the assumed 'norm' of white racial identities, so too have scholars of masculinity sought to problematize the assumed norm of maleness. Masculinity was the assumed normative starting point, and it was women, not men, who were 'gendered' in the same way that non-whites were 'raced.' John Tosh commented in 1994 that "in the historical record it is as though masculinity is everywhere but nowhere."[6] The problem has been overcome, in theory if not always in practice, by treating men as being equally 'gendered' to women, in the same way that whiteness studies seeks to treat whites as 'raced.'

There are more than parallels here—there are fundamental intersections, especially in the colonial context where the constructions of colonial masculinity invariably involved the colonized 'other' of the non-white male, as well as the 'other' of colonial femininity, as an oppositional construct against which the colonial male was defined. In the metropolitan centers of Empire the whiteness of the British male could be safely assumed. In the colonial context it was rather different. Indigenous peoples and other non-whites, such as Chinese gold miners, loomed as threats to the racial and cultural purity of the British colonizers. Matters were further complicated by the growing desire of Australian colonists to mark themselves off from the British towards the end of the nineteenth century—to construct themselves as a new and better race, products of the new world and a counter to the degeneracy of modern Europe.[7]

Constructions of Australian masculinity in colonial juvenile adventure stories almost always included Indigenous Australians. The colonizing male could not be defined without reference to the colonized, though the terms of reference and the nature of the relationship changed over the last quarter of the nineteenth century and the first two decades of the twentieth. Aileen Moreton-Robinson has noted that by "conceptualising 'race' as a socially constructed and relational concept it is possible to explore how the shaping power of the racialized 'other' is fundamental to the construction of the white self."[8] The same applies in reverse. Depictions of the Aboriginal 'other' certainly influenced the construction of Australian colonial 'whiteness.' But as the nature of the idealized Australian white 'race' changed, in accordance with imperatives such as the growing influence of social Darwinism and the desire for a distinct Australian racial identity, so too did the depiction, deployment and use of the Aboriginal 'other.'

This chapter examines the evolving relationship between whiteness and Aboriginality as revealed in the Australian juvenile adventure story in three principle sections. It firstly considers some typical boys' adventure novels from the period between approximately 1875 and 1920 and shows that although whiteness studies might be a new or recent departure in academic writing, the question of what it means to be "white" and to be Australian has been debated in Australian literature, and specifically Australian juvenile fiction, ever since the colonial period. It argues that that in these stories there were moves from exterminatory discourses towards Indigenous people, aimed at preserving the purity of colonial whiteness prior to about 1900, toward, in the early twentieth century, incorporating or appropriating elements of imagined Aboriginality into notions of Australian whiteness. The chapter secondly considers some of the possible reasons for this important change, and concludes by considering some of the possible effects and implications of such a shift in how Australian whiteness was constructed.

Juvenile adventure stories might appear to be a rather odd source for an examination of such themes, especially when weighed up against colonial art, adult fiction, or serious nonfiction contemplations of the future of the white 'races' in Australia and of the nature of the Indigenous peoples. Their plot lines are thin, they are often simplistic, and they were often written by authors with little or no experience of Australia and its Indigenous people. Such stories are easily characterized as simplistic and ignorant. But juvenile adventure stories can yield rich pickings. They appeal as a source for three main reasons.

The first is that any European colonial encounter in the 'new world' involved a necessary meeting of whiteness with colonial blackness, and forced the colonizing peoples to confront the issue of hybridity—how would whiteness fare in a black environment, and what were the possibilities and dangers of the whites 'going native,' whether in lifestyle or in 'breeding.' As Robert Dixon, Richard Phillips and others have argued, colonial literature was the site where the anxieties, concerns hopes and dreams of what this encounter might produce, if anything, were announced, played out and resolved. The most famous contemporary example of this is found in Rider Haggard's landmark *King Solomon's Mines* of 1885, where the whiteness of the explorers is only just maintained as the threat of descent into the black 'other,' represented by the danger of emasculation by a feminized and sexualized landscape, is narrowly averted.[9] This takes place in juvenile literature as well as in adult fiction.

The second is that because of the intended audience of juvenile literature—children—there is little room in these texts for irony, nor for subversion. These are didactic texts. As such, children's literature thus offers a very clear window onto the adult consciousness and value systems that created it. If such stories were not so reflective of dominant or hegemonic values, they would not have been written, they would not have been published and they would not have been purchased or borrowed and read. We can thus examine these stories for the discourses they contain and use them as windows onto colonial ideas about race—specifically, in this instance, what should happen to whiteness in the colonial encounter.

The third reason why juvenile literature appeals as a source lies its effect on young minds. No readers can be assumed to be empty vessels into which authors can pour their meanings and world views, but young readers are likely to be less critical than most. Martin Green has suggested that English adventure stories were "collectively, the story England told itself as it went to sleep at night" and has suggested that such stories "charged England's will with the energy to go out into the world and explore, conquer and rule."[10] Green's rhetorical flourishes are based on the reality that such stories were avidly consumed in England, and they were similarly popular in Australia.[11] Initially, Australian boys could read the works of English authors who used Australia as a site for manly derring-do against treacherous Aborigines, bushrangers and the Australian environment, but toward the end of the century and in the early years of the twentieth there was an increased availability of works authored by Australians, or at least by British authors who had spent some time in Australia. Between 1875 and 1920 there were some twenty to twenty-five books published in this newly popular boys' adventure genre that were set in Australia and which sought to grapple with the issue of relations between the colonizers and the colonized.

AUSTRALIAN ADVENTURE STORIES— W. H. G. KINGSTON TO JOSEPH BOWES

The early stories, in the 1870s and 1880s, fairly predictably cast Indigenous people as the villains who need to be evaded, overcome, or exterminated. There is little or no accommodation possible between the 'civilized' Australian whites and the uncivilized or uncivilizable Indigenous Australian blacks. To the extent that there is any accommodation, it rests on Aboriginal 'faithfulness' to their white overlords, and on white generosity towards Indigenous peoples. There is no suggestion of any major alliance or intermingling— Australian whiteness retains its purity by maintaining hard and fast boundaries against a black 'other.' Australian whiteness is purely British; there is little indication in these early adventure stories of an emergent sense of Australian nationalism, so the emphasis is on remaining as purely British as possible and thus on displacing and resisting the Indigenous people rather than reaching any understanding or arrangements for coexistence with them.

W. H. G. Kingston's Australian adventure stories, titled *Twice Lost: A Story of Shipwreck and Adventure in the Wilds of Australia* (1876) and *Australian Adventures* (1884) exemplify the desire to impose an unmitigated British whiteness as the essence of Australian civilization. In both stories English civilization is represented by settlers seeking to establish new homes in the colonies. In the process they displace Indigenous people and overcome any resistance, triumph over bushrangers who represent the possible descent into lawlessness and barbarism, and survive being lost in the Australian bush.

In *Twice Lost* the Indigenous people are represented as savage, heathen and untrustworthy. They horrify the principal characters (the Raynor family) by the manner in which they devour a rotting whale that they have found on the beach, thus illustrating their savagery and lack of civilization. In the words of the narrator:

> As they cut out pieces of the flesh, they rammed them into their mouths. Tearing them with their teeth like a pack of famishing wolves; some of them literally forcing their way into the carcass, out of which they emerged carrying huge pieces of dripping flesh, covering their bodies with blood. Even the women, some of them young, and, as seen from a distance, far from ill-looking, attacked the whale in the same fashion as the men, and appeared again dripping all over with blood. When I thought of the putrid state of the flesh, it made me almost sick to look at them, and disgusted at seeing human beings so degraded.[12]

Their lack of trustworthiness and the impossibility of redemption is represented by the Raynors' Aboriginal guide, who deserts them when the call of the wild becomes too strong for him.

Kingston was not entirely unsympathetic to Australia's Indigenous peoples. One character is made to remind another that "we are the trespassers" and that as such they are obliged "to treat them with humanity, and to take every pains not to injure them or deprive them of their means of existence." But there was nothing desirable to be found in Aboriginality, and no suggestion that whiteness and blackness could reach much of an accommodation in the Australian setting. The Aborigines are classed as "ignorant savages," a black 'other' to white civilization, and whites "have, of course, a perfect right to be here."[13]

Such ideas are further developed in Kingston's rather unimaginatively titled *Australian Adventures* of 1884. Two brothers are settling in Australia to make their fortunes and provide for their mother and siblings back in England. There are, as one would expect in a story of this genre, a myriad of dangers to be overcome, but the principal human enemies are bushrangers and Aborigines, both of whom are deployed as 'others' to the civilized values embodied by the Thornton brothers. From early in the story, and early in the brothers' adventures, the danger presented by Aborigines is clear. As one brother states in the narrator's voice:

> We heard that they had at different times murdered a number of unfortunate hut-keepers and shepherds up the country, so that we were inclined to form very

unfavourable opinions of the aborigines. Toby [our black guide], to be sure, was faithful enough, but then he was semi-civilized.[14]

There are frequent attacks from the 'blacks,' which are successfully fought off, and there is no criticism of what is in effect a massacre. After a gang of blacks have been caught and imprisoned in a hut, the narrator tells us: "Some tried to get out of the window on one side of the hut, but Guy, Hector and I shot them down as they reached the ground."[15] Whiteness and blackness were to be kept distinct, and there is no doubt that the former is to triumph over the latter.

Similar themes and attitudes are evinced in other Kingston novels set in Australia, and in those by his great contemporary rival, G. A. Henty.[16] The bearers of whiteness are the bearers of civilization, religion and decency, qualities they are imposing on a black land where the Indigenous blackness represents savagery, barbarism, cruelty and superstition. Indigenous people are frequently described in the most disparaging of terms, often likened to dogs, are seen as barely civilizable, if at all, and are forced, with only the odd pang of minor regret, to make way for the whiteness of their colonizers. Indigenous people are depicted as an obstacle and a threat to an idealized, civilized British whiteness transferred and maintained in its 'purest' form possible in an Australian setting. In this regard the stories reflect the logics of imperialism, where the agents of Christian civilization who practiced agriculture were granted moral authority to displace those who appeared below them on an imagined evolutionary—peoples who practised hunting and gathering, non-Christian spirituality, and who lacked clothes, towns, churches, roads, courts of law and other markers of western civilization.

Henty and Kingston refused to even seriously confront the issue of 'hybridity'—of what would happen to British whiteness when transferred to an Australian setting where it could be influenced by the Indigenous people and by the Australian environment. Both were English authors and neither visited Australia. Without exposure to the Australian environment and the Indigenous peoples, the shapes hybridity might have taken would have been hard for them to imagine, but a stronger explanation is probably related simply to their perspective—they were English, outsiders looking in, and were uninterested in Australia as anything other than a field for the deeds of British adventurers. Later generations of Australian adventure story writers, however, men who were born, or who at least spent long period of their lives in Australia, gave the issue more attention.

Issues surrounding hybridity are, for example, explored in Ernest Favenc's *The Secret of the Australian Desert* of 1896. This is essentially about a white expedition, though with a black guide, into the Australian desert and a number of encounters with Indigenous people. Some of the Indigenous tribes are, if not to be admired, at least bearable for the whites, partly because they are prepared to learn new skills and new values—to effectively whiten themselves by abandoning primitiveness and adopting 'civilization.' Others, however, are depicted as savage cannibals, and the whites massacre them, shooting down the last members of the tribe, described as 'the bloodthirsty Warlattas,' from horseback. Along the way they come across the journals of an earlier expedition of discovery into the deserts. In them the stories of Stuart and Murphy, both now dead, are revealed. Stuart and Murphy represent the extremes of the hybridity issue. Murphy sinks to the level of his Indigenous captors and partakes in cannibalism—he has surrendered his whiteness for blackness. Stuart, on the other hand, has recorded in his diary that: "I thank God that though I have lived so long amongst these savages, I have not sunk down to be one of them in their habits, but rather have taught them better things."[17] Murphy represents whiteness that has turned black—a failure of the colonial project—whereas Stuart represents whiteness lightening the Australian blackness—the ideal of colonization. In such a narrative the problem of hybridity is announced and overcome, if only through the rejection of any hybridization between the white colonizers and the black colonized. Indigenous Australians remain the dangerous 'other' to colonizing whiteness.

All of this is directed at an explication of what the white Australian, and particularly the white Australian male, should be. The ideal was that norms of 'Britishness' should be maintained in the colonial environment, that the colonial surrounds should be uninfluential. Civilized values, defined by religion, racial purity, domesticity and so on were to be transported to the colonies and maintained in the face of the threateningly savage environment.

This might be regarded as nothing more or less than could be expected in nineteenth-century settler societies as they went about the process of colonizing the land and its people. But there is a significant shift that takes place in the early years of the twentieth century, evidenced in at least three adventure stories published between 1911 and 1918. The shift is that in two of these stories Aborigines and whites team up and combine, to some degree at least, to defeat Asian enemies—in the form of Malay coastal raiders in one story, and the Chinese in another. The stereotypical dichotomies of white versus black are thus upset somewhat by white and black combining to defeat the 'Yellow Peril.'[18] This does not result in favourable portraits of Indigenous Australians who are still portrayed as savage and uncivilized, but they are regarded as the lesser of two evils and it is suggested that, unlike Asians, they at least belong in Australia. The main effect of the narrative shift is to emphasize the white sense of belonging, to turn them into defenders of their territory rather than the conquerors of Aboriginal land. Fighting for Australia emphasizes their connectedness.

But the most interesting shift takes place in a third story, Joseph Bowes'
1918 adventure, *The Young Anzacs*, the first of a trilogy about Australians
fighting in the Middle East.[19] The central figure in the story is Jack Smith
who, as the title of the story would suggest, enlists immediately when the war
is declared and serves bravely and successfully at Gallipoli where he wins a
commission, and, in later stories, in the Middle East where he is promoted
to Major. Jack is the idealized Australian male from the period—bush-bred,
physically powerful, egalitarian, patriotic and militarily willing and capable.
The most significant and interesting feature about Jack, however, is that he is
part-Aboriginal, for his grandmother was a 'half-caste.'

Jack's part-Aboriginality serves him well, giving him, we are told, a
superior sense of instinct to aid his powers of logic, and apparently also
giving him greater physical aptitude for the demands of Middle Eastern
warfare. The keen eyesight Aboriginal people were thought to possess allows
Jack to see over greater distances than his fellows, he is a crack shot, and
the desert is not so much a stranger to him as it is to city-bred Australians.
Both the story and the hero are formulaic and overly stylized, and the plot is
frankly embarrassing to a twenty-first-century reader. But the important point
is that Australianness is constructed by Bowes as something other than purely
white. Aboriginality is embraced by and allied to whiteness, producing an
idealized Australian white man who is in fact partly black.

This is a subtle but reasonably clear shift. The earlier hard lines of the
late nineteenth century that demarcated white and black in the making of an
idealized Australian male are blurred by the 1910s. Read in the context of the
publication of other contemporary children's stories that celebrated, or at least
expressed some admiration for elements of Aboriginality, it is tempting to see
this as reflective and constitutive of a more open and enlightened version
of Australian whiteness, one that discarded previously hostile attitudes and
moved instead to engage with and embrace Indigeneity.

To what extent is this the case? To what extent can we read these evolving
constructions as signs of a willingness to lower the fences that were supposed
to keep Australian whiteness safe from the influence of the native? In my
view, the new openness was more apparent than real, something that becomes
clearer if we consider the reasons behind, and the extent and impact of, this
change the idealized construction of Australian whiteness.

WHY THE CHANGE?

To be sure, the literature of the 1910s differs noticeably from the literature of
the 1870s and 1880s in its depiction of Indigenous Australians. The alleged
barbarities, Godlessness and treachery of Aboriginal people is markedly less

evident in later stories. It is a more sympathetic construction of Aboriginality that allows elements of it to be incorporated into Australian whiteness. This was part of a general trend in children's literature of the time, most notably seen in Mary Grant Bruce's Billabong stories where one of the principal characters, 'Billy,' is Aboriginal, albeit that Billy is certainly at the bottom of the hierarchy on Billabong Station. It is also evident in other children's books, but is most explicitly detailed by Bruce in the foreword to her book *The Stone Axe of Burkamukk* (1922):

> We are apt to look on the blacks as utter barbarians, but, as we read their own old stories, we see that they were boys and girls, men and women, not so unlike us in many ways, and that they could admire what we admire in each other, and condemn what we would condemn.[20]

Aboriginal people are not as feared or fearsome in later stories as in the earlier ones, so one of the reasons for the change in the composition of Australian whiteness appears to be a gentler outlook on racial questions, a softening of the marginalizing discourses of racism as it applied to Indigenous Australians.

Other reasons are, however, more self-serving, more about the needs of the colonizers than the rights or aspirations of the colonized. When the shift from completely marginalizing Aboriginality to embracing elements of it is placed in the context of the general remodelling of Australian masculine ideals over this same period, it becomes clear that the reasons and motives for constructing an Australian whiteness that incorporated elements of Australian blackness in such a way had little to do with a more generous attitude toward Aboriginality per se that with the changing needs and anxieties about the fortunes of Australian whites.

Firstly, colonization of Aboriginal peoples was still proceeding apace in the period from the 1870s through to the 1890s when Kingston, Henty and Favenc wrote their stories. European settlers were still moving into new areas and Indigenous Australians were still mounting a determined resistance. By the 1910s, however, this stage of the colonial project had been largely completed. It was lot easier to be generous, even romantic, toward a displaced Indigenous population in the 1910s when the frontier wars were all but over, in eastern Australia particularly, and when Aboriginal resistance was changing character and form, than in the late nineteenth century in the midst of ongoing armed conflict.

Secondly, and connected to this, the concerns of Australian nation builders had radically changed. In the 1870s and 1880s it was about making colonial Australia; by the 1910s it was about defending the new nation state of Australia and the British Empire as a whole against external enemies. Writers such as Joseph Bowes and Alexander MacDonald thus looked outward in the 1910s, whereas earlier generations had looked inward. Aboriginal people were thus enlisted as allies rather than hunted as enemies not because of new racial sensibilities, but because the perceived enemies were now external in the form of potential Asian invaders and the Central Powers. Invasion scares and imperial wars had a completely different dynamic to colonialism, and consequently encouraged different forms of whiteness. The part-Aboriginalizing of Australian whiteness helped make the colonizers Indigenous to some extent, thus reinforcing their claim to the continent at a time when it was feared that white Australians' moral right to occupy an entire continent was questionable.[21]

Moreover, I think Jack's part-Aboriginality and the alliance with Aborigines in other stories function as little more than Australian motifs. Jack's Aboriginality is akin to the adoption of wattle as the national flower, the institution of Wattle Day, the adoption of green and gold as the national colors, the cry of 'coo-ee,' or the kangaroo and the emu on the coat of arms, or the outback origins of virtually all of the hero figures of children's adventure stories in this period. When Australians looked to what made them culturally and racially distinctive in the late nineteenth and early twentieth centuries, they looked to the Australian environment, and this included the colonized Indigenous peoples as well as the sun, the bush and conditions on the frontiers of settlement. Part Aboriginality is thus deployed by Bowes not to make Jack actually part Aboriginal, but more to make him more distinctively and unequivocally Australian.

More generally, the more open attitudes toward Aboriginal people and the breaking down of the hard boundaries between a civilized whiteness and an uncivilized Aboriginality probably owed more to European concerns about modernism and the softening influences of modern urban life. The desire to rediscover a little savagery, as some commentators put it, and the increasing attention to Herbert Spencer's famous dictum that "the first requisite to success in life is to be a good animal" encouraged some idealization of premodern cultures, peoples and ways of living.[22] Efforts to fight the deleterious effects of modernity found expression in the growing emphasis on physical training in schools, in the Boy Scouts and in the bush legend, as well as a partial, and limited, identification with Aboriginality.[23]

Finally, the later authors, such as Bowes and Macdonald, tended to be Australian-born or to have spent most of their adult lives in Australia, whereas the earlier authors were British-born, and some of them had never even set foot in Australia. Authors such as Kingston and Henty deployed Aborigines much as they deployed black Africans, or Indians—all opponents of Britain's great imperial civilizing mission. Their perspective, not surprisingly, differed greatly from authors who grew up in Australia, who did not see it as savage or uncivilized space, and who were less prone to knee-jerk depictions of native peoples as representing anti-civilization. Moreover, for these later Australian-born authors, who generally wrote in a nationalistic trope, simple dichotomies of civilized British whiteness and an uncivilized Australian blackness were not sufficient; they sought out a hybrid space where Australian whiteness was, if not Aboriginal, then certainly not British either. Britishness was deployed as an 'other' alongside Aboriginality, rather than something that was to quash or defy Aboriginality. Robert Dixon has described the problem and challenges of such an identity formation:

> Australian identity is produced by a contradictory structure that condemns it to an ongoing state of hybridity or bastardry. On the one hand Australia is the 'other' of England, asserting itself as an independent identity through an assumed relation to England's others—the land, Aborigines, Asia, Woman. Yet these others must also be kept beyond the boundaries of the new Australian civility if it is to remain pure and self-consistent.[24]

The new category of Australian whiteness, as defined by these authors, was to include elements of both British whiteness and Australian blackness, but to reject others.

The fact that the shift had more to do with addressing colonial anxieties and the need for a distinctive Australian identity rather than generosity toward the Indigenous is reflected in, and evidenced by, the terms of the alliance or intermingling with Indigenous peoples, by the way in which the problem of hybridity as identified by Dixon is negotiated. Jack Smith, for example, the part-Aboriginal hero of Joseph Bowes' wartime trilogy, is, in the terminology of the time, only one-eighth Aboriginal. He is enough of a 'white' to go to Melbourne Grammar School and captain both the football and cricket teams and to feel great loyalty to Australia and the British Empire. There is nothing Aboriginal or non-white about him at all—except his grandparentage and his supposedly primitive instinct. The problem of hybridity is thus managed by giving Jack Aboriginal descent, and nothing more. Similarly, those Aborigines who form alliances with the colonists against external enemies are defined as heroic or friendly or allied purely and precisely because they fight against Asians—a white preoccupation of the late nineteenth and early twentieth centuries if ever there was one.

EXTERMINATION TO ASSIMILATION

What then, can we conclude about the 'white mind' and its attitudes toward whiteness and blackness in this period as revealed through an examination of Australian juvenile adventure stories? It is clear that the writers of these stories were concerned about the issue of hybridity with white people occupying black lands and coming into contact with non-white peoples, and the stratagems they advocated for addressing the problem *did* clearly undergo a subtle but substantial change—from extermination of Australian blackness to its incorporation. This did have a positive side in that it opened up a space for the continued expression of Aboriginality as part of Australian culture, in particular its manhood. But it was essentially an appropriation of certain aspects of constructed Aboriginality to ease non-Indigenous anxieties about place, belonging and racial fitness rather than a genuine desire to embrace Aboriginality.

Moreover, the effects and implications of 'incorporation' or assimilation of the black into an Australian version of whiteness could be just as destructive of Aboriginality as physical extermination. If we accept Raphael Lemkin's definition of genocide as being a two-stage process commonly associated with colonialism, where the patterns and bases of collective life of the oppressed are destroyed, and then the patterns and bases of collective life of the oppressor are imposed, then the shift from the earlier constructions of whiteness to the later ones can be seen as simply a case of moving from one stage of the process to the other.[25]

Patrick Wolfe has written insightfully about processes of biological absorption in colonial societies, and has argued that in settler societies the denoting of part-Indigenous people as 'white' suited the colonizers because it lowered the Indigenous population and thereby left the land open to be claimed, with less competition from the numerically reduced Indigenous peoples, by the colonizers.[26] Moreover, if the colonizers could attach themselves to the land as 'natives' by virtue of Indigenous blood, the special claims of the colonized lost much of their force. The process is easy to see in Australia around the early twentieth century in the form of state-sponsored child removal policies, and is also evident in the cultural realm of children's adventure stories. In the later adventure stories, for example, Aboriginal 'blood' lives on, albeit in diluted form, but Aboriginality does not survive in any sense of an ongoing and distinct people, culture or way of life. Blackness is whitened, rather than the reverse. In this respect the adventure stories and their changing depictions of Australian whiteness resonate with the shift in race relations from dispossession and extermination to the not-much-less benign practices of child removal and forced assimilation.

And yet, despite such severe limitations, the shift in what Graham Dawson calls "cultural imaginaries" from entirely non-Aboriginal British whiteness as the colonial ideal to a party Aboriginal Australian whiteness did have at least some positive implications.[27] For all its shortcomings, this type of reconstruction of the imagined Australian whiteness did at least open up a space for the survival of Aboriginal people and Aboriginality, however circumscribed, within the Australian body politic. Tenuous though this was, it was at least an advance on the exterminatory outlook that preceded it, and at least offered a basis from which later renaissance could proceed.

NOTES

1. Aileen Moreton-Robinson, "Whiteness Matters: Australian Studies and Indigenous Studies" in *Thinking Australian Studies: Teaching Across Cultures*, ed. David Carter, Kate Darian-Smith and Gus Worby (Brisbane: University of Queensland Press, 2004), 136–37.

2. Moreton-Robinson, "Whiteness Matters.

3. Moreton-Robinson, "Whiteness Matters," 137.

4. Joan Wallach Scott, *Gender and the Politics of History* (New York: Columbia University Press, 1988), 29.

5. See, for example: Gisela Bock, "Women's History and Gender History: Aspects of an International Debate," *Gender and History* 1, no. 1 (1988): 13; R. W. Connell, *Gender and Power: Society, the Person, and Sexual Politics* (Stanford: Stanford University Press, 1987), 78–79; Robert A. Nye, *Masculinity and Male Codes of Honour in Modern France* (Oxford: Oxford University Press, 1993), 5; Kay Schaffer, *Women and the Bush: Forces of Desire in the Australian Cultural Tradition* (Melbourne: Cambridge University Press, 1988), 13; Scott Coltrane, "Theorizing Masculinities in Contemporary Social Science," in *Theorizing Masculinities*, ed. Harry Brod and Michael Kaufman (Thousand Oaks, Calif: Sage, 1994), 45. See also David D. Gilmore, *Manhood in the Making: Cultural Concepts of Masculinity* (New Haven: Yale University Press, 1989), 4–5, 230.

6. John Tosh, "What Should Historians do with Masculinity?: Reflections on Nineteenth-Century Britain," *History Workshop Journal*, no. 38 (1994): 180.

7. See, for example, Robert H. MacDonald, *Sons of the Empire: The Frontier and the Boy Scout Movement, 1890–1918* (Toronto: University of Toronto Press, 1993), 4.

8. Moreton-Robinson, "Whiteness Matters," 40.

9. See: Rebecca Stott, "The Dark Continent: Africa as Female Body in Haggard's Adventure Fiction," *Feminist Review*, no. 32 (Spring, 1989): 69–89; Anne McClintock, *Imperial Leather: Race, Gender and Sexuality in the Colonial Contest* (New York: Routledge, 1995), 1–24.

10. Martin Green, *Dreams of Adventure, Deeds of Empire* (New York: Basic Books, 1979), 224.

11. Jackie Hollingworth, "The Call of Empire: Children's Literature Revisited" in *Mother State and Her Little Ones*, ed. Bob Bessant (Melbourne: Centre for Youth and Community Studies, Phillip Institute of Technology, 1987), 93.

12. W. H. G. Kingston, *Twice Lost: A Story of Shipwreck and Adventure in the Wilds of Australia* (London: Thomas Nelson, 1876), 277–78.

13. Kingston, *Twice Lost*, 331–32.

14. W. H. G. Kingston, *Australian Adventures* (London: George, Routledge and Sons, 1884), 9–10.

15. Kingston, *Australian Adventures*, 152.

16. See, for example, W. H. G. Kingston, *The Young Berringtons; Or, the Boy Explorers* (London: Cassell, 1880); and G. A. Henty, *A Final Reckoning: A Tale of Bush Life in Australia* (London: Blackie and Son, 1887).

17. Ernest Favenc, *The Secret of the Australian Desert* (London: Blackie and Son, 1896), 150.

18. See: Alexander Macdonald, *The Invisible Island: A Story of the Far North of Queensland* (London: Blackie and Son, 1911); Joseph Bowes, *Comrades: A Story of the Australian Bush* (London: Henry Froude, Hodder and Stoughton, 1912).

19. Joseph Bowes, *The Young Anzacs* (London: Humphrey Milford, Oxford University Press, 1918); *the Anzac war-Trail: With the Light Horse in Sinai* (London: Humphrey Milford, Oxford University Press, 1919); and *The Aussie Crusaders* (London: Humphrey Milford, Oxford University Press, 1919).

20. Mary Grant Bruce, *The Stone Axe of Burkamukk* (Melbourne: Ward, Lock and Co., 1922), 5–6.

21. On such fears see: David Walker, *Anxious Nation: Australia and the Rise of Asia, 1850–1939* (Brisbane: University of Queensland Press, 1999), especially chapters 8 and 9.

22. Herbert Spencer, *Education: Intellectual, Moral and Physical* (New York: D. Appleton, 1900 (1860)), 95.

23. See, for example: Martin Crotty, *Making the Australian male: Middle-Class Masculinity 1870–1920* (Melbourne: Melbourne University Press, 2001), especially chapters 6 and 7, and Richard White, *Inventing Australia: Images and Identity, 1688–1980* (Sydney: George Allen and Unwin, 1981), especially chapters 5–7.

24. Robert Dixon, *Writing the Colonial Adventure: Race, Gender and Nation in Anglo-Australian Popular Fiction, 1875–1914* (New York: Cambridge University Press, 1995), 11.

25. R. Lemkin, *Axis Rule in Occupied Europe* (Washington: Carnegie Endowment for International Peace, 1944), cited in Henry Reynolds, *An Indelible Stain: The Question of Genocide in Australia's History* (Melbourne: Viking, 2001), 14.

26. Patrick Wolfe, "Land, Labour and Difference: Elementary Structures of Race," *American Historical Review*, 106, no. 3 (2001).

27. Graham Dawson, *Soldier Heroes: British Adventure, Empire and the Imagining of Masculinities* (London: Routledge, 1994).

Chapter Nine

Laura Bush and Dan Brown: Whiteness, Feminism and the Politics of Vulnerability

Tanya Serisier

In the years since the publication of Samuel Huntington's influential and controversial *Foreign Affairs* article in 1993, the idea of a 'Clash of Civilizations' between the West and Islam has shaped much public discourse within the West.[1] It has provided the major explanatory narrative for the destruction of the twin towers in New York and the subsequent launching of the 'war on terror.'[2] The violence and bloodshed of this war, however, makes it easy to forget that it occurs within a rhetoric of a wider cultural 'clash' that both surrounds and predates it. This clash has focused variously in Australia and other Western nations on anxieties around immigration, asylum seekers, multiculturalism and ethnic crime, as well as terrorism.[3] In essence, proponents of this clash argue, in the words of George W. Bush that the values of white/Western civilization must be defended against those who "hate us" and especially hate "our freedoms".[4]

Who exactly constitutes 'us' and 'them' within this logic is rarely explicitly defined, but instead built up through repeated cultural tropes and representations to the point where the categories seem transparently self-evident. In this chapter I examine these representations as a contemporary form of Orientalism that provides much of the discursive basis and justification for the war on terror. As Edward Said noted, Orientalism, and its construction of the 'Oriental' as an object of knowledge, cannot be separated from what he referred to as the "idea of Europe, a collective notion identifying 'us' Europeans as against all 'those' non-Europeans."[5] Within the context of the War on Terror however, this idea of 'Europe' has been largely supplanted by the West, or what Osuri and Bannerjee have referred to as the "white diaspora."[6] This "white diaspora," however, shares what Said referred to as the "major component" of European culture, "the idea of European identity as a superior one in comparison with all the non-European peoples

and cultures," and this idea continues to underlie Western constructions of the
'clash of cultures' between the white diaspora and the Islamic other.[7]

Analyses of these discourses often focus on the linked tropes of culture,
race, civilization and progress. However, in the words of Meyda Yegenoglu:
"the question of sexual difference" is often relegated "to a sub-field in the
analysis of colonial discourse." She insists on the need to recognize "how
representations of sexual and cultural difference are constitutive of each
other."[8] Therefore, this paper focuses on exploring the ways in which the above
discourses are intrinsically bound up with politics of gender and sexuality.[9]

As Said was careful to emphasize in his work, Orientalist discourse
permeated, and continues to permeate Western culture. Dominant Orientalist
discourses are hegemonic, and rely for their reproduction on multiple levels of
representation, and highly disparate generic sources. So, these representations
can be found in the official realm of politics, academia, literature, and also
within popular or 'low' culture. Indeed, the interplay and reinforcement
between these different genres and spheres is an important aspect of the
"durability and strength" of Orientalist discourse. For these reasons, I have
chosen to focus my exploration on two highly disparate texts that give an
example of the resonance between these different cultural domains, Laura
Bush's national radio address of November 2001 following the invasion
of Afghanistan, and Dan Brown's best-selling novel, *Angels and Demons*,
published in 2000.[10] These texts both occupy a highly significant position in
contemporary Western culture, and are therefore well-placed to illuminate the
issues under exploration.

Laura Bush's radio address represented the first time in US history that
a First Lady delivered the weekly National Presidential radio address. This
fact alone is testament to its symbolic and political importance for the Bush
Administration, and it remains to date the Administration's most calculated
and deliberate articulation of the relationships among gender, race and
civilization. Her speech drew explicit links between issues of women's rights,
and the 'War on Terror,' specifically in relation to the invasion of Afghanistan.
Indeed, in her speech, Bush suggested that the two were causally related.
The speech also symbolized the Bush Administration's *rapprochement* with
feminist organizations, coinciding with the first high-level meetings between
Administration officials and representatives of groups such as the Feminist
Majority Foundation. As a result of these meetings, the State Department
decided to fill a high-level position to promote women's rights overseas,
which had been left vacant since the Republicans came to office.[11]

The success of Dan Brown's novels, which have dominated the best-seller
lists in North America, Australia and Europe, makes them significant cultural

artefacts. Their enduring popularity indicates the cultural resonance of his work and themes. *Angels and Demons*, a worldwide best seller, is the first in a trilogy centered on the American religious and art historian, Robert Langdon. The second book in this series is Brown's most famous work, *The Da Vinci Code*. Published in 2000, it provides a useful illustration of the ways in which cultural motifs and anxieties of the War on Terror predate, and provide the preconditions for, the War on Terror.[12]

SEX, VIOLENCE AND MUSLIM MEN

"Seeing terror in a woman's eyes was his ultimate aphrodisiac . . ."

Angels and Demons is primarily focused around a plot to destroy the Vatican, engineered by the Catholic Church's ancient enemy, the science-worshipping Illuminati. The mastermind of this plot, and the ultimate villain of the book, turns out to be a rather unbalanced Catholic priest, Carlo Ventresca. However, in the grand tradition of last minute twists, the priest is not revealed as a villain until the final chapters of the novel. Rather, the face of evil throughout this book is a "mahogany-skinned" Muslim, known only as "the Hassassin." This villain is motivated by an ancient cultural hatred of Christianity, expressed in his first appearance in the book as he contemplates the successful completion of his first of many murders:

> As the killer walked, he imagined his ancestors smiling down on him. Today he was fighting *their* battle, he was fighting the same enemy they had fought for ages, as far back as the eleventh century.[13]

He is a remorseless killer, a fanatical and vicious Muslim driven by hatred for the Christian west. This figure has become a familiar trope, not just in mass-produced 'low-brow' fiction, but in contemporary representations of the good and evil of international and domestic politics. Brown's Hassassin could easily be an agent of Osama Bin Laden, or the man himself. Similarly, this character is reminiscent of the fears conjured in Western nations around the potential dangers of illegal immigrants, refugees, and Muslim immigration more broadly.

However, while this villain is undoubtedly racialized, he is also decisively male, and lasciviously sexual. In a familiar move in hegemonic Western constructions of non-white men, he is a sexual animal.[14] The connections between this animalistic sexuality and non-Western otherness are emphasized throughout Brown's book, such as this description of the Hassassin's visit to a brothel:

> An appetite for hedonistic pleasure was something bred into him by his ancestors. His ascendants had indulged in hashish, but he preferred a different kind of gratification. . . . Although his people did not celebrate Christmas, he imagined that this is what it must feel like to be a Christian child, sitting before a stack of Christmas presents, about to discover the miracles inside. He opened the album and examined the photos. A lifetime of sexual fantasies stared back at him. . . .[15]

Brown continually reinforces the 'cultural' nature of the Hassassin's predilections, making it clear that his sexual behaviour is not unrepresentative of masculine Muslim sexuality more generally. Towards the climax of the novel, "the Hassassin" contemplates what he will do to the recently abducted heroine, Vittoria:

> She was a spoil of war, and when he was finished with her, he would pull her from the divan and force her to her knees. She would service him again. *The ultimate submission*. Then, at the moment of his own climax, he would slit her throat.
> *Ghayat assa'adah*, they called it. *The ultimate pleasure*.[16]

In Brown's book, the sexual practice of murdering women as the climax to fellatio is culturally common enough in the unspecified Muslim homeland of the Hassassin to have a commonly used name.

The connection of this masculine Muslim sexuality to animalistic violence is continually rearticulated. Brown informs us of the Hassassin, that "seeing terror in a woman's eyes was his ultimate aphrodisiac."[17] This extreme sadomasochism is, however, particularly racially focused toward white women, and is connected to his hatred for Western culture more generally. The Hassassin's brothel visit, mentioned above, continues:

> When he saw his selection, he knew he had chosen well. She was exactly as he had requested . . . nude, lying on her back, her arms tied to the bedposts with thick velvet cords.
> He crossed the room and ran a dark finger across her ivory abdomen. *I killed last night*, he thought. *You are my reward*.[18]

Indeed, the only pursuits we see the Hassassin engaged in are his work for the Illuminati and his private pursuit of sexual domination of European women, of whom Brown states, "[f]orcing them into physical submission was a gratification he always enjoyed."[19] The 'animalistic' nature of the

Hassassin's pleasures is reinforced throughout *Angels and Demons* by the lack of strategic agency attributed to the Hassassin. He is an exotic savage, carrying out orders, or perhaps, a dangerous animal kept on a carefully controlled leash. In Brown's world, the Hassassin requires the direction of the Western, scientific, Illuminati, embodied in the criminally brilliant priest. Although, there is a large thematic opposition between religion and science in Brown's novel, Carlo Ventresca's ability to operate as a key figure in the scientific Illuminati and the Catholic Church ultimately complicates this distinction. Indeed, the only character to remain firmly outside the realm of Western rationality is the Hassassin.

This image of a sexualized, violent, racialized masculinity, uncontrollably desirous of white women, is a recurrent feature of dominant Western portrayals of non-western sexuality. This construction and the racial violence that is its practical counterpart are most infamous in relation to the construction of black men as rapists of white women in the post-Reconstruction South of the United States, and in the extra-legal but officially sanctioned record of lynching that accompanied it.[20] However, the construction of Muslim society as uncivilized also goes beyond the realm of individual sexuality and racist stereotyping, and into the field of international politics and the relationship of the West to societies seen to be comprised of individuals who share fundamental sexual attitudes with Brown's Hassassin.

CIVILIZATION, PROGRESS AND WOMEN'S RIGHTS

"Civilized people throughout the world are speaking out in horror"

On November 17, 2001, Laura Bush became the first person other than the President to give the weekly Presidential radio address. While her speech was explicitly concerned with the invasion of Afghanistan, her comments were clearly focused on a wider engagement with the 'Clash of Civilizations.' The stated goal of her address was nothing less than "to kick off a world wide effort to focus on the brutality and terror against women and children by the al-Qaeda terrorist network." The "brutality" of al-Qaeda was contrasted with the reactions of "civilized people throughout the world," who were, according to Bush, "speaking out in horror." The connections that Bush was attempting to draw were made even more explicit when she stated that "the fight against terrorism is also a fight for the rights and dignity of women."[21]

Perhaps even more explicitly than Brown's novel, Bush's speech illustrates the deployment of elements of gender, race and progress, in contemporary discourses of civilization. Historically, dominant Western conceptions of civilization have been premised on women's exclusion from the public sphere and relegation to domestic and feminine duties.[22] However, here, the Taliban and al-Qaeda are condemned as uncivilized for this very same exclusion and particularly for refusing women the rights to education and work. According to Bush, civilization is not only opposed to this exclusion, but horrified by it. Indeed, by equating civilization with "the rights and dignity of women," Bush deliberately rhetorically connects the 'Clash of Civilization' with western feminism. Indeed, she does this in a way that equates the West with women's rights, and the Muslim Other, personified in the Taliban, as the absolute negation of women's emancipation. It is not necessary to argue that there is no difference between the status of women's rights within Bush's America and the Taliban's Afghanistan to critique this argument. Rather, it simply requires noting that women's rights remain a complex and contradictory field of struggles, gains and losses, within both the 'West' and the 'Muslim world.' Indeed, the diverse conditions of gender politics within different communities and nations within both these monolithic constructions points to their absurdity. The problem with Bush's speech is in its attempt to incorporate women's rights, as defined by Bush, within a dichotomous economy of white superiority.

Bush is hardly original in making this argument. It is one that was propagated in the late 19th and early 20th century by both socialists and advocates of women's rights.[23] Neither is this the first time that Western feminist arguments or projects have been enlisted towards the ends of Western or white supremacy. Indeed, complicity in politics of racism and Imperialism have been an enduring complication of feminism's status as an emancipatory political project.[24] However, Laura Bush's use of feminist discourse in this way seems to signal a discursive shift between the politics of feminism and whiteness.[25] From being a feature of critical and oppositional discourses such as feminism and socialism, the rhetorical connection between feminist emancipation and civilization has been adopted as mainstream official doctrine, in the person of a Republican First Lady.[26]

It is of course necessary to remain cognizant of the context of Bush's speech. Far from an exercise in abstract rhetoric, this was a justification of both a specific invasion and the ongoing use of force in the War on Terror. Women's rights are not only a benchmark of Western cultural superiority, but their removal, and the "brutal oppression of women," is "a central goal of the terrorists." It seems that while for her husband, the terrorists simply hate "our" freedoms, for Laura Bush it is freedoms of women particularly that attract the ire of Islamic militants. The War on Terror must be supported then, "not only because our hearts break for the women and children in Afghanistan, but also because in Afghanistan we see the world the terrorists would like to impose on the rest of us."[27] There is within Bush's speech a direct exhortation on western feminists and women more generally, to choose the right side. By the end of Bush's speech the invasion of Afghanistan has been transformed into a quest "to ensure that dignity and opportunity will be secured for all the women and children in Afghanistan."[28] And really, who could be opposed to that?

FICTION AND REALITY:
THE WORLDS OF BUSH AND BROWN

It is fitting at this point to briefly note the disjunctions between fiction and reality, or politics and literature. At an obvious level, despite the resonances between the worlds of culture and politics, there is a distinction between a novel and a political radio address, a difference between a fictional plot to destroy the Vatican, and a factual successful attempt to destroy the World Trade Center. At another level, both texts may be seen to blur the absolute boundaries between fiction and reality. Both tell the story of a world that is in one sense 'real,' and, in another, imagined. The popularity and notoriety of Brown's novels is in large part based on their blending of the fictional and the historical, or at least the historically possible. Both *Angels and Demons* and its more notorious sequel discuss real historical institutions and figures, such as the Vatican, the European Organisation for Nuclear Research (CERN), Leonardo Da Vinci, Galileo Galilei, and Gian Lorenzo Bernini. Indeed, Brown's works have not been read as purely fictional but as historical, and occupy a place within both the genres of fiction and historical conspiracy theory. On the other hand, while Bush's speech is clearly located within the reality of contemporary warfare, it too may be read as a form of fiction. The story told by Bush, and the stories told by her husband, of an American military strategy driven by concern for women and children, is one that could be described as a justificatory fiction.[29] More specifically, the story of Afghani women discarding the oppressive strictures imposed by their fanatical terrorist Muslim rulers was quickly revealed to be entirely fictional.[30] Indeed, it is by no means established that the women of Afghanistan are any better off post-invasion than they were before it.

Bush's speech and Brown's book are, however, quite different texts, and occupy very different positions socially and generically, and as such have differing rationales, structures and purposes. Moreover, Bush's speech is significant in many ways because it was exceptional. Its very existence, a radio address by the First Lady, was designed to give an added sense of urgency and authority to Bush's words. Brown's book, on the other hand, is notable in many ways for its lack of exceptionality. It is a conventional thriller with no pretensions to disrupting the conventions of the genre. The significance of Brown, and of *Angels and Demons*, is rather to be found in its 'generic' nature.[31] Brown is, as his official website puts it, "one of the best-selling authors of all time." My purpose here is not to argue that Bush's speech and Brown's novel are the same, but rather that a juxtaposition of them as highly different, but culturally significant texts, is useful in exploring the hegemonic nature of the cultural tropes I am examining here.

However, there are significant differences between Brown's fictional pre-September 11th universe, and Laura Bush's post-September 11th reality. As mentioned above, the vision of Muslim masculinity presented in *Angels and Demons* is almost entirely animalistic and with very little strategic agency. The Hassassin, who does not even merit an individual name, carries out orders with a bloodthirsty pleasure, and indulges in his passions for the sexual degradation of white women. His lack of respect for women is simply a further mark of his animal nature. But as an animal, the Hassassin is ultimately revealed to be simply a tool of the master villain of the novel, a priest with aspirations to both become Pope, and to bring about the ultimate triumph of (Catholic) religion over science. The most notable distinction between Brown's novel and Bush's reality then, is that the Hassassin's, while still bloodthirsty misogynists, can no longer be simply dismissed as nameless animals. Osama bin Laden is not a slave to his passions, requiring direction from a white puppet-master. Rather, it is the Hassassins themselves who have a strategic vision, and that is to impose the reality of 'Afghanistan' on the rest of the world. Bush's terrorists share the bloodthirsty and misogynist desires long associated with Western constructions of Arab masculinity, but they have no white master pulling the strings.[32] Indeed, it is this pairing of desire with the rationality and capacity for strategic thought that has often been seen as its diametric opposite, that creates the sense of threat in Bush's speech. Not only do these Muslim men desire the subjugation of women, and white women particularly, but they have finally achieved the rational capacity to carry it out. It is this that gives the sense of an urgent imperative to Bush's exhortations to white women to fall in line in the war against those who would oppress them.

MUSLIM WOMEN AS THE SILENT OTHER

"In *his* country women were possessions"

If the reality of September 11 has altered cultural constructions of Muslim masculinity however, it seems to have done little to change Western images of Muslim women. Within Bush and Brown's texts, Muslim women are noticeable more for their absence as active or speaking subjects. In Brown's novel, Muslim women are simply referred to as "possessions" or "chattel." They are submissive, "they know their place," and do not fight against it.[33] A similar conception is at work in Bush's speech, which portrays the women of Afghanistan as already and absolutely, subjugated. Indeed, the only function Muslim women perform in Brown's narrative is as a contrast to the independent and strong Western women. The only mention of the women of the Hassassin's country is in order to explain his sexual desire to subjugate women who do not think of themselves as "weak."[34] While the comparison is not as implicit in Bush's speech, it is clear that the image of women's lives in Afghanistan is contrasted with the supposed lives of Bush's listeners. The image of Muslim women presented in both texts functions ultimately as a tribute to the superiority of Western civilization. The superior rights and agency of white women, strong and independent and capable of action comes to stand in for the superiority of white civilization as a whole.

Muslim women are therefore not only oppressed but incapable of resistance to oppression, or of acting to change their status. By calling on the 'civilized' world to act on behalf of Muslim women, Bush erases the history of Afghani women's resistance to their subjugation. Further, she discounts the very possibility of this resistance occurring. Within Bush's world, the only possibility of change in Muslim women's status comes from the actions of white supporters of women's rights. In particular, it is because of "recent military gains" in Iraq that women have acquired some level of autonomy. This conception of liberation means that Muslim women continue to be voiceless and entirely lacking in agency. Rather, they depend ultimately on white supporters of liberal feminism to ensure their freedom through military intervention. In drawing these links between women's liberation and Western invasion and occupation of a third world country, Bush could be accused of subverting feminist arguments to her own ends. The historical context however, does not allow white feminism such an easy way out. Historians such as Louise Newman have traced the ways in which participation in the Imperialist project allowed white women to claim their equality with white men through their assertion of superiority over non-white men and women. Newman further argues that crucial to these claims was the role white women could play in rescuing and civilizing non-white women through their gradual assimilation into white norms and values.[35] Newman also makes the valuable point that contemporary western understandings of the relationship between gender and civilization continue to draw on this legacy, and it is this legacy that provides the context for Bush's speech.

What perhaps most sharply distinguishes Bush's speech from this legacy is its profound element of anxiety, a feature shared by Brown's characterization.

Both texts engage in the familiar processes of presenting the 'Oriental' woman as a helpless object of pity, and requiring salvation. However, in both of these contemporary texts she is also a representation of imminent threat, and the precarious nature of white women's freedoms. This is most clear in Bush's summary of why the civilized world must speak out:

> [N]ot only because our hearts break for the women and children in Afghanistan, but also because in Afghanistan we see the world the terrorists would like to impose on the rest of us.

So, we see that the more traditional construction of the Muslim woman as an object requiring the rescue of enlightened white women is made to sit alongside the Muslim woman as the potential marker of white women's future, unless we act now. So, finally, what Bush is asking of us is support for a kind of preemptive defensive strike for women's rights. If the West fails to act, white women will quickly find themselves in the same position as their subjugated sisters. Rather than the West engaged in exporting feminism to the subjugated women of the world, white women are portrayed as defending their freedoms from the invading Muslims who would take it away from them. Similarly, in *Angels and Demons*, the Hassassin has come to Europe in order to force European women into submission. Again, Brown's description of the state of Muslim women serves as a warning of the kind of world the Hassassin wishes to impose upon Europe.

WHITENESS AND THE DESIRABILITY OF FEMINISM

"I thought you said she was a *physicist*!"

In many ways therefore, the constructions of Muslim women within the two texts do not depict subjects in their own right, but rather the spectre of the potential subjugation of white women. The white woman is presented as the opposite of this, free from oppression. She is indeed presented as a model of liberated femininity, and therefore as a feminine ideal, the focus of desire for both white and non-white men alike. The clearest illustration of this construction is found in Brown's heroine, Vittoria Vetra. It is worth noting therefore, that she is depicted in the book almost exclusively from the point of view of Robert Langdon, the hero. Therefore, much of her perceived value comes from his admiration of her. When Vittoria first appears, all Robert knows about her is that she is a physicist. However, surprisingly, the first sign of her presence is deep-sea diving gear:

'I thought you said she was a *physicist!*'

'She is. She's a Bio Entanglement Physicist. She studies interconnectivity of life systems. . . . Recently she disproved one of Einstein's fundamental theories by using atomically synchronized cameras to observe a school of tuna fish.' . . .

Descending from the chopper in her khaki shorts and white sleeveless top, Vittoria Vetra looked nothing like the bookish physicist he had expected. Lithe and graceful, she was tall with chestnut skin and long black hair that swirled in the backwind of the rotors . . . As the air currents buffeted her body, her clothes clung, accentuating her slender torso and small breasts.[36]

Brown's heroine then is a brilliant physicist who deep-sea dives, wears revealing clothing, looks anything but bookish, and is, we discover momentarily, also a guru of Hatha yoga. Brown goes to great length to demonstrate that education and independence have made Vittoria no less feminine or desirable. This logic was perhaps summarized most famously and succinctly in George Bush's first speech after the attacks of September 11. In answer to his own rhetorical question as to why 'they' hate 'us,' he responded emphatically, "they hate our freedoms." Vittoria's emancipated version of white womanhood is clearly coded with feminist undercurrents such as education and independence, setting her apart from the Muslim woman depicted by both Bush and Brown who lacks access to these resources. At the same time, her accomplishments include a tribute to the cosmopolitan nature of the modern white woman. As an accomplished exemplar of white femininity, Vittoria has not only mastered the ancient Eastern discipline of yoga, but is able to use it to enhance her sexual appeal to her white male partner.

It is made clear in the book that a key aspect of Vittoria's exemplary model of white womanhood is her ability to provoke desire in men. This is as true for the valorized white masculinity embodied in the novel's hero, Robert Langdon, as for the debased Muslim masculinity of the Hassassin. In contrast to the Hassassin however, Robert's desire is expressed as an urge to protect Vittoria, and therefore she becomes the medium for distinguishing between Robert, the good white man, and the Hassassin, the bad Oriental. In contrast to the Hassassin who revels in the pain of white women, once Robert learns of his heroine's abduction, "his initial instinct was for Vittoria."[37] Indeed, even whilst Robert is in imminent danger of being shot, "he thought of Vittoria and ached to help her."[38] The urge to protect becomes overwhelming for Langdon:

A new compulsion had ignited within him. It was simple. Stark. Primal. Find Vittoria.[39]

In distinction to 'the Hassassin,' who acquired his violent lust from his ancestors, Langdon's 'primal' regression unearths the white man's instinct toward chivalry.

Vittoria as an idealized model of white womanhood cannot be read separately from the model of Western gender relations that is presented in the novel through the development of her and Robert's relationship. Founded as it is on the notion of equality, liberal Western feminism is focused primarily on the relative status of women to men in a given society. So, the 'equal' white woman is contrasted to the subordinated Muslim woman, and it is the supposedly equal relationship between men and women in the West that is seen as the primary evidence of women's emancipation. The claim to equality is therefore central to the distinction that both Bush and Brown make between Western and Islamic societies. In Laura Bush's radio address, the absolute nature of that distinction is demonstrated rhetorically through the gendering of the Islamic subjects and the universalizing of the Western or "civilized" subjects. "Women" are referred to specifically only in the context of Afghanistan or as the objects of desire of the terrorists. Western subjects are referred to only as "people" or "families," universal and nongendered categories that are used to emphasize the lack of gender hierarchy and division within the West. This assertion of equality can also be seen in the format of the address itself. Although, as was mentioned above, this radio address was the first time in American history that a First Lady had performed the weekly Presidential radio address, and therefore the first time that a woman had performed it, Bush makes no mention of this fact, and gives no explanation for her presence. The structure of her speech therefore implies that there is nothing unusual in a woman giving the Presidential radio speech.[40] Women are, after all, equal in the United States of America.

The equality that is claimed to exist between men and women in the West then also becomes an integral part of implicit claims to white superiority. Dan Brown demonstrates this clearly in the climactic battle scene in which the Hassassin is eventually defeated and killed. The battle begins with the Hassassin at a clear advantage. He has already defeated Robert in close combat on several occasions and finally left him for dead. At the same time he has captured Vittoria, who lies before him bound and helpless. He has just begun the process of removing her clothes with a knife, when Robert, not dead after all, arrives to rescue her. The ensuing duel between the two men is patently uneven and the Hassassin maintains the upper hand for the duration of the contest. He is just about to send Robert plunging off a balcony 100 feet in the air, when Vittoria intervenes. She has used her yoga skills and her captor's distraction to escape and her intervention allows Robert to move to safety. Working together, the two of them overwhelm the Hassassin until finally:

[T]he Hassassin stumbled back against the railing. Langdon and Vittoria went for him at the same instant, both heaving and pushing. The Hassassin's body sailed backward over the banister into the night.

Clearly, it is Robert and Vittoria's ability to work together and in partnership that enables them to defeat the Hassassin. This is a victory made possible by the workings of Western gender relations, enabled by Vittoria's enlightened white womanhood, and Robert's complementary Western masculinity. The Hassassin, who can only see women as objects of perverse desire, would have been incapable of such a feat, as would his female counterparts, identified only as chattel and property.

A FEMINIST WHITENESS?—TOWARD A CRITIQUE

The texts under consideration here give insight into the ways in which gender and race intersect within dominant contemporary discourses surrounding relations between the West and the Islamic world. These discourses are dominated by the linked constructions of the 'Clash of Civilization' and the 'War on Terror.' Within these discourses there is a presentation of white civilization as marked by gender equality, and enlightened masculinity and educated and accomplished femininity. This stands in explicit contrast to the conception of Muslim society as marked by profound gender hierarchy and domination, and masculinity marked by brutality and sexualized violence, and femininity equated with absolute passivity. In short, this dichotomy represents a claiming of the gains and benefits of liberal Western feminism within a racialized discourse of white supremacy. However, by highlighting the workings of these discourses, analysis of these texts can also begin to point to contradictions and tensions contained within them.

Within this discourse there is an attempt to construct an absolute dichotomy between the West, and Islamic society. It is this dichotomy that epistemologically enables the relationship between the two to be portrayed as a 'clash' or 'war.' Perhaps the most obvious application of this dichotomous logic to questions of gender is the counter-posing of the chivalrous white masculinity of Robert to the debased, animalistic masculinity of the Hassassin, in *Angels and Demons.* However, on closer inspection, the differences between them appear to be not so fundamental. Robert's white masculinity means he is able to appreciate Vittoria's brilliance as a physicist. However, this appreciation by no means diminishes the power of Robert's masculine gaze to assess and evaluate Vittoria physically. At their first meeting he notes approvingly that she is nothing like the "bookish physicist" he had expected.

Instead, Robert notices that she is not "overly beautiful" but exudes a "raw sensuality," and also that the helicopter backwind shows off her breasts.[41] It is clear, therefore, that Robert, like the Hassassin, both desires *and* objectifies Vittoria. However, his objectifying gaze is coded by Brown as acceptable and unproblematic, validating and reinforcing the existence of gender hierarchies within Western society.

This reinforcement of gender hierarchy unsettles attempts within the texts to depict equality as the defining feature of Western sexual politics. Indeed, the resolution of Robert and Vittoria's relationship within the novel demonstrates that the recodification of discourses of gender and civilization need not threaten Western male dominance. Even their joint triumph over the Hassassin occurs following a string of events that only reinforce their gender inequality. Despite the fact that Vittoria spends "months at a time working in dangerous ecological locations" and is proficient with weapons, while Robert is an academic who has never held a gun before, it is still Vittoria who is abducted and Robert who enters at the 11th hour to rescue her from a "fate worse than death."[42] The consummation of their relationship similarly reinforces the patriarchal division between the active male and passive female that Western feminists have consistently critiqued.[43] Vittoria's seduction attempts are described this way:

> She seemed to be willing him to set down his fork and carry her off in his arms.[44]

Robert teases her by not responding, exploiting his surety that nothing can happen between them without his initiation, while despite her expertise in physics, yoga, and various other skills, Vittoria can only wait frustrated. Her seemingly emancipated model of white womanhood does nothing to disrupt traditional western gendered relations of power.

The contradictions are if anything even more apparent upon close examination of Bush's radio address. Even the unprecedented nature of the First Lady delivering the weekly Presidential address belies the image of a sexually equal Western society that Bush is attempting to present. The fact that a woman has never before given the address points to the limited nature of women's participation in the American public sphere, particularly in prominent roles. Additionally, it is significant that Bush was speaking in her capacity as the *wife* of the President, and not as a public figure in her own right. The mediation of Bush's ability to speak through the figure of her husband hardly acts as an exemplar of liberated white womanhood. Even more telling perhaps, is the domestic record of the Bush Administration on women's rights. Domestically, the Republicans are opposed by the major women's rights organizations, such as the National Organization for Women, and the Feminist Majority Foundation, on almost every issue, from abortion to equal opportunity legislation. Rather than representing a commitment to the advancement of women's rights, Bush's speech represents a validation of feminist criticisms of non-Western societies, and occurs within the ongoing and systemic denial of the validity of these critiques domestically. It should not be surprising that the most senior women's rights appointment to come out of this administration was of an office specifically focused on women's rights overseas.

The ultimate effect of constructions of gender within these texts is to negate feminism as an oppositional practice within Western societies. There is no suggestion here that gender relations in the west or normative models of white heterosexuality could become an object of critique or even questioning. Rather, they are posited as the apex of civilized relations between the sexes. By combining discourses of women's rights and civilization, and contrasting liberated Western women with their subjugated Islamic counterparts, these discourses seek to elide contestations and critiques of the dominant institutions of gender and family that have emerged from within Western societies. The logical conclusion to these discourses then is to transform support for women's rights from an oppositional practice within white society to Laura Bush's missionary exhortation to conquest.

NOTES

1. For the original and influential use of this phrase, see Samuel P. Huntington, "The Clash of Civilizations," *Foreign Affairs* 72, no. 3 (1993): 22–28. This phrase, as well as its meanings and connotations has subsequently been used by many and various authors. Engaging with this debate almost of necessity requires accepting the problematically totalizing and homogenous categories of 'the West' and 'Islam.' They are deployed here not as useful terms of analysis in the their own right, but as fictional constructs which are required in order to render the 'Clash of Civilizations' discourse meaningful. It is, of course, important to note the way that repeated use of these terms both creates and reinforces them as meaningful identities.

2. Here I refer of course both to the invasions of Afghanistan and Iraq, and to domestic security measures which have primarily focused on suspect domestic populations within Western nations, most particularly Muslim communities.

3. For a valuable discussion of the white Australian nationalism and its accompanying anxieties see: Ghassan Hage, *White Nation: Fantasies of White Supremacy in a Multicultural Society* (Sydney: Pluto Press, 1998).

4. George W. Bush, *Address to a Joint Session of Congress and the American People*, Washington, September 20, 2001 (Speech Transcript).

5. Edward W. Said, *Orientalism* (New York: Pantheon Books, 1978), 7.

6. Goldie Osuri and Subhabrata Bobby Bannerjee, "White Diasporas: Media Representations of September 11 and the Unbearable Whiteness of Being in Australia," *Social Semiotics* 14, no. 2 (August, 2004).

7. Said, *Orientalism*, 7–9.

8. Meyda Yegenoglu, *Colonial Fantasies: Toward a Feminist Reading of Orientalism* (Cambridge: Cambridge University Press, 1998), 1.

9. My discussion of the contemporary discursive connections between 'civilization,' 'race,' 'gender' and 'progress' is indebted to Gail Bedermann's excellent historical exploration of the connections between these terms in the United States in the Victorian era. See: Gail Bedermann, *Manliness and Civilization: A Cultural History of Gender and Race in the United States, 1880–1917* (Chicago: Chicago University Press, 1996).

10. Laura Bush, *Radio Address by Mrs. Bush*, United States of America, The White House, November 17, 2001 (Radio Broadcast); Dan Brown, *Angels and Demons* (London: Corgi Books, 2000).

11. Martha Brant, "Periscope (Women's Issues in the War on Terrorism)," *Newsweek*, November 26, 2001.

12. At the same time, it is important to note that *Angels and Demons* only became a best seller in its own right following the phenomenal success of *The Da Vinci Code*. This raises important and interesting questions about the ways in which the War on Terror may have increased cultural resonances and therefore audiences for cultural works centered around these themes. However, the fact that the book was written prior to the attack on the World Trade Center continues to point to historical continuities.

13. Brown, *Angels and Demons*, 31.

14. For a discussion of the construction of non-white masculine sexuality as primitive or animal-like, see: Christopher Frayling, "The House that Jack Built: Some Stereotypes of the Rapist in the History of Popular Culture," in *Rape*, ed. Sylvana Tomaselli and Roy Porter (Oxford: Basil Blackwell, 1986).

15. Brown, *Angels and Demons*, 53–54. This particular scene found numerous echoes in American media's descriptions of the alleged strip club visits of the September 11th hijackers shortly before the attacks occurred. Interesting in both of these cases is the attempt to disavow the brothel and strip clubs as Western cultural and economic institutions and instead project them as part of the depraved sexual terrain of the Oriental other.

16. Brown, *Angels and Demons*, 476.

17. Brown, *Angels and Demons*, 432.

18. Brown, *Angels and Demons*, 55.

19. Brown, *Angels and Demons*, 86.

20. See: Angela Davis, *Women Race and Class* (New York: Vintage Books, 1983), 190–94; Sandra Gunning, *Race, Rape and Lynching: The Red Record of American Literature, 1890–1912* (New York: Oxford University Press, 1996).

21. Bush, *Radio Address by Mrs. Bush*.

22. See, for example: Bedermann, *Manliness and Civilization*, 28.

23. A prominent socialist example is August Bebel, *Woman in the Past, Present and Future*, trans. H. B. Adams Walther (London: William Reeves, c. 1900). For a discussion of this logic within the history of American feminism see: Louise Newman, *White Women's Rights: The Racial Origins of Feminism in the United States* (New York: Oxford University Press, 1999).

24. The fraught relationship between the politics of women's liberation and white racial supremacy have been the topic of much excellent analysis and discussion. For example, see: Ruth Frankenberg, *White Women, Race Matters: The Social Construction of Whiteness* (Minneapolis: University of Minnesota Press, 1993); Newman, *White Women's Rights*. Particularly influential in the Australian context in this regard is the work of Aileen Moreton-Robinson. See: Aileen Moreton-Robinson, *Talkin' Up to the White Woman: Aboriginal Women and Feminism* (Brisbane: University of Queensland Press, 2000).

25. For a particularly insightful example of this type of analysis, see Jessica Rutter, "'Saving' Women in Algeria and Afghanistan: (Neo)Colonialism, Liberation and the Veil," *Eruditio Online* 24 (2004), http://www.duke.edu/web/eruditio/Rutter.html (accessed September 6, 2005).

26. Critics of Laura Bush's speech have been quick to point out that this feminist consciousness has failed to find its way into policy, and domestic policy particularly. Indeed, the Bush administration continues to pursue an explicitly anti-feminist agenda. This contradiction will be discussed below. At this point it is sufficient to note that the use of feminist rhetoric is significant.

27. Bush, *Radio Address by Mrs. Bush*.

28. Bush, *Radio Address by Mrs. Bush*.

29. For a discussion of the interplay between truth and fiction in public discussion of the War on Terror, see Stuart Croft, *Culture, Crisis, and America's War on Terror* (Cambridge: Cambridge University Press, 2006).

30. Dana L. Cloud, "'To Veil the Threat of Terror': Afghan Women and the Clash of Civilizations in the Imagery of the U.S. War on Terrorism," *Quarterly Journal of Speech* 90, no. 3 (2004).

31. As one reader of this chapter pointed out, racism has historically been a feature of the popular thriller genre, and Brown's Hassassin can be read as the latest example of this tradition. However, it is precisely the historical particularity of Brown's use of these conventions that makes the text worth reading in this context. In a similar vein, it is the historical particularity of Bush's use of the archetypal appeal to the safety of women and children to justify wars that makes her speech an illuminating text in this instance. A discussion of the political and cultural significance of the 'thriller' genre in relation to the racial politics of Brown's work would be useful. However, it is outside the scope of this chapter. For an interesting historical discussion of the 'thriller' genre in relation to the war on terror, see Begona Aretxaga, "Terror as 'Thrill': First Thoughts on the 'War on Terrorism,'" *Anthropological Quarterly* 75, no. 1 (2002).

32. It is interesting to note then that it is precisely this point that seems most unpalatable to conspiracy theorists of the far-right and the far-left. The reality of

Brown's novel is more easily assimilable to the logic of the numerous websites and internet forums which declare that the Bush administration must have known, or that the fact that the mujahadeen were originally funded by the U.S.A. means that Bin Laden is merely a puppet of the Pentagon. The idea that the Hassassins could be directing the course of events does not fit with constructions of Muslim masculinity that leaves rationality and strategic agency in the hands of white men.

33. Brown, *Angels and Demons*, 85.

34. Brown, *Angels and Demons*, 85.

35. Newman, *White Women's Rights*, 14–20.

36. Brown, *Angels and Demons*, 68–69.

37. Brown, *Angels and Demons*, 411.

38. Brown, *Angels and Demons*, 416.

39. Brown, *Angels and Demons*, 439.

40. This is despite the fact that the role of the First Lady has become increasingly controversial in the past decade. In particular, Laura Bush's predecessor, Hillary Clinton, faced extensive public criticism for overstepping the boundaries of her role. For a contemporary comment on the irony of this in relation to Bush's radio speech, see Katha Pollitt, "After the Taliban," *Nation*, December 17, 2001.

41. Brown, *Angels and Demons*.

42. Brown, *Angels and Demons*, 411.

43. For a recent and particularly insightful expose of the implications of these Western cultural norms, see Nicole Gavey, *Just Sex? The Cultural Scaffolding of Rape* (London and New York: Routledge, 2005).

44. Brown, *Angels and Demons*, 619.

Chapter Ten

Marking the White Body: Tattooing in the White Colonial Literary Imagination

Annie Werner

In 1857, Adrien Paul published a sequel to the classic shipwreck adventure story, *The Swiss Family Robinson*. This book, *Willis the Pilot, a Book for Boys*, follows the continuing adventures of Becker and his family, who, after 15 years on the "unknown coast in the Pacific Ocean"[1] find themselves in the company of the crew of the English dispatch sloop, the Nelson. The boatswain of this sloop, Willis, emerges as something of a hero in the book, though the Swiss family remains central to the action. This illustration accompanies a scene in which Jack is accosted by two "ferocious-looking savages."[2] Jack assumes, "from the aspect of the men who held him, that they were cannibals, and consequently that his fate was sealed."[3] The illustration depicts "Jack's victory over the savages," which occurs as soon as he regains control over his rifle. The "aspect" from which Jack makes his deduction of anthropophagy is ultimately a rendition of several stereotypical motifs, deployed in popular representations of white/indigenous relations in the colonial Pacific, all of which point to the subject's cannibalistic tendencies. The Indigenous body is signified by a number of easily-recognized, though generically "savage" markers—dark(er) skin, a grass headdress (remarkably reminiscent of the feathered headdresses depicted in contemporary representations of Native Americans), a necklace of flowers, a loincloth and a body and face full of dark, 'primitive' tattooing. The interaction between the two men similarly reiterates the colonial relationship, and the discrepancies between the text and the illustration indicate the extent to which visual representations provide a kind of parallel narrative that simultaneously supports and contradicts the literary depiction. According to the text, the savages "tore off his upper garments," yet in the pictorial representation of "Jack's victory over the savages" he has been miraculously re-clothed, the whiteness of his garments further emphasizing the brown nakedness of the "supplicated" savage.[4] When Jack fires his rifle, "the frightened wretch pressed his hands together in an attitude of supplication."[5] The "copper-colored devil"[6] is fearful of the stern, rifle-toting Jack, and assumes an attitude of prayer, thereby promoting Jack to a God-like status, 'justifying' to readers and viewers alike the superiority of the white man in such encounters.

Central to this encounter is Jack's assumption that the men he encounters are cannibals, and that his "fate was sealed." The possibility of being consumed provides Jack with the impetus to fight, and ultimately subdue this threat. The basis for this assumption is a reading of the motifs that render his opponent as 'savage,' most notably the color of his attacker's skin, which is emphasized by the tattooed marks. In this chapter, I will address the problematic nature of tattooing as an artificial pigmentation of skin that necessarily, though at times subtly, complicates notions of race and whiteness. I argue that popular colonial representations of Indigenous tattooing such as the illustration discussed above have shaped the West's understanding of the term: the word *tattoo*, and the multitude of images and connotations it suggests, is inextricably linked to the history of colonial exploration. I will provide an overview of the way that tattoos have been represented in a selection of colonial texts, and consider some of the following questions: What happens when the corporeal boundary becomes inscribed, literally, with a 'savage' text? How does this text complicate the notion of 'whiteness' and race? What does this inscription 'do' to the binary of self and other? How can one embody an inscribed self, one with connotations of primitivism and non-whiteness, yet still remain, in essence, 'white'? My objective is to explicate the way that Indigenous tattoos problematize and complicate racial categorization by offering to readers an imposed non-whitening or "voluntary stigma."[7]

Jane Caplan's anthology *Written on the Body* represents a significant body of work that has recently been done regarding the geographical, chronological and political histories of tattooing. Many of the chapters interrogate the extent to which various representations of tattooing/tattooed bodies interact with and respond to the impact of colonialism. As with other significant works in the same area such as the anthology *Tattoo: Bodies, Art, and Exchange in the Pacific and the West, Written on the Body* works to dispel the myth that Captain Cook 'discovered' tattooing, explaining instead that he was responsible for re-introducing the practice to a Western audience. Prior to European 'discovery' of the islands of the Pacific, the practice of tattooing in Europe had been all but forgotten. As is pointed out in several chapters of Caplan's anthology, the practice of permanently marking the skin by injecting some kind of pigment had been practiced on the continent for centuries, the earliest-known tattooed person being Ötzi the 'Ice Man,' found in the alps near the border of Austria and Italy in 1991. It is estimated that Ötzi died between 3300 and 3200BC, making him not only the oldest known tattooed specimen, but possibly the oldest known human mummy.[8]

While it is patently clear from Caplan's anthology that Cook was not responsible for 'discovering' tattooing, what is significant about Cook's voyages to the Pacific and his published journals and accounts of these events, is that he adapted the term *tattoo* from the Polynesian *ta tau*, and introduced it to the English language. As C. P. Jones has pointed out, Cook's description of the practice of "tattowing" on Tahiti in 1769 is the first appearance of the word in English. By introducing the term within an explicit context of colonial expansion and exploration, Cook was responsible for embedding the European use of the term within the discourse of colonialism that was dependent upon popular representation of the supplication of Indigenous people by whites. Within this discourse, tattooing and, perhaps more significantly, tattooed people, took on a meaning that was far more complicated than just a suggestion that the individual's skin was permanently marked. People in Europe had been injecting ink under their skin for various reasons for centuries—the practice in itself was nothing new. Cook's invoking of a new term for the practice, however, as well as a depiction of a different kind of people engaging the practice—exotic, tawny savages—meant that the new terminology was fully loaded with racialized, exoticized, and necessarily imperialist overtones.

The distinction between 'white' and 'colored,' relates not only to the 'natural' color of the skin, but also to any imposed coloring, such as tattooing, that also impacts upon the perceived identity of the 'colored' subject. In 'Post-Bourgeois Tattoo,' Marc Blanchard suggests that:

> there seems to be a link between the reception of tattooing in Europe and the ideology of colonization. Not only because Western man does *not* customarily tattoo his body,[9] but precisely because tattoos are the mark of the colonized other: the difference between the colonizer and the colonized is in the texture of the skin. The former's skin is white and transparent. The latter's is made opaque by the designs in it.[10]

From the time when the practice of tattooing was re-introduced to the West tattooing and tattooed bodies have been located within a discourse that engages repeatedly with notions of whiteness and non-whiteness. In particular, the process of tattooing a civilized, white body with a primitive, non-white text has complicated processes of identity definition on the colonial frontiers.

A METAPHORIC TRANSGRESSION
OF A CORPOREAL FRONTIER?

> The surface of the body seems everywhere to be treated, not only as the
> boundary of the individual as a biological and psychological entity, but as the
> *frontier* of the social self as well.[11]

As this quote from Terence Turner's "The Social Skin" articulates, in studies
of the body, the image of the skin as a mediation point between the self and
the social, or the self and the Other, is pronounced, making a parallel between
the skin as frontier and the frontier of colonialism. Richard Dyer's work on
whiteness is also useful here, as he highlights the notion that white skin can
be seen as an *invisible* boundary in that it is taken for granted. He asserts that
"whites must be seen to be white, yet whiteness as race resides in invisible
properties and whiteness as power is maintained by being unseen. To be seen
as white is to have one's corporeality registered, yet true whiteness resides in
the non-corporeal."[12] Dyer suggests that white skin is perceived as invisible
until it is colored, in his work, by racial signification, thereby rendering the
colored person as Other to the invisible, unmentionable whiteness of the
'unmarked' white individual. Essentially however, he asserts that whiteness
is racialized, because of this very process.

  Dyer's emphasis on highlighting the corporeality of the white person is
interesting within the context of my discussion, in that tattoos, like other
'racial' coloring, compromise whiteness, and bring into focus the existence of
the corporeal boundary that is the skin. When he suggests that "the frontier"
is all about bringing boundaries and borders to a country and people that had
none,[13] he reminds us that the frontier of colonialism is also about introducing
the concept of boundaries, both corporeal and geographic. Early colonial
representations of tattooing in the west are not only concerned with the fact
that tattooing highlights and transforms the skin, but also that it *invades*, and
violates the skin. The act of transgressing and 'tainting' the skin-boundary
with the tattoo—particularly in the case of a white person being marked by
an Indigenous tattoo—brings the boundary into focus, and simultaneously
emphasizes the vulnerability of that boundary.

  Richard Slotkin defines a mythology as "a complex of narratives that
dramatizes the world vision and historical sense of a people or culture, reducing
centuries of experience into a constellation of compelling metaphors."[14] When
contemplating the mythology of the tattoo, and specifically the mythology
of the Indigenous tattoo, the complex of narratives of which one needs to
take stock is dominated by accounts by those western writers who first
encountered the practice. In the colonial history of the Pacific, Indigenous

tattooing operated as a way of defining the self (white, colonizing) from the Other (Indigenous, colonized).

For colonial settlers, the metaphorical implications of this suggestion and the potential vulnerability it evoked were threatening, as they witnessed not only 'primitive' Indigenous people practicing tattooing, but also renegade white men—beachcombers and other dissenters—also being marked as Other. The threat to white identity, and, by extension, to the boundaries of the white colony, is all too clearly exemplified by the process of tattooing.

Coinciding with the (re)introduction into the European consciousness of tattooing as a cultural practice, was the emergence of the genre of beachcomber narratives. Beachcombers, those men who deserted ships, escaped convict settlements or rejected the colony, crossed beaches into the Indigenous culture of the islands they inhabited. For many of these men, tattooing was an outward symbol of assimilation to their adopted culture and rejection of their own. They were deserters and renegades, and the tattooed white man is a fixture of beachcomber literature from the Pacific.

As I. C. Campbell explains,

> Contemporary observers had both a fascination and a horror of the tattooed white man, regarding the native tattoo as a sign of extreme degradation and depravity. Nothing else seemed to symbolize so evocatively the extent to which a white man had 'let himself go' or 'sunk' than having his skin marked in the manner of 'savages.'[15]

Beachcomber narratives were a powerful and popular force in the eighteenth century, and were responsible for conveying many attitudes and understandings about the people of the Pacific. In many cases, narratives about these men centered on the extent to which they had 'become' savage, and crossed the boundary between 'us' and 'them.' Most significantly, however, beachcombers were often positioned as intermediary, transgressive figures who complicated and problematized many binaries that were essential to the maintenance of the 'civilized' identity. This is particularly the case in the narratives of beachcombers who were tattooed in the Indigenous style of the islanders amongst whom they resided. The presence of tattooing upon the white body represented a kind of racialization that simultaneously problematized and reinforced notions of whiteness and cultural, national and racial boundaries. It also troubled the attempts of colonists to maintain a strong, definable sense of 'us' and 'them' by complicating an otherwise simplistic symbol of Otherness. In *Carnal Knowledge and Imperial Power: Race and the Intimate in Colonial Rule*, Ann Laura Stoler suggests that the fear of the Other that was maintained by the colonizers was not as simple as maintaining European supremacy or justification. She suggests that this was part of a "critical, class-based logic; not only statements about Indigenous subversives, but directives aimed at dissenting European underlings."[16] Generation of a fear of Otherness forms an integral part of the apparatus that keeps potential dissenters in line, thereby maintaining the boundaries *within* white society as well since, as she explains, "Colonisers themselves were not by nature unified."[17] Stoler's point here is integral to a consideration of the presentation of tattooing in beachcomber narratives, since interactions between tattoos and whiteness are often central to representations of Indigenous tattooing.

Representations of tattooing in beachcomber narratives are almost unanimously negative. The tattooing process is frequently framed as a torturous procedure, inflicted by savages upon the passive, victimized body of the innocent white person. James O'Connell, a beachcomber on Ponape in the Caroline Islands, describes his tattooers as "savage printers." The woman who tattoos his hand is referred to as his "executioner," and the process itself is described as a "battering" and a "punishment."[18] Many other beachcombers engaged with this discourse that equated tattooing with torture, yet some took the connection even further, indicating that the truly barbaric aspect of the process was the corporeal transformation it entailed. Edward Robarts, a beachcomber in the Marquesas in the early 1800s offers a description of Joseph Cabris, another beachcomber living on the same island, which exemplifies this attitude. In his journal, Robarts comments on his first meeting with Cabris after the latter has had his face tattooed. "I lookt at him, but did not Know him. The face was tattooed all over [and this] disguised the features. When he spoke, I drew my hand from him. I Knew him to be the french boy."[19] In this interaction, Cabris is transformed by his facial tattoo, and this transformation renders him unrecognizable to Robarts. The denial of visual recognition—in Robarts' terms, visual 'Knowledge'—indicates the removal of Cabris from Robarts' visual perception of his fellow white man, and Robarts recoils from this transformed individual. Robarts' reaction to Cabris' transformed identity is virtually standard in beachcomber narratives of the nineteenth century. Indigenous tattooing was depicted as an irreversible act of violence against the 'white' identity of the 'victim,' and the beachcomber narratives helped to establish this perception in the minds of the reading public.

In many cases, it is likely that the narrators of these texts engaged the trope of 'tattoo torture' in order to absolve themselves of the responsibility of being marked in such a 'savage' manner. The beachcombers who published their narratives had invariably returned to Europe or America, and therefore had a vested interest in re-integrating themselves into white society. Additionally, many of these men were forced to make a living from their experiences, either by selling their stories and/or performing in circuses and sideshows, so the maintenance of a 'civilized' and white identity was preferable to being labeled a 'renegade.' Given the general public's perception of tattooing as a 'primitive' or 'barbaric' practice, it would have been difficult for a beach-comber to admit to having willingly succumbed to such transformation. Torture, or forcible tattooing, therefore, became a frequently used excuse. As Campbell points out, "Returning and fitting back in turned out to be more dif-ficult than might be expected and, in many cases, appears to have been more difficult than the adaption to Polynesian life had been."[20] The physical, cor-poreal, geographic, and cultural border crossings that these men experienced defined and irreversibly dictated the way that they were able to re-integrate into European and American society. The permanent visibility of some of the beachcombers' tattoos meant that their return 'home' was stigmatized by the marks they wore. Campbell indicates that "the term [beachcomber] generally had connotations of opprobrium because a man who chose to 'live among natives' was not merely an emigrant; he was regarded in European society as a renegade."[21] For tattooed beachcombers, this opprobrium was made im-mediately visually apparent.

The dehumanizing effect of this opprobrium is evident in descriptions of tattooed people from the Pacific, thereby linking the process of tattooing with the process of objectification. O'Connell draws an animal likeness, claiming that after receiving his tattoos he resembled a "rhinoceros," and writing that "I came from the tattoo hospital a bird of much more diversified plumage than when I entered."[22] Horace Holden, a beachcomber on Palau, indicates that the tattooed people he encountered were no longer human: he was "filled with horror by the sight of being apparently human, and yet almost destitute of the ordinary marks of humanity. . . . They were fantastically tattooed on different parts of their bodies."[23] Frank Coffee, a traveler who published his journal as *Forty Years in the Pacific: A Book of Reference for the Traveller and Pleasure for the Stay-at-Home*, likens the tattooed faces of elderly Maori to "plaques of old wood."[24] Tattoos are seldom represented as having no effect upon the *character* of the tattooed individual, entrenching the notion that the tattoo—and in particular the *Indigenous* tattoo—is a transformative process that is able to alter the intrinsic identity of the tattooed person.[25]

Later, more popular and even canonical texts such as Herman Melville's novels further emphasized and embedded this notion. Melville's first novel, *Typee*, and its sequel, *Omoo*, are perhaps some of the most famous beachcomber narratives and, like Robarts before him, Melville expresses an extreme fear and abhorrence of the "transformation" that tattooing would signal. When first faced with the threat of being tattooed like the Marquesans he resides amongst in *Typee*, Melville is "Horrified at the bare thought of being rendered hideous for life."[26] It is the permanence of the act that is truly

horrendous to Melville—the thought of being made indelibly 'monstrous'—
and he "shudders" at the "ruin the tattooist might inflict upon [his] figure-
head."[27] As Karky, the tattooist, motions toward making three parallel lines
on Melville's face, "the flesh fairly crawl[s] upon [his] bones."[28] The incident
is significant because it betrays Melville's horror of the "violence to identity"
that tattooing represents in a very profound and personal way.[29] Melville's
paralyzing and at times inordinate horror at being tattooed is linked to his
fear of being eaten, most obviously by his abhorrence for the Indigenously
tattooed white men he encounters, whom he views as being 'consumed' by
their marks. Malini Johar Schueller describes Melville's reaction as a fear of
the "permanent visible impress of the other on his whiteness."[30] It is important
to remember here that cannibalism and tattooing are both mythologized,
savage practices that represent a transgression of the skin—the boundary of
identity. Melville's inordinate fear of being tattooed suggests that he is much
more fearful of this transformation than of the possibility of being eaten. The
thought of actually *living* with a deformed and objectified face, a face that is
no longer his, consumed as it were by Karky's inks, is much more horrendous
than being consumed by death. He writes:

> This incident opened my eyes to a new danger; and I now felt that in some
> luckless hour I should be disfigured in such a manner as never more to have the
> *face* to return to my countrymen, even should an opportunity offer. . . . What an
> object he would have made of me![31]

The consumption of his "face divine" is the site of the ultimate objectification,
whereby even on escaping the island, he would have been so transformed as
to render it impossible to assimilate back into white society. For Melville,
the irreversible bodily transgression of ink through skin becomes an
important mark(er): a permanent, living symbol of the native's simultaneous
consumption and invasion of the white body. His fears, whether of
cannibalism or tattooing, represent a fear of physical alteration, disfigurement
or mutilation. It is not a specific fear, but a general fear that his body—his
corporeal identity—will be irreparably damaged or altered, thereby "leaving
the social order completely to become . . . what Melville would call an
'isolato,' a permanent object of horror and disgust."[32] Leonard Cassuto argues
that Melville's fear of tattooing is based on the racial othering that it would
entail. Cassuto claims that:

> Tommo's fear in *Typee* of becoming a racial freak . . . stands as an individual
> manifestation of an increasing tension that permeated American culture generally
> in the 1840s, a tension linked to the unravelling of the racial distinctions central
> to American social organization and the meaning of being 'white'. . . . Tattooing

in *Typee* embodies this tension, acting as a code for racial difference that visibly links color to freak status.[33]

Cassuto's argument specifically focuses on the threat to whiteness that tattooing poses.

Melville's awareness of the break from whiteness that tattooing would symbolize is articulated clearly in his descriptions of those white men who were tattooed in the Marquesan style. In *Omoo*, Melville describes a:

> renegado from Christendom and humanity—a white man, in the south seas girdle, and tattooed in the face . . . Some of us gazed upon this man with a feeling akin to horror, no ways abated when informed that he had voluntarily submitted to this embellishment of his countenance.[34]

The main source of horror at the appearance of this man is, of course, his tattooed face, the tattooed white body already having been established as a source of horror throughout *Typee*. Additionally, Melville informs the reader with disgust, this man had been tattooed *voluntarily*. This beachcomber is objectified by his facial tattoo, and is rendered a *"renegado from humanity"* implying that, in being so literally de-faced, he has forfeited his status as human. Similarly, in the epilogue to *Typee*,[35] Melville describes another beachcomber character who goes by the name of Jimmy, and resides on the beach at Nukuheva. Jimmy is a "grizzled sailor" who "lived a devil-may-care life in the household of Mowanna the king."[36] He knows the language of the Marquesans, and, like the renegado in *Omoo*, wears their national dress and native tattoos. Melville's distaste for the character is evident, and he is portrayed in the account as a dishonest and mercenary "heartless villain."[37] Schueller indicates that the inclusion of the story of Jimmy serves as a warning of the consequences of 'going native,' and suggests that this section "might well have been titled 'The Moral of Jimmy: The Results of Savagery'" instead of "The Story of Toby" as it appears in the book.[38] Indeed, Melville's horror of the tattooed white man is both pronounced, and intrinsically linked to his own anxieties surrounding his identity while on the beach. My reading of *Typee*, and *Omoo*, reveals that Melville's fear is not only linked to his perception of whiteness, but also identity as it is figured through the literary 'types' of the captive and beachcomber. Given the context of this literature within a colonial, expansionist framework, Melville's novels participate in the movement that situated the tattoo as a mark of the *colonized* Other, thereby implicating a power relationship that is not merely tied to notions of color and race.

The anxieties articulated in Melville's first novels are not, however, peculiar to the experiences of beachcombers in the Pacific, and the concept of tattooing as a transformative process for racial and cultural identity is also apparent in the captivity narratives that formed the cultural foundation of what was to become the United States of America. In 1856, a decade after the publication of *Typee*, *The Captivity of the Oatman Girls* was published in Los Angeles. Olive Oatman, 13, and her sister Mary Ann, 8, members of a Mormon emigrant party crossing the desert on their way to California, were captured by a group of Yavapais. After a year of captivity, they were sold to the Mojave. Mary Ann, along with many Mojave people, died of starvation during a drought-induced famine, but Olive continued to live amongst the Mojave for four years, until she was again purchased by a General at Fort Yuma. After her release, Oatman's story was published by the Methodist minister, Reverend Royal B. Stratton, and the book and subsequent lecture tour subjected Olive to intense moral scrutiny, much of which was centered on the Mojave tattoos that she had received in captivity.

Captivity narratives, such as Oatman's, were a powerful ideological tool for defining the boundaries of Euro-American society on the frontier. Christopher Castiglia suggests that "captivity narratives were circulated to create what Lauren Berlant has called a national symbolic, rendering the borders of America as the boundaries of the white, female body."[39] When considering this metaphor of the white female body as national body, the transgressions expressed in Oatman's narrative—tattoos primarily, as well as the linked categories of miscegenation and childbearing—mark yet another symbolic violation.

Reverend Stratton utilized, and indeed exploited, Oatman's captivity and tattoos to exemplify the savagery of the Southwestern Indians, and his book was a flagrant piece of anti-Indian propaganda. Oatman's Mojave tattoos however, disrupted and complicated her whiteness, and fuelled rumors that she had been married to and had borne the children of a Mojave chief. Though most contemporary anthropological studies conclude that the tattoos Oatman received did in fact symbolize marriage and/or childbearing, at the time of Olive's return from captivity, no anthropological understanding of her marks was available. For the reading and viewing public, the marks were literally unreadable, interpretable only as marks of savagery and primitivism within the context provided by the colonial discourse that surrounded their representation. Ironically then, the marks were a tabula rasa upon which the viewing public could project their own meanings. The public's desire to 'read' the tattoos led to many interpretations, including those that suggested familial associations with the Mojave.

Implications of miscegenation and moral corruption were obviously contrary to Stratton's agenda, and he emphatically denied any suggestions that Olive had had any sexual relationship during her captivity. He stressed both in the narrative and in newspaper accounts that the tattoos were "slave marks," applied so that Olive could not escape and, as in the beachcomber accounts discussed earlier, the Oatman girls' tattooing is framed as a torturous experience. In Stratton's account, Olive "pleads" with the Indians that they not put "those ugly marks" on her and Mary Ann. "To all our expostulations they only replied in substance—that they knew why we objected to it; that we expected to return to the whites, and we would be ashamed of it then; but that it was their resolution we should never return, and that as we belonged to them we should wear their 'Ki-e-chook.'"[40] In addition to positioning the marks as those of slaves and captives, this account also suggests the break from whiteness that the marks represent. According to Stratton, the Mojave were aware that the tattooed marks would make it difficult for Olive and Mary Ann to return to white society, and so applied them in order to ensure the obstruction and complication of their white identity.

The depiction of the tattooing process also fulfilled a significant literary function for Stratton. Female captivity narratives almost unanimously contained suggestions or representations of rape and/or sexual abuse. Even when no actual sexual violation is mentioned, rape imagery was frequently included in stories of female captivity. Levernier and Stodola, in their book *The Indian Captivity Narrative 1550—1900* cite various examples of such imagery. One such example is found in *An Affecting Narrative of the Captivity and Sufferings of? Mrs. Mary Smith* (1815). In this narrative, Smith's two daughters, aged eleven and nineteen "were stripped, tied hands above head to saplings, pierced with pine splinters dipped in turpentine."[41] The girls' bodies are described as being "pierced" by the "erect" needles of the Indians, and the description is indicative of the way that bodily violation is equated with sexual transgression within the captivity narratives of the eighteenth and nineteenth centuries.

In *Captivity of the Oatman Girls*, Stratton employs a similar tactic; his representation of the puncturing of the girls' skin and his description of the tattoo operation echoes the description of the pine needle incident in the Smith narrative. The Indians "pricked the skin" on the girls' faces "until they bled freely" then repeated the pricking action a second time after dipping the sticks into the coloring substance and administering it to the "lacerated parts of the face."[42] The opening of the girls' faces and the insertion of ink by way of the intrusion of "sharp sticks" under the skin certainly suggests a rape scenario. Contradictorily however, elsewhere in the text Stratton is keen to deny the suggestion of any kind of actual sexual transgression. Stratton's contradiction indicates that he was uneasy with the possibility of Olive's transculturation. He maintains the evocation of violence and transgression, yet he must simultaneously establish Olive as a site of strength and redemption, not a symbol of weakness and potential racial pollution. Olive's tattoos, therefore, were a handy alternative to the depiction of any actual sexual relationship between Olive and her captors, either forced or voluntary, since they represent a similar kind of transgression yet without the moral compromise that was implied by marriage or childbearing. Her body was penetrated, her white skin tainted, yet her chastity remained intact, thus rendering her the perfect example of God's deliverance.

In popular representation, the tattoos on Olive's body signified a violation of sacred boundaries—of race, gender and 'American' identity. The mutilation that is visually apparent upon the captive body in the form of the Indigenous tattoo instantaneously signified for the Euro-American public the transgressive violation of which the Indians were capable: a white female body is compromised and a fraught and—most significantly—colored and racialized body is born. Notions of whiteness are problematized by the presence of her tattoos, which are inherently sexualized within the context of the narrative. These complications of her white identity, including the physical disruption of her whiteness by the colored tattoos, and the implied complications arising from the associated suggestions of miscegenation are directly related to her role as a white woman: the bearer and reproducer of stable and coherent whiteness.

The Captivity of the Oatman Girls is a complex narrative that is full of contradictions. Stratton's confused rendering of the narrative within the quite rigid, formulaic genre of the North American captivity narrative, meant that he struggled to incorporate the tattoo marks she received in captivity. No other captive, female or male, had included tattooing in her or his narrative, so Stratton had no benchmark within the captivity narratives of the early United States. Separate from this genre however, tattoos had already been well established within European and American consciousness, and the colonial context of their reception and meaning was maintained and expanded by representations of tattooing that reiterated these implications. For this reason, Stratton's framing of Oatman's tattoos in his own narrative was already determined to a certain degree by the representations that preceded his.

Stratton's text, the early beachcomber narratives from the Pacific, and Melville's *Typee* and *Omoo*, provide only a superficial glimpse at the literary representations of tattooing since 1800. These representations have significantly impacted the way that tattooing—particularly Indigenous, Other tattooing—has been perceived by the west. Most notably, early colonial representations have dictated and entrenched the degree to which the tattoo is seen as a complication of whiteness. This complication is intrinsically linked to the colonial context within which 'tattoo' has been most significantly represented. Additionally, the tattoo's position(ing) as a transgressive violation of the skin—the boundary of corporeality and, more significantly *identity*—responds to and interacts with the ambiguities and anxieties of colonialism as a whole. My purpose in this chapter has been to open up for discussion the colonial history of tattooing, its literary history, and its complicated relationship to notions of whiteness within the colonial agenda.

NOTES

1. Adrien Paul, *Willis the Pilot: A Sequel to the Swiss Family Robinson* (London: F. Warne, 1866), 9.

2. Adrien Paul, *Willis the Pilot*, 260.

3. Adrien Paul, *Willis the Pilot*.

4. Adrien Paul, *Willis the Pilot*, 261.

5. Adrien Paul, *Willis the Pilot*.

6. Adrien Paul, *Willis the Pilot*, 262.

7. Clinton R. Sanders, "Marks of Mischief: Becoming and Being Tattooed," *Journal of Contemporary Ethnography* 16, no. 4 (1988).

8. For more information on Otzi's tattoos, see C. P. Jones, "Stigma and Tattoo," in *Written on the Body*, ed. Jane Caplan (Princeton: University of California Press, 2000), 1–16.

9. Presumably, Blanchard is here referring to the fact that in the period of colonization in the Pacific white people were not commonly tattooed.

10. Marc Blanchard, "Post-Bourgeois Tattoo: Reflections on Skin Writing in Late Capitalist Societies," *Visual Anthropology Review* 7 no. 2 (1991): 13.

11. Terence Turner "The Social Skin," in *Not Work Alone: A Cross-cultural View of Activities Superfluous to Survival*, ed. J. Cherfas and R. Lewin (London: Temple Smith, 1980), 112.

12. Richard Dyer, *White* (London and New York: Routledge, 1997), 49.

13. Dyer, *White*, 35.

14. Richard Slotkin, *Regeneration Through Violence: The Mythology of the American Frontier, 1600–1860* (Middletown, Conn.: Wesleyan University Press, 1973), 6.

15. I. C. Campbell *"Gone Native" in Polynesia: Captivity Narratives and Experiences from the South Pacific* (Westport: Greenwood Press, 1998), 99.

16. Ann Laura Stoler, *Carnal Knowledge and Imperial Power: Race and the Intimate in Colonial Rule* (Berkeley: University of California Press, 2002) 25.

17. Stoler, *Carnal Knowledge and Imperial Power*, 24.

18. James O'Connell, *A Residence of Eleven Years in New Holland and the Caroline Islands: Being the Adventures of James F. O'Connell; Edited from his Verbal Narration* (Ann Arbor, Michigan: UMI, 2004).

19. Edward Robarts, *The Marquesan Journal of Edward Robarts, 1797–1824: Edited, with an introduction by Greg Dening* (Canberra: Australian National University Press, 1974), 97.

20. Campbell, *"Gone Native" in Polynesia*, 99.

21. Campbell, *"Gone Native" in Polynesia*, 4.

22. O'Connell, *A Residence of Eleven Years in New Holland and the Caroline Islands*, 116.

23. Horace Holden, *A Narrative of the Shipwreck, Captivity and Sufferings of Horace Holden and Benj. H. Nute; Who Were Cast Away in the American Ship Mentor, on the Pelew Islands, in the Year 1832; and for Two Years Afterwards Were Subjected to Unheard of Sufferings Among the Barbarous Inhabitants of Lord North's Island* (Boston: Russell, Shattuck, and co., 1836), 32.

24. Frank Coffee, *Forty Years in the Pacific: A Book of Reference for the Traveller and Pleasure for the Stay-at-home* (New York and Sydney: Oceanic Publishing Co., c1920), 179.

25. For a more detailed discussion of beachcombers and tattoos, see Annie Werner, "Savage Skins: The Freakish Subject of Tattooed Beachcombers," *Kunapipi* 27, no. 1 (2005).

26. Herman Melville, *Typee* (London and Glasgow: Collins Clear-Type Press c1905), 297.

27. Melville, *Typee*, 297.

28. Melville, *Typee*, 298.

29. John Evelev, "Made in the Marquesas: Tattooing and Melville's Critique of the Marketplace," *Arizona Quarterly* 48, no. 4 (1992): 20.

30. Malini Johar Schueller, "Colonialism and Melville's South Seas Journeys," *Studies in American Fiction* 22, no. 1 (1994): 11.

31. Melville, *Typee*, p. 298. My emphasis.

32. Dan Latimer, "Oedipus in the South Seas: The Case of Herman Melville's Typee," *Essays in Literature* 21, no. 2 (1994): 218–33: 221.

33. Leonard Cassuto, "'What an object he would have made of me!': Tattooing and the Racial Freak in Melville's Typee," in *Freakery: Cultural Spectacles of the Extraordinary Body*, ed. Rosemary Garland Thomson (New York: New York University Press, 1996), 234–48: 235.

34. Herman Melville, *Omoo: A Narrative of Adventures in the South Seas* (London: J. M. Dent and Co. c1910), 26.

35. This section is actually referred to as the 'sequel' to *Typee*, however since I am referring to *Omoo* as the sequel, I shall refer to this as the epilogue.

36. Melville, *Typee*, 354.

37. Melville, *Typee*, 357.

38. Schueller, "Colonialism and Melville's South Seas Journeys," 10.

39. Christopher Castiglia, *Bound and Determined: Captivity, Culture-Crossing, and White Womanhood from Mary Rowlandson to Patty Hearst* (Chicago: University of Chicago Press, 1996), 9.

40. Royal B. Stratton, *Captivity of the Oatman Girls Among the Apache and Mojave Indians* (New York: Dover Publications, 1994), 134.

41. James A. Levernier and Katherine Zabelle Derounian-Stodola, *The Indian Captivity Narrative, 1550–1900* (New York: Maxwell, Macmillan International, 1993), 130.

42. Stratton, *Captivity of the Oatman Girls*, 134.

Bibliography

Allen, Theodore. *The Invention of the White Race: Volume One, Racial Oppression and Social Control* (London: Verso, 1994).

Althusser, Louis. "Ideological State Apparatuses," in *Mapping Ideology*, edited by Slavoj Žižek (London: Verso, 1994).

Anderson, Benedict. *Imaginary Communities: Reflections on the Origins and Spread of Nationalism* (London: Verso, 1983).

Anderson, Haithe. "On the Limits of Liberalism and Multiculturalism," *Teachers CollegeRecord* August 12 (2002), http://www.tcrecord.org/Content.asp?Content ID=11009 (accessed August 20, 2002).

Anderson, Warwick. *The Cultivation of Whiteness: Science, Health and Racial Identity in Australia* (Melbourne: Melbourne University Press, 2002).

Appiah, Anthony. "The Uncompleted Argument: Du Bois and the Illusion of Race," in *"Race," Writing and Difference* edited by Henry Louis Gates, Jr. (Chicago: University of Chicago Press, 1985).

Appiah, Kwame. "The Postcolonial and the Postmodern," in *The Post-Colonial Studies Reader*, eds. Bill Ashcroft, Gareth Griffiths and Helen Tiffin (New York: Routledge, 1995).

Aretxaga, Begona. "Terror as 'Thrill': First Thoughts on the 'War on Terrorism,'" *Anthropological Quarterly* 75, no. 1 (2002): 138–50.

Attwood, Bain. *Telling the Truth about Aboriginal History* (Crows Nest, NSW: Allen & Unwin, 2005).

Attwood, Bain. "Learning about the Truth: The Stolen Generations Narrative," in *Telling Stories: Indigenous History and Memory in Australia and New Zealand*, ed. Bain Attwood and Fiona Magowan (Crows Nest, NSW: Allen and Unwin, 2001), 183–212.

Attwood, Bain. "The Burden of the Past in the Present," in *Reconciliation: Essays on Australian Reconciliation*, edited by Michelle Grattan (Melbourne: Bookman Press, 2000), 254–59.

Attwood, Bain. "The Past as Future: Aborigines, Australia and the (Dis)course of History," *Australian humanities Review* Issue 13 (April–June 1996): 1–4.

Attwood, Bain, ed. *In the Age of Mabo: History, Aborigines and Australia* (St. Leonards, NSW: Allen & Unwin, 1996).

Attwood, Bain. "Making History, Imagining Aborigines and Australia," *Prehistory to Politics; John Mulvaney, the Humanities and the Public Intellectual*, edited by Tim Bonyhady and Tom Griffiths (Carlton, VIC: Melbourne University Press, 1996): 98–116.

Attwood, Bain. "The Paradox of Australian Aboriginal History" *Thesis Eleven* 38, no. 1 (1994): 118–37.

Attwood, Bain. "Aborigines and Academic Historians: Some Recent Encounters," *Australian Historical Studies* 24, no. 94 (April 1990): 123–35.

Attwood, Bain and Andrew Markus, "(The) 1967 (Referendum) and All That: Narrative and Myth, Aborigines and Australia," *Australian Historical Studies* 29, no. 111 (Oct 1998): 267–88.

Babb, Valerie. *Whiteness Visible: The Meaning of Whiteness in American Literature and Culture* (New York: New York University Press, 1998).

Ballhatchet, Kenneth. *Race, Sex and Class under the Raj* (London: Weidenfeld and Nicholson, 1980).

Barker, Joanne. *Sovereignty Matters: Locations of Contestation and Possibility in Indigenous Struggles for Self-Determination* (Lincoln: University of Nebraska Press, 2005).

Barua, D. K. "Kipling's *Kim*: A Parable of Imperial Hope," *Rabindra Bharati Patrika* (2000–2001): 8–18.

Bawer, Bruce. "Edward W. Said, Intellectual," *The Hudson Review* 54, no. 4 (Winter 2002).

Bay, Mia. *The White Image in the Black Mind* (New York: Oxford University Press, 2000).

Bebel, August. *Woman in the Past, Present and Future*, trans. H. B. Adams Walther (London: William Reeves, c. 1900).

Bedermann, Gail. *Manliness and Civilization: A Cultural History of Gender and Race in the United States, 1880–1917* (Chicago: Chicago University Press, 1996).

Benjamin, Walter. "On the Concept of History," trans. Harry Zohn *Selected Writing, Volume 4: 1938–1940* (Cambridge: Harvard University Press, 2003).

Berger, John. *Ways of Seeing* (Harmondsworth: Penguin, 1972).

Berger, Maurece. *Whiteness and Race in Contemporary Art*, Center for Art and Visual Culture (Baltimore: University of Maryland, 2004).

Bernstein, Hilda. *The World that Was Ours* (London: Persephone Books, 2004).

Biko, Steve. *Black Consciousness in South Africa* (New York: Random House, 1978).

Blanchard, Marc. "Post-Bourgeois Tattoo: Reflections on Skin Writing in Late Capitalist Societies," *Visual Anthropology Review* 7, no. 2 (1991): 11–21.

Blixen, Karen. *Out of Africa* (Harmondsworth: Penguin, 1980).

Bock, Gisela. "Women's History and Gender History: Aspects of an International Debate," *Gender and History* 1, no. 1 (1988).

Bonnett, Alistair. "A White World? Whiteness and Meaning of Modernity in Latin America and Japan," in *Working through Whiteness: International Perspectives*, edited by Cynthia Levine-Rasky (Albany, USA: State University of New York, 2002).

Bowes, Joseph. *The Anzac War-Trail: With the Light Horse in Sinai* (London: Humphrey Milford, Oxford University Press, 1919).

Bowes, Joseph. *The Aussie Crusaders* (London: Humphrey Milford, Oxford University Press, 1919).

Bowes, Joseph. *The Young Anzacs* (London: Humphrey Milford, Oxford University Press, 1918).

Bowes, Joseph. *Comrades: A Story of the Australian Bush* (London: Henry Froude, Hodder and Stoughton, 1912).

Brant, Martha. "Periscope (Women's Issues in the War on Terrorism)," *Newsweek*, November 26, 2001.

Breytenbach, Breyton. *Dog Heart: A Memoir* (Cape Town, Johannesburg, Pretoria: Human and Rousseau, 1998).

Breytenbach, Breyton. *A Season in Paradise* (New York: Persea Books, 1980), translated by Rike Vaughan.

Brodkin, Karen. *How Jews Became White Folk* (New Brunswick: Rutgers University Press, 1999).

Brown, Dan. *Angels and Demons* (London: Corgi Books, 2000).

Bruce, Mary Grant. *The Stone Axe of Burkamukk* (Melbourne: Ward, Lock and Co., 1922).

Bruyneel, Kevin. *The Third Space of Sovereignty, the Postcolonial Politics of US–Indigenous Relations* (Minneapolis: University of Minnesota Press, 2007).

Bush, George W. "Address to a Joint Session of Congress and the American People," Washington, September 20, 2001 (Speech Transcript).

Bush, Laura. "Radio Address by Mrs. Bush," United States of America, The White House, November 17, 2001 (Radio Broadcast).

Butler, Judith. *Precarious Life: The Powers of Mourning and Violence* (London: Verso, 2004).

Campbell, I. C. *"Gone Native" in Polynesia: Captivity Narratives and Experiences from the South Pacific* (Westport: Greenwood Press, 1998).

Carlson, Nancy. *There's a Big, Beautiful World Out There!* (New York: Viking, 2002).

Carter, David. "Multicultural Australia or Australian Multiculturalism?" in *Dispossession, Dreams & Diversity*, edited by David Carter (Frenchs Forest, NSW: Pearson, 2006), 332–55.

Casey, Maryrose. *Creating Frames: Contemporary Indigenous Theatre* (St. Lucia, QLD: University of Queensland Press, 2004).

Casey, Maryrose. "After Mabo: What's at Stake?" *Australian Screen Education* 32 (2003).

Cassuto, Leonard. *The Inhuman Race: The Racial Grotesque in American Literature and Culture* (New York: Columbia University Press, 1997).

Cassuto, Leonard. "'What an object he would have made of me!': Tattooing and the Racial Freak in Melville's Typee," in *Freakery: Cultural Spectacles of the*

Extraordinary Body, edited by Rosemary Garland Thomson (New York: New York University Press, 1996), 234–48.

Castiglia, Christopher. *Bound and Determined: Captivity, Culture-Crossing, and White Womanhood from Mary Rowlandson to Patty Hearst* (Chicago: University of Chicago Press, 1996).

Césaire, Aimé. *Discourse on Colonialism* (New York: MR, 1972).

Chatterjee, Partha. *The Nation and Its Fragments: Colonial and Postcolonial Histories* (Delhi: Oxford University Press, 1995).

Chaudhuri, Nirad. *The Autobiography of an Unknown Indian* (Bombay: Jaico Publishing House, 1991).

Chaudhuri, Nirad. *The Continent of Circe: Being an Essay on the Peoples of India* (Mumbai: Jaico, 2000).

Cheetham, Deborah. "White Baptist Abba Fan," *Wimmin's Business* Festival of the Dreaming, Opera House (Sydney, September 27, 1997).

Cloud, Dana L. "'To Veil the Threat of Terror': Afghan Women and the Clash of Civilizations in the Imagery of the U.S. War on Terrorism," *Quarterly Journal of Speech* 90, no. 3 (2004): 285–87.

Coetzee, J. M. *Boyhood* (London: Vintage, 1998).

Coffee, Frank. *Forty Years in the Pacific: A Book of Reference for the Traveller and Pleasure for the Stay-at-home* (New York and Sydney: Oceanic Publishing Co., c1920).

Cohen, David. *People who have Stolen From Me: Rough Justice in the New South Africa* (New York: St. Martin's Press, 2004).

Coltrane, Scott. "Theorizing Masculinities in Contemporary Social Science," in *Theorizing Masculinities*, edited by Harry Brod and Michael Kaufman (Thousand Oaks, Calif.: Sage, 1994).

Connell, R. W. *Gender and Power: Society, the Person, and Sexual Politics* (Stanford: Stanford University Press, 1987).

Cope, Bill and Mary Kalantzis, ed. *Reconciliation, Multiculturalism, Identities: Difficult Dialogues, Sensible Solutions* (Altona, Victoria: Common Ground, 2001).

Crafts, Hannah. *The Bondwoman's Narrative*, edited by Henry Louis Gates Jr. (New York: Time Warner, 2002).

Crenshaw, Kimberle, Neil Gotanda, Gary Peller and Thomas Kendall, ed. *Critical Race Theory: The Key Writings that Formed the Movement* (New York: The New Press, 1995).

Croft, Stuart. *Culture, Crisis, and America's War on Terror* (Cambridge: Cambridge University Press, 2006).

Crotty, Martin. *Making the Australian Male: Middle-Class Masculinity 1870–1920* (Melbourne: Melbourne University Press, 2001).

Cuomo, Chris and Kim Hall, ed. *Whiteness: Feminist Philosophical Reflections* (Lanham, MD: Rowman & Littlefield, 1999).

Dalrymple, William. *White Mughals: Love and Betrayal in Eighteenth-Century India* (New Delhi: Penguin, 2002).

Daniels, Jessie. *White Lies: Race, Class, Gender and Sexuality in White Supremacist Discourse* (London: Routledge, 1997).

Davies, Margaret and Ngaire Naffine. *Are Persons Property? Legal Debates about Property and Personality* (Aldershot, Dartmouth Publishing, 2001).

Davis, Angela. *Women Race and Class* (New York: Vintage Books, 1983).

Dawson, Graham. *Soldier Heroes: British Adventure, Empire and the Imagining of Masculinities* (London: Routledge, 1994).

Delgado, Richard and Jean Stefancic, ed. *Critical Whiteness Studies: Looking Behind the Mirror* (Philadelphia: Temple University Press, 1997).

Deloria, Phillip. *Playing Indian* (Michigan: Yale University Press, 1998).

Deloria, Vine Jr. *Red Earth, White Lies: Native Americans and the Myth of Scientific Fact* (New York: Scibner, 1995).

Deloria, Vine Jr. *Custer Died for Your Sins: An Indian Manifesto* (Oklahoma: University of Oklahoma Press, 1988).

Deloria, Vine Jr. and Clifford Lytle. *American Indians: American Justice* (Austin: University of Texas Press, 1983).

Demetra, George. *Mysteries of the Dark Moon: The Healing Power of the Dark Goddess* (San Francisco: HarperSanFrancisco, 1992).

Dixon, Robert. *Writing the Colonial Adventure: Race, Gender and Nation in Anglo-Australian Popular Fiction, 1875–1914* (New York: Cambridge University Press, 1995).

Doane, Ashley and Eduardo Bonilla-Silva, ed. *White Out: The Continuing Significance of Racism* (New York and London: Routledge, 2003).

Downing, John and Charles Husband. *Representing "Race": Racisms, Ethnicities and Media* (London: Sage, 2005).

During, Simon. "Introduction," in *The Cultural Studies Reader* (New York: Routledge, 1993).

Dyer, Richard. "The Matter of Whiteness," in *White Privilege: Essential Readings on the Other Side of Racism*, edited by Paula Rothenberg (New York: Worth Publishers, 2002).

Dyer, Richard. *White* (London and New York: Routledge, 1997).

Evelev, John. "Made in the Marquesas: Tattooing and Melville's Critique of the Marketplace," *Arizona Quarterly* 48, no. 4 (1992): 19–45.

Fanon, Frantz. *Black Skin White Masks* (New York: Grove Press, 1991).

Farred, Grant. "First Stop Port-au-Prince: Mapping Postcolonial Africa through Toussaint L'Ouverture and His Black Jacobins," in *The Politics of Culture in the Shadow of Capital*, ed. David Lloyd and Lisa Lowe (Durham, NC: Duke University Press, 1997).

Favenc, Ernest. *The Secret of the Australian Desert* (London: Blackie and Son, 1896).

Fine, Michelle, Lois Weis, Linda Powell and L. Mun Wong, eds., *Off White; Readings on Race, Power and Society* (New York: Routledge, 1997).

Flagg, Barbara. *Was Blind but Now I See: White Race Consciousness and the Law* (New York: New York University Press, 1998).

Foster, Frances Smith. *Witnessing Slavery* (Westport: Greenwood Press, 1976).

Foucault, Michel, *History of Sexuality, Vol. 1* (London: Penguin Books, 1998).

Frankenberg, Ruth, ed. *Displacing Whiteness: Essays in Social and Cultural Criticism* (London: Duke University Press, 1997).

Frankenberg, Ruth. *White Women, Race Matters: The Social Construction of White-ness* (Minneapolis: University of Minnesota Press, 1993).

Fraser, Robert. *Lifting the Sentence: A Poetics of Postcolonial Fiction* (Manchester: Manchester University Press, 2000).

Frayling, Christopher. "The House that Jack Built: Some Stereotypes of the Rapist in the History of Popular Culture," in *Rape*, edited by Sylvana Tomaselli and Roy Porter (Oxford: Basil Blackwell, 1986).

Fuller, Alexandra. *Let's Not go to the Dogs Tonight* (London: Random House, 2002).

Gardner, Marilyn. "Families see a subtle, lasting shift in values," *Christian Science Monitor* 94, no. 23 (December 6, 2001).

Gates, Henry Louis, Jr. and Hollis Robbins, eds. *In Search of Hannah Crafts: Critical Essays on The Bondwoman's Narrative* (Cambridge, MA: BasicCivitas, 2004).

Gavey, Nicole. *Just Sex? The Cultural Scaffolding of Rape* (London and New York: Routledge, 2005).

Gavron, Jeremy. *Moon* (London: Viking, 1996).

Geha, Joseph. "Alone and all Together," in *Big City Cool: Short Stories About Urban Youth*, edited by M. Jerry Weiss and Helen S. Weiss (New York: Persea Books, 2002), 51–64.

Gerstein, Moricai. *The Man Who Walked Between the Towers* (Brookfield, Connecti-cut: Roaring Brook Press, 2003).

Gilmore, David. *Manhood in the Making: Cultural Concepts of Masculinity* (New Haven: Yale University Press, 1989).

Gilmore, Leigh. *The Limits of Autobiography: Trauma and Testimony* (Ithaca, New York and London: Cornell University Press, 2001).

Gilmore, Leigh. *Autobiographics: A Feminist Theory of Women's Self-Representation* (Ithica: Cornell University Press, 1994).

Godwin, Peter. *Mukiwa* (London: Picador, 1996).

Goldberg, David Theo. *The Racial State* (Malden, MA: Blackwell Press, 2002).

Gooneratne, Yasmine. *A Change of Skies* (New Delhi: Penguin, 1992).

Green, Martin. *Dreams of Adventure, Deeds of Empire* (New York: Basic Books, 1979).

Grounds, Richard A., George E. Tinker, and David E. Wilkins, eds. *Native Voices: American Indian Identity and Resistance* (Kansas, University Press of Kansas, 2003).

Gunning, Sandra. *Race, Rape and Lynching: The Red Record of American Literature, 1890–1912* (New York: Oxford University Press, 1996).

Hacking, Ian. *Rewriting the Soul: Multiple Personality and the Sciences of Memory* (Princeton: Princeton University Press, 1995).

Hage, Ghassan. *Against Paranoid Nationalism: Searching for Hope in a Shrinking Society* (Sydney: Pluto Press, 2003).

Hage, Ghassan. *White Nation: Fantasies of White Supremacy in a Multicultural So-ciety* (Sydney: Pluto Press, 1998).

Haggis, Jane and Susan Schech. "Migrancy, Multiculturalism and Whiteness: Re-charting Core Identities in Australia," *Communal/Plural: Journal of Transnational & Cross-Cultural Studies* 9, no. 2 (2001).

Haggis, Jane and Susanne Schech. "Incoherence and Whiteness," *Unmasking Whiteness: Race Relations and Reconciliation* (Nathan, QLD: Griffith University, 1999), 45–51.

Hall, Stuart. "The Spectacle of the Other," *Cultural Representations and Signifying Practices* (London: Sage, 1997).

Hall, Stuart. "The Social Production of News," in *Policing the Crisis: Mugging, the State, and Law and Order* (London: Palgrave Macmillan, 1978).

Hall, Stuart and Paul Du Gay, eds. *Questions of Cultural Identity* (London: Sage, 1996).

Haney-Lopez, Ian. *White by Law: The Legal Construction of Race* (New York: New York University Press, 1996).

Harris, Cheryl. "Whiteness as Property," in *Critical Race Theory: The Key Writings that Formed the Movement*, edited by Kimberle Crenshaw, Neil Gotanda, Gary Peller and Thomas Kendall (New York: The New Press, 1995), 276–91.

Hartley, John. "An Aboriginal Public Sphere in the Era of Media Citizenship," *Cultural Policy* 8, no. 2 (1997).

Hawthorne, Susan and Bronwyn Winter. "Introduction" in *September 11, 2001: Feminist Perspectives* (Melbourne: Spinifex, 2002).

Heabich, Anna. "The Noongar stolen generations" (notes for paper presented to Albany seminar *Impressions—Albany's History and Heritage* April 24, 1997) http://wwwmcc.murdoch.edu.au/ReadingRoom/CRCC/fellows/haebich/stolen.html (accessed April 24, 2001).

Henty, G. A. *A Final Reckoning: A Tale of Bush Life in Australia* (London: Blackie and Son, 1887).

Hibbs, Thomas S. "Film and TV in Anxious Times," *The New Atlantis: A Journal of Technology and Science* (Summer 2004): 1–11.

Hill, Mike, ed. *Whiteness: A Critical Reader* (New York: New York University Press, 1997).

Hill, Mike. *After Whiteness: Unmaking an American Majority* (New York: New York University Press, 2004).

Holden, Horace, *A Narrative of the Shipwreck, Captivity and Sufferings of Horace Holden and Benj. H. Nute; Who Were Cast Away in the American Ship Mentor, on the Pelew Islands, in the Year 1832; and for Two Years Afterwards Were Subjected to Unheard of Sufferings Among the Barbarous Inhabitants of Lord North's Island* (Boston: Russell, Shattuck, and Co., 1836).

Hollingworth, Jackie. "The Call of Empire: Children's Literature Revisited" in *Mother State and Her Little Ones*, edited by Bob Bessant (Melbourne: Centre for Youth and Community Studies, Phillip Institute of Technology, 1987).

hooks, bell. *Black Looks: Race and Representation* (Boston: South End Press, 1992).

Hope, Christopher. *White Boy Running* (London: Abacus, 1988).

Human Rights and Equal Opportunity Commission, 'Bringing Them Home: The "Stolen Children" Report' http://www.hreoc.gov.au/social_justice/stolen_children/index.html (accessed April 24, 2001).

Huntington, Samuel. P. "The Clash of Civilizations," *Foreign Affairs* 72, no. 3 (1993): 22–28.

Ignatiev, Noel. *How the Irish Became White* (New York: Routledge, 1995).

Jacobs, Harriet. *Incidents in the Life of a Slave Girl* (Boston: Published for the Author, 1861).

Jacobson, Matthew F. *Whiteness of a Different Color: European Immigrants and the Alchemy of Race* (Cambridge: Harvard University Press, 1998).

Jones, C. P. "Stigma and Tattoo," in *Written on the Body*, ed. Jane Caplan (Princeton: University of California Press, 2000), 1–16.

Jordan, Glen and Chris Weedon. *Cultural Politics: Class, Gender, Race and the Postmodern World* (Oxford: Blackwell, 1995).

Joseph, Helen. *Tomorrow's Sun: a Smuggled Journal from South Africa* (London: Hutchinson, 1966).

Joseph, Helen. *If This Be Treason* (London: Deutsch, 1963).

Jürgens, Richard. *The Many Houses of Exile* (Pretoria: Clarke's Books, 2002).

Kauanui, Kehulani. "Diasporic Deracination and 'Off-Island' Hawaiians," *The Contemporary Pacific* 19, no. 1 (2007): 137–60.

Keeton, Patricia. "Reevaluating the 'Old' Cold War: A Dialectical Reading of Two 9/11 Narratives," *Cinema Journal*, 43, no. 4 (Summer 2004): 114–21.

Kennedy, Roseanne. "The Affective Work of Stolen Generations Testimony: From the Archives to the Classroom" *Biography* 27, no. 1 (2004): 48–77.

Kennedy, Rosanne. "Stolen Generations Testimony: Trauma, Historiography, and the Question of 'Truth,'" *Aboriginal History* 25 (2001) 116–31.

Keohane, Sonja. "Continuing thoughts on 'A Presidential Sham,'" *We The People* 2001, http://www.dickshovel.com/sonsham.html (accessed March 9, 2008).

Kidd, Rosaline. *The Way We Civilize* (Brisbane: University of Queensland Press, 1997).

Kipling, Rudyard "To the Native-Born," *DayPoems*, http://www.daypoems.net/poems/1836.html (accessed September 5, 2005).

Kipling, Rudyard. *Kim* (New Delhi: Rupa & Co, 2004).

Kipling, Rudyard. *The Naulahka: a Story of West and East*, 2nd ed. (London: W. Heinemann, 1892).

Kincheloe, Joe L., Shirley Steinberg, Nelson M. Rodriguez and Ronald Chennault, eds., *White Reign: Deploying Whiteness in America* (New York: St. Martin's Griffin, 2000).

Kingston, W. H. G. *Australian Adventures* (London: George, Routledge and Sons, 1884).

Kingston, W. H. G. *The Young Berringtons; Or, the Boy Explorers* (London: Cassell, 1880).

Kingston, W. H. G. *Twice Lost: A Story of Shipwreck and Adventure in the Wilds of Australia* (London: Thomas Nelson, 1876).

Knadler, Stephen P. *The Fugitive Race: Minority Writers Resisting Whiteness* (Jackson: University Press of Mississippi, 2002).

Kolchin, Peter. "Whiteness Studies: the New History of Race in America," *Journal of American History* 89, no.1 (June 2002).

Kristeva, Julia. *The Kristeva Reader*, ed. Toril Moi (New York: Columbia University Press, 1986).

Krog, Antjie. *A Change of Tongue* (Johannesburg: Random House, 2003).

Krog, Antjie. *Country of My Skull* (London: Jonathan Cape, 1997).

Kumar, Amitava. "Conditions of Immigration," in *Whiteness: A Critical Reader*, ed. Mike Hill (New York: New York University Press, 1997).

LaCapra, Dominick. *History, Politics and the Novel* (Ithaca: Cornell University Press, 1987).

Lampert, Jo. "Teach Your Children Well (Or Not): Children, Media and War," in *Terrorism Media Society*, edited by Tomasz Pludowski (Torun, Poland: Cellgium Civitas, 2006), 287–97.

Latimer, Dan. "Oedipus in the South Seas: The Case of Herman Melville's Typee," *Essays in Literature* 21, no. 2 (1994): 218–33.

Lessing, Doris. *African Laughter: Four Visits to Zimbabwe* (London: HarperCollins, 1992).

Levernier, James A. and Katherine Zabelle Derounian-Stodola. *The Indian Captivity Narrative, 1550–1900* (New York: Maxwell, Macmillan International, 1993).

Levine-Rasky, Cynthia, ed. *Working through Whiteness: International Perspectives* (Albany: State University of New York Press, 2002).

Lewis, Simon. "Culture, Cultivation and Colonialism in *Out of Africa* and Beyond." *Research in African Literatures* 31, no. 1 (Spring, 2000): 63–79.

Lipsitz, George. *The Possessive Investment in Whiteness: How White People Profit from Identity Politics* (Philadelphia: Temple University Press, 1998).

Lindsay, Elaine. *Spirituality in Australian Women's Fiction* (Amsterdam: Rodopi, 2000).

Loomba, Ania. *Colonialism/Postcolonialism* (London: Routledge, 1999, New Critical Idion Series).

Macdonald, Alexander. *The Invisible Island: A Story of the Far North of Queensland* (London: Blackie and Son, 1911).

MacDonald, Robert. *Sons of the Empire: The Frontier and the Boy Scout Movement, 1890–1918* (Toronto: University of Toronto Press, 1993).

Majaj, Lisa Suhair. "Arab-Americans and the Meanings of Race" in *Postcolonial Theory and the United States: Race, Ethnicty, and Literature*, edited by Amritjit Singh and Peter Schmidt (Jackson: University Press of Mississipi, 2000).

Majid, Anourar. "The Failure of Postcolonial Theory After 9/11," *The Chronicle of Higher Education* 49, no. 10 (2002): B11.

Malan, Rian. *My Traitor's Heart* (London: Vintage, 1990).

Manne, Robert. *Australian Quarterly Essay: In Denial the Stolen Generations and the Right* (Melbourne: Schwarz Publishing, 2001).

Mannoni, O. *Prospero and Caliban: The Psychology of Colonization* (London: Methuen, 1956).

Marrouchi, Mustapha. "Introduction: Colonialism, Islamism, Terrorism," *College Literature* 30, no. 1 (Winter 2003): 6–55.

Martin, R. K. *Hero, Captain and Stranger: Male Friendship, Social Critique, and Literary Form in the Sea Novels of Herman Melville* (Chapel Hill: University of North Carolina Press, 1986).

McClintock, Anne. *Imperial Leather: Race, Gender and Sexuality in the Colonial Contest* (New York: Routledge, 1995).

McGillis, Roderick. "The Delights of Impossibility: No Children, No Books, Only Theory," *Children's Literature Association Quarterly* 23, no. 4 (1999).

Meadows, Michael. "A 10-point Plan and a Treaty," in *Unmasking Whiteness* edited by Belinda McKay (Nathan, QLD: Griffith University, 1999).

Melville, Herman. *Omoo: A Narrative of Adventures in the South Seas* (London: J. M. Dent and Co. c1910).

Melville, Herman. *Typee* (London and Glasgow: Collins Clear-Type Press c1905).

Memmi, Albert. *The Colonizer and Colonized* (Boston: Beacon Press, 1991).

Mickler, Steve. *The Myth of Privilege: Aboriginal Status, Media Visions, Public ideas* (Perth: Freemantle University Press, 1998).

Mihesuah, Devon A. *American Indians: Stereotypes and Realities* (Atlanta: Clarity Press, 1996).

Mills, Charles W. "Racial Exploitation and the Wages of Whiteness," in *What White Looks Like: African American Philosophers on the Whiteness Question*, edited by George Yancy (New York: Routledge, 2004).

Moreton-Robinson, Aileen, "Writing Off Indigenous Sovereignty: The Discourse of Security and Patriarchal White Sovereignty," in *Sovereign Subjects* edited by Aileen Moreton-Robinson (Sydney, Allen&Unwin, 2007).

Moreton-Robinson, Aileen. "Whiteness Matters: Implications of Talkin' up to the White Woman," *Australian Feminist Studies* 21, no. 50 (July 2006).

Moreton-Robinson, Aileen. "The House that Jack Built: Britishness and White Possession," *Journal of the Australian Critical Race and Whiteness Studies Association* 1 (2005): 21–29.

Moreton-Robinson, Aileen. "The Possessive Logic of Patriarchal White Sovereignty: The High Court and the Yorta Yorta Decision," *Borderlands E-Journal* 3, no. 2 (October 2004), http://www.borderlands.net.au/vol3no2_2004/moreton_possessive.htm (accessed June 10, 2008).

Moreton-Robinson, Aileen. "Whiteness Matters: Australian Studies and Indigenous Studies" in *Thinking Australian Studies: Teaching Across Cultures*, edited by David Carter, Kate Darian-Smith and Gus Worby (Brisbane: University of Queensland Press, 2004).

Moreton-Robinson, Aileen, ed. *Whitening Race: Essays in Social and Cultural Criticism* (Canberra: Aboriginal Studies Press, 2004).

Moreton-Robinson, Aileen. "I Still Call Australia Home: Indigenous Belonging and Place in a White Postcolonizing Society," *Uprootings/Regroundings: Questions of Home and Migration*, edited by Sara Ahmed, Claudia Castañeda, Anne-Marie Fortier, Mimi Sheller (Oxford: Berg, 2003).

Moreton-Robinson, Aileen. *Talkin' Up to the White Woman: Aboriginal Women and Feminism* (Brisbane: University of Queensland Press, 2000).

Moreton-Robinson, Aileen and Fiona Nicoll, "'We Will Fight Them on the Beaches': Protesting Cultures of White Possession," *Journal of Australian Studies* no. 89 (2006): 149–60.

Morgan, Edward. *A Passage to India* (London: Dent, 1961).

Morris, Pam ed. *The Bakhtin Reader: Selected Writings of Bakhtin, Medvedev, Voloshinov* (Sydney: Edward Arnold, 1997).

Morrison, Toni. "Black Matters," in *Race Critical Theories: Text and Context*, edited by Philomina Essed and David Theo Goldberg (Massachusetts: Blackwell Publishers, 2002).

Morrison, Toni. *Playing in the Dark: Whiteness and the Literary Imagination* (Cambridge: Harvard University Press, 1992).

Nakayama, Thomas K. and Judith N. Martin, ed. *Whiteness: The Communication of Social Identity* (Thousand Oaks: Sage, 1999).

Nandy, Ashis. *The Illegitimacy of Nationalism: Rabindranath Tagore and the Politics of Self* (New Delhi: Oxford University Press, 1994).

Nandy, Ashis. *The Intimate Enemy: Loss and Recovery of Self Under Colonialism* (Delhi: Oxford University Press, 1999).

Ndebele, Nhlanhla. "The African National Congress and the Policy of Non-Racialism: a Study of the Membership Issue. Politikon" 29, no. 2 (November 2002): 133–46.

Newman, Louise. *White Women's Rights: The Racial Origins of Feminism in the United States* (New York: Oxford University Press, 1999).

Nicolacopoulos, Toula and George Vassilacopoulos. "Racism, Foreigner Communities and the Onto-pathology of White Australian Subjectivity," in *Whitening Race: Essays in Social and Cultural Criticism*, edited by Aileen Moreton-Robinson (Canberra: Aboriginal Studies Press, 2004).

Nicoll, Fiona. "Reconciliation in and out of Perspective: White Knowing, Seeing, Curating and Being at Home in and Against Indigenous Sovereignty," in *Whitening Race: Essays in Social and Cultural Criticism*, edited by Aileen Moreton-Robinson (Canberra: Aboriginal Studies Press, 2004).

Nicoll, Fiona. "De-facing *Terra Nullius* and Facing the Public Secret of Indigenous Sovereignty in Australia," *Borderlands eJournal* 1, no. 2 (December 2002) http://www.borderlandsejournal.adelaide.edu.au/vol1no2_2002/nicoll_defacing.html (accessed May 28, 2008).

Nuttall, Sarah and Carli Coetzee, eds. *Negotiating the Past: The Making of Memory in South Africa* (Oxford: Oxford University Press, 2002).

Nye, Robert. *Masculinity and Male Codes of Honour in Modern France* (Oxford: Oxford University Press, 1993).

O'Connell, James. *A Residence of Eleven Years in New Holland and the Caroline Islands: Being the Adventures of James F. O'Connell; Edited from his Verbal Narration* (Ann Arbor, Michigan: UMI, 2004).

Osuri, Goldie and Subhabrata Bobby Bannerjee, "White Diasporas: Media Representations of September 11 and the Unbearable Whiteness of Being in Australia," *Social Semiotics* 14, no. 2 (August, 2004), 151–71.

Parry, Benita. "The Contents and Discontents of Kipling's Imperialism," in *Postcolonial Studies: A Materialist Critique* (London: Routledge, 2005).

Patel, Andrea. *On That Day: A Book of Hope for Children.* (Toronto: Tricycle Press, 2001).

Paul, Adrien. *Willis the Pilot: A Sequel to the Swiss Family Robinson* (London: F. Warne, 1866).

Perera, Suvendrini. "Race, Terror, Sydney, December 2005," *Borderlands E-journal* 5, no. 1 http://www.borderlandsejournal.adelaide.edu.au, 2006 (accessed May 26, 2008).

Perera, Suvendrini. "Who will I become? The Multiple Formations of Australian Whiteness," *Journal of Australian Critical Race and Whiteness Studies Association* 1, no.1 (2005): 30–39.

Petrilli, Susan, ed. "Whiteness Matters/Il Bianco Al Centro Della Questione," *Athanor: Semiotica, Filosofia, Arte, Letteratura* Anno XVII, nuova serie, n. 10 2006/2007.

Pifer, Drury. *Innocents in Africa: An American Family's Story* (New York: Harcourt Brace & Company, 1994).

Pollitt, Katha. "After the Taliban," *Nation*, December 17, 2001.

Polya, Gideon. "Body Count: the Awful Truth," *National Indigenous Times*, June 14, 2007, http://www.nit.com.au/news/story.aspx?id=11552 (accessed June 8, 2007).

President's Advisory Board on Race, "Executive Order 13050," *The Multiracial Activist* June 13, 1997, http://www.multiracial.com/government/whitehouse-eo13050 .html (accessed March 7, 2008).

Fiona Probyn, "Playing chicken at the Intersection: The White Critic of Whiteness," *Borderlands EJournal* 3, no. 2 (2004), http://www.borderlandsejournal.adelaide .edu.au/vol3no2_2004/probyn_playing.htm (accessed June 10, 2008).

Rains, Francis V. "Is the Benign Really Harmless?: Deconstructing Some 'Benign' Manifestations of Operationalised White Privilege," in *White Reign: Deploying Whiteness in America*, edited by Joe L. Kincheloe, Shirley Steinberg, Nelson M. Rodriguez and Ronald Chennault (New York: St. Martin's Griffin, 2000).

Rasmussen, Birgit, Eric Kleinberg, Irene Nexica and Matt Wray, ed. *The Making and Unmaking of Whiteness* (Durham: Duke University Press, 2001).

Reynolds, Henry. "From Armband to Blindfold," *Australian Review of Books* (March 2001), 8–9, 26.

Reynolds, Henry. *An Indelible Stain: The Question of Genocide in Australia's History* (Melbourne: Viking, 2001).

Robarts, Edward. *The Marquesan Journal of Edward Robarts, 1797–1824: Edited, with an Introduction by Greg Dening* (Canberra: Australian National University Press, 1974).

Roediger, David. *Working Toward Whiteness: How America's Immigrants Became White* (New York: Basic Books, 2005).

Roediger, David. *The Wages of Whiteness: Race and the Making of The American Working Class* (New York: Verso, 1999).

Roediger, David. *Towards the Abolition of Whiteness* (London: Verso, 1994).

Roy, Parama. *Indian Traffic: Identities in Question in Colonial and Postcolonial India* (Berkeley: University of California Press, 1998).

Rutter, Jessica. "'Saving' Women in Algeria and Afghanistan: (Neo)Colonialism, Liberation and the Veil," *Eruditio Online* 24 (2004), http://www.duke.edu/web/ eruditio/Rutter.html (accessed September 6, 2005).

Said, Edward, "White Price Oslo?" *Al-Ahram On-line* 2002, http://weekly.ahram.org .eg/2002/577/op2.htm (accessed March 20, 2002).

Said, Edward W. *Orientalism* (New York: Pantheon Books, 1978).

Sanders, Clinton. "Marks of Mischief: Becoming and Being Tattooed," *Journal of Contemporary Ethnography* 16, no. 4 (1988): 395–432.

Schaffer, Kay. *Women and the Bush: Forces of Desire in the Australian Cultural Tradition* (Melbourne: Cambridge University Press, 1988).

Schapper, Henry P. *Aboriginal Advancement to Integration: Conditions and Plans for WA* (Canberra: Australian National University Press, 1970).

Schueller, Malini. "Colonialism and Melville's South Seas Journeys," *Studies in American Fiction* 22, no. 1 (1994): 3–19.

Scott, Joan. *Gender and the Politics of History* (New York: Columbia University Press, 1988).

Scott, Paul. *The Jewel in the Crown* (London: Heinemann, 1966).

Seshadri-Crooks, Kalpana. *Desiring Whiteness: A Lacanian Analysis of Race* (New York: Routledge, 2000).

Sherman, Joseph. "Serving the Natives: Whiteness as the Price of Hospitality in South African Yiddish Literature," *Journal of Southern African Studies* 26, no. 3 (September 2000): 505–21.

Shogren, Elizabeth. "Clinton Calls for New Approach to 'Affirmative Action,'" *AAD Project*, 1998, http://aad.english.ucsb.edu/docs/PBS-july98.html (accessed March 9, 2008).

Showalter, Elaine. *Hystories: Hysterical Epidemics and Modern Culture* (London: Picador, 1998).

Silva, Noenoe. *Aloha Betrayed: Native Hawaiian Resistance to American Colonialism*, 4th printing (Durham: Duke University Press, 2006).

Slotkin, Richard. *Regeneration Through Violence: The Mythology of the American Frontier, 1600–1860* (Middletown, Conn.: Wesleyan University Press, 1973).

Slovo, Gillian. *Every Secret Thing: My Family, My Country* (London: Little, Brown, 1997).

Spencer, Herbert. *Education: Intellectual, Moral and Physical* (New York: D. Appleton, 1900 (1860)).

Spivak, Gayatri Chakravorty. "The Burden of English," in *The Lie of the Land: English Literary Studies in India*, edited by Rajeswari Sunder Rajan (Delhi: Oxford University Press, 1993), 275–99.

Spivak, Gayatri Chakravorty. "Can the Subaltern Speak?" in *Marxism and the Interpretation of Culture*, edited by C. Nelson and L. Grossberg (Basinstoke: Macmillan Education, 1988).

Standaert, Michael. *Skipping Towards Armageddon: The Politics and Propaganda of the Left* (New York: Soft Skull Press, 2006).

Stepan, Nancy Leys. "Race and Gender: The Role of Analogy in Science" in *The Anatomy of Racism*, edited by D. T. Goldberg (Minneapolis: University of Minnesota Press, 1990).

Stoler, Anne. *Carnal Knowledge and Imperial Power: Race and the Intimate in Colonial Rule* (Berkeley: University of California Press, 2002).

Stott, Rebecca. "The Dark Continent: Africa as Female Body in Haggard's Adventure Fiction," *Feminist Review*, no. 32 (1989): 69–89.

Stowe, Harriet Beecher. *Uncle Tom's Cabin* (London: Blackie, 1979).

Stratton, Jon. "Before Holocaust Memory: Making Sense of Trauma Between Post Memory and Cultural Memory," *Journal of Australian Critical Race and Whiteness Studies Association* 1, no. 1 (2005): 54–70.

Stratton, Jon. "Two Rescues, One History: Everyday Racism in Australia," *Social Identities* 12, no. 6 (November 2005).

Stratton, Royal. *Captivity of the Oatman Girls Among the Apache and Mojave Indians* (New York: Dover Publications, 1994).

Sutton, Peter. "The Politics of Suffering: Indigenous Policy in Australia since the 1970s," *Anthropological Forum* 11, no. 2 (November, 2001): 125–73.

Suzman, Helen. *In No Uncertain Terms: The Memoir of Helen Suzman* (Johannesburg: Jonathan Ball, 1993).

Tagore, Rabindranath. *Gora. Rabindra-Rachanabali*, Centenary Edition (Calcutta: West Bengal Government, Bengali year 1368 [1961]).

Taxel, Joel. "Multicultural Literature and the Politics of Reaction," *Teachers College Record* 98, no. 3 (1997) http://www.tcrecord.org/content.asp?contentid=9617 (accessed June 8, 2008).

Tosh, John. "What Should Historians do with Masculinity?: Reflections on Nineteenth-Century Britain," *History Workshop Journal* no. 38 (1994).

Transcript: "Barack Obama's Speech on Race," *New York Times* (March 18, 2008) http://www.nytimes.com/2008/03/18/us/politics/18text-obama.html?ei=5070&en=eeb9fd47e9f2bd55 (accessed March 25, 2008).

Turner, Terence. "The Social Skin," in *Not Work Alone: A Cross-cultural View of Activities Superfluous to Survival*, edited by J. Cherfas and R. Lewin (London: Temple Smith, 1980).

Walker, David. *Anxious Nation: Australia and the Rise of Asia, 1850–1939* (Brisbane: University of Queensland Press, 1999).

Warrior, Robert. "Tribal Secrets: Recovering American Indian Intellectual Traditions" (Minnesota: University of Minnesota Press, 1995).

Watson, Irene. "Settled and Unsettled Spaces: Are We Free to Roam?" in Aileen Moreton-Robinson's "Writing Off Indigenous Sovereignty: The Discourse of Security and Patriarchal White Sovereignty," *Sovereign Subjects: Indigenous Sovereignty Matters* edited by Aileen Moreton-Robinson (Sydney: Allen&Unwin, 2007).

Webb, Janeen and Andrew Enstice. *Aliens & Savages* (Sydney: Harper Collins, 1998).

Werner, Annie. "Savage Skins: The Freakish Subject of Tattooed Beachcombers," *Kunapipi* 27, no. 1 (2005).

West, Cornel. "The New Cultural Politics of Difference," in *The Cultural Studies Reader*, edited by Simon During (New York: Routledge, 1993).

Wiegman, R. "Whiteness Studies and the Paradox of Particularity," *Boundary* 2, no. 28 (3) (1999).

Wildman, Stephanie M and Adrienne D. Davis. "Making Systems of Privilege Visible," in *White Privilege: Essential Readings on the Other Side of Racism*, edited by Paula Rothenberg (New York: Worth Publishers, 2002).

Williams, Patrick. "Kim and Orientalism," in *Kipling Reconsidered*, edited by Phillip Mallett (London: Macmillan, 1989).

Williams, Raymond. *Like a Loaded Weapon: The Rehnquist Court, Indian Rights and the Legal History of Racism in America* (Minneapolis: University of Minnesota Press, 2005).

Windschuttle, Keith. *The Fabrication of Aboriginal History Volume One, Van Die-men's Land 1803–1847* (Sydney: MacLeay Press, 2002).

Windschuttle, Keith. "The Break Up of Australia," *Quadrant* 44, no. 9 (September 2000): 8–16.

Windshuttle, Keith. "The Myths of Frontier Massacres in Australian History," Parts 1, 2 and 3, *Quadrant October* 44, nos. 10–12 (November and December, 2000): 8–21, 17–24, 6–20.

White, Richard. *Inventing Australia: Images and Identity, 1688–1980* (Sydney: George Allen and Unwin, 1981).

Whitlock, Gillian. *The Intimate Empire: Reading Women's Autobiography* (Oxford: Cassell, 2000).

Wolfe, Patrick. "Land, Labor and Difference: Elementary Structures of Race," *American Historical Review* 106, no. 3 (2001): 866–905.

Yancy, George, ed. *What White Looks Like: African American Philosophers on the Whiteness Question.* (New York and London: Routledge, 2004).

Yegenoglu, Meyda. *Colonial Fantasies: Toward a Feminist Reading of Orientalism* (Cambridge: Cambridge University Press, 1998).

Yellin, Jean Fagin. *"The Bondwoman's Narrative* and *Uncle Tom's Cabin"* in *In Search of Hannah Crafts: Critical Essays on The Bondwoman's Narrative*, ed. Henry Louis Gates, Jr. and Hollis Robbins (Cambridge, MA: BasicCivitas, 2004), 106–16.

Index

About the Contributors

Urbashi Barat is professor and head, Department of Postgraduate Studies & Research in English, and Director, Centre for Gandhian Studies and Director, Centre for Ambedkar Studies, Rani Durgavati University, Jabalpur, India. She has taught undergraduate and postgraduate English courses for more than 25 years, and has published widely on English-Language Teaching in India, postcolonial literatures, and women's studies. At present she is working on three research projects: a comparison between Indian Dalit, Australian aboriginal and Canadian "First Nation" women's lifewriting, contemporary Indian women's drama, and the differences in women's fiction in English in settler colonies (Australia, New Zealand, Canada) and "invaded" colonies (India, Pakistan, Sri Lanka).

Maryrose Casey is a lecturer with the Centre for Drama and Theatre Studies at Monash University. Her publications include articles and book chapters on contemporary Australian theatre practice, primarily focused on contemporary Indigenous theatre. She has also published on Indigenous Australian protests as performed and performative acts. Her publications include the multi award-winning monograph *Creating Frames: Contemporary Indigenous Theatre 1967–1997* (University of Queensland Press, 2004). Her current projects include *Telling the Story: Aboriginal and Torres Strait Islander Theatre Practices* for Routledge's *Theatres of the World* series and a book on Indigenous Australian protests across the last hundred years for University of Queensland Press.

Martin Crotty is a senior lecturer in History at the University of Queensland. His interest in whiteness studies grow out of his work on Australian masculinity, published as *Making the Australian Male: Middle-Class Masculinity*

1870–1920. He is currently researching and writing on the history of the RSL, and co-edits the *Journal of Australian Studies* with Melissa Harper.

Jo Lampert is a lecturer in the School of Cultural and Language Studies at the Queensland University of Technology in Brisbane Australia. Though originally from Canada she has lived in Australia for the past thirteen years, teaching literature, sociology and Indigenous education. Her doctoral thesis, on children's literature about September 11, will be published as a book in 2009.

Suzanne Lynch is a graduate of Hunter College City University of New York and is currently completing a doctorate at the University of Illinois at Urbana-Champaign. She teaches English at Hillsborough Community College and is the recent recipient of a National Endowment for the Humanities summer Institute award.

Aileen Moreton-Robinson is a *Goenpul* woman from *Minjerribah* (Stradbroke Island), *Quandamooka* First Nation (Moreton Bay) in Queensland, Australia. She is Professor of Indigenous Studies, Indigenous Studies Research Network, at the Queensland University of Technology. Prior to this appointment she taught Women's Studies at Flinders University and Indigenous studies at Griffith University and the University of South Australia. Her books include *Talkin' Up to the White Woman: Indigenous Women and Feminism* (2000), University of Queensland Press, St Lucia and two edited collections entitled *Whitening Race: Essays in Social and Cultural Criticism* (2004), Aboriginal Studies Press, Canberra and *Sovereign Subjects: Indigenous Sovereignty Matters* (2007), Allen & Unwin, Sydney. Her work in progress is a book on white possession. Professor Moreton-Robinson has been involved in the struggle for Indigenous rights at local, state and national levels and has worked for a number of Indigenous organizations. She was the founding President of the Australian Critical Race and Whiteness Studies Association which can be accessed at www.acrawsa.org.au. Her research interests include Whiteness, Gender and Race within Law, Nation, Society and Knowledge Production and she has published in journals and anthologies in Australia and abroad. Professor Moreton-Robinson is recognized as one of Australia's leading theorists in the field of Critical Race and Whiteness Studies.

Fiona Nicoll is a lecturer in cultural studies at the University in Queensland and the author of *From Diggers to Drag Queens: Configurations of Australian National Identity* (Pluto Press, 2001) as well as publications in the area of queer theory, critical race and whiteness studies and gambling studies. She is also a founding member of the Australian Critical Race and Whiteness Studies Association.

Tanya Serisier is a doctoral student in the Centre for Comparative Literature and Cultural Studies at Monash University, Australia. She has written primarily on questions of race and representation in feminist discourse around sexual violence. Her PhD thesis focuses particularly on practices of textuality and narration in feminist anti-rape politics.

Tony Simoes da Silva teaches English Literatures at the University of Wollongong. His research spans Anglophone and Lusophone postcolonial writing and theory; contemporary writing in English more generally; postcolonial life writing and cultural critical theories. Recent or forthcoming publications include essays in *Connecting Cultures* (ed. Emma Bainbridge, Routledge, 2008), *Partial Answers* (2007), *Third World Quarterly* (2005), *Kunapipi* (2008) and *ARIEL*.

Annie Werner is nearing the end of her doctoral candidature in the school of English Literature, Philosophy and Languages at the University of Wollongong. Her thesis examines representations of Indigenous tattooing in colonial and postcolonial literature from the Pacific and North America, and she has presented her work at conferences in Australia and the United States. In 2006 she co-convened the Fabulous Risk circus conference, in association with the CCAS, ACAPTA and Circus Monoxide, and sections of her thesis appear in *Kunapipi* and a forthcoming anthology, *Something Rich and Strange*.